# CHRISTIANITY

## LOST IN TRANSLATION

## A CRITICAL LOOK AT CHRISTIANITY

Charles E. Kpodzo

# ACKNOWLEDGMENT

This book is a reflection of my personal journey and experiences, enriched and guided by extensive research into the Scriptures, aligning with my deep faith in Jesus Christ. I owe a debt of gratitude to many who have offered encouragement and support in various forms, contributing significantly to this project. Special thanks are extended to those who motivated me to embark on this writing endeavor and have provided material, spiritual, and academic support.

Above all, I express my profound gratitude to the LORD God Almighty, whose inspiration through the Holy Spirit propelled me to initiate and complete this work for His Glory. It is my hope that this book, grounded in the Word of God, will uplift the Body of Christ and contribute to the Salvation of the Saints.

> **1 Corinthians 14:3 (KJV)** But he that prophesieth speaketh unto men *to* edification, and exhortation, and comfort.

> **2 Corinthians 10:8 (KJV)** For though I should boast somewhat more of our authority, which the Lord hath given us for edification, and not for your destruction, I should not be ashamed:

> **2 Corinthians 13:10 (KJV)** Therefore I write these things being absent, lest being present I should use sharpness, according to the power which the Lord hath given me to edification, and not to destruction.

Furthermore, I draw upon the wisdom of Scripture, aligning seamlessly with God's Truth, free from any distortion or suggestion. This impartation of Truth, referring specifically to the knowledge of God, is central to my message. The Gospel of Christ stands unequivocally, capable of either offending or defending, inherent in its essence. It naturally challenges sinners, the wayward, the obstinate, and anyone straying from the path of Truth. Thus, the Gospel of Christ is also aptly known as "The Offense of the Cross."

> **Galatians 1:8 (KJV)** But though we, or an angel from heaven, preach any other gospel unto you than that which we have preached unto you, let him be accursed.

> **Galatians 1:9 (KJV)** As we said before, so say I now again, If any *man* preach any other gospel unto you than that ye have received, let him be accursed.

> **Galatians 1:10 (KJV)** For do I now persuade men, or God? or do I seek to please men? for if I yet pleased men, I should not be the servant of Christ.

**Galatians 5:11 (KJV)** And I, brethren, if I yet preach circumcision, why do I yet suffer persecution? then is the offence of the cross ceased.

The pursuit of God's knowledge through my myriad life experiences and interactions with individuals and groups, both within and outside the Body of Christ, has laid the foundational conviction for writing this book. To those whose names I may not remember but whose stories have left a lasting imprint on me, your interactions, questions, or actions have all fueled my motivation to write.

To the local church and the ministers of God, your deeds and omissions have provided compelling reasons for my writing. To the believer, your personal engagements with me, your behavior towards others, and your conduct within your community have all inspired me to pen down these words.

Lastly, to you, the reader on the verge of exploring this book, I extend my gratitude. You have been in my thoughts frequently and for many significant reasons.

1.  There exists a profound scarcity and longing for the Word of God, characterized by a deficit in accurate spiritual comprehension and interpretation:

    **Amos 8:11 (KJV)** Behold, the days come, saith the Lord GOD, that I will send a famine in the land, not a famine of bread, nor a thirst for water, but of hearing the words of the LORD:

    **Amos 8:12 (KJV)** And they shall wander from sea to sea, and from the north even to the east, they shall run to and fro to seek the word of the LORD, and shall not find *it*.

    **Amos 8:13 (KJV)** In that day shall the fair virgins and young men faint for thirst.

2.  The Gospel of the LORD Jesus Christ, the Word of God, is not being conveyed and instructed with the correct teachings of Holiness, Truth, and Righteousness:

    **2 Timothy 4:1 (KJV)** I charge *thee* therefore before God, and the Lord Jesus Christ, who shall judge the quick and the dead at his appearing and his kingdom;

    **2 Timothy 4:2 (KJV)** Preach the word; be instant in season, out of season; reprove, rebuke, exhort with all longsuffering and doctrine.

    **2 Timothy 4:3 (KJV)** For the time will come when they will not endure sound doctrine; but after their own lusts shall they heap to themselves teachers, having itching ears;

    **2 Timothy 4:4 (KJV)** And they shall turn away *their* ears from the truth, and shall be turned unto fables.

3.  The Word has been misinterpreted to you in a manner not aligned with Scripture itself!

    **2 Corinthians 2:17 (KJV)** states, "For we are not like so many, who peddle the word of God for profit; but in sincerity, as from God, in the sight of God, we speak in Christ."

4. The message of Scripture has been inaccurately conveyed to you, contrary to what the Scriptures themselves dictate!

> **2 Corinthians 2:17 (KJV)** For we are not as many, which corrupt the word of God: but as of sincerity, but as of God, in the sight of God speak we in Christ.

5. The Word should serve as your daily sustenance engage with it to nourish your soul and spirit each day.

6. The Word of God is the sustenance of the soul! A soul devoid of the Word of God is essentially lifeless. Thus, to revive a lifeless soul, one must impart the Word of God, the Gospel of the LORD Jesus Christ!

> **Proverbs 24:13 (KJV)** My son, eat thou honey, because *it is* good; and the honeycomb, *which is* sweet to thy taste:

> **Proverbs 24:14 (KJV)** So *shall* the knowledge of wisdom *be* unto thy soul: when thou hast found *it*, then there shall be a reward, and thy expectation shall not be cut off.

> **Matthew 10:8 (KJV)** Heal the sick, cleanse the lepers, raise the dead, cast out devils: freely ye have received, freely give.

7. The Word of God acts as sweet nourishment to the soul, much like honey enriches the palate. It brings comfort and delight, infusing the spirit with its rich, profound sweetness. Just as honey is known for its healing properties and its ability to energize and soothe, so too does the Word of God rejuvenate the soul, mend spiritual wounds, and provide peace and vitality to those who partake in its wisdom. Engaging with the Word is akin to savoring the pure, natural essence of honey, offering a deep, satisfying spiritual sustenance that enriches one's inner being.

> **Ezekiel 3:1 (KJV)** Moreover he said unto me, Son of man, eat that thou findest; eat this roll, and go speak unto the house of Israel.

> **Ezekiel 3:2 (KJV)** So I opened my mouth, and he caused me to eat that roll.

> **Ezekiel 3:3 (KJV)** And he said unto me, Son of man, cause thy belly to eat, and fill thy bowels with this roll that I give thee. Then did I eat *it*; and it was in my mouth as honey for sweetness.

> **Ezekiel 3:4 (KJV)** And he said unto me, Son of man, go, get thee unto the house of Israel, and speak with my words unto them.

> **Revelation 10:8 (KJV)** And the voice which I heard from heaven spake unto me again, and said, Go *and* take the little book which is open in the hand of the angel which standeth upon the sea and upon the earth.

> **Revelation 10:9 (KJV)** And I went unto the angel, and said unto him, Give me the little book. And he said unto me, Take *it*, and eat it up; and it shall make thy belly bitter, but it shall be in thy mouth sweet as honey.

> **Revelation 10:10 (KJV)** And I took the little book out of the angel's hand, and ate it up; and it was in my mouth sweet as honey: and as soon as I had eaten it, my belly was bitter.

> **Revelation 10:11 (KJV)** And he said unto me, Thou must prophesy again before many peoples, and nations, and tongues, and kings.

8. Drawing from **Proverbs 24:13-14 (KJV),** it's evident that the Holy Bible, embodying the Word of God and the Gospel of the LORD Jesus Christ, stands unparalleled as the sole scripture across the globe offering the promise of Salvation to those who diligently pursue the Word of God

9. Any faith that does not offer its followers the assurance of salvation and an eternal place in Heaven alongside God Almighty is fundamentally misaligned and originates from malevolent forces.

   > **Matthew 11:28 (KJV)** Come unto me, all ye that labour and are heavy laden, and I will give you rest.

   > **Matthew 11:29 (KJV)** Take my yoke upon you, and learn of me; for I am meek and lowly in heart: and ye shall find rest unto your souls.

   > **Matthew 11:30 (KJV)** For my yoke is easy, and my burden is light.

10. Every visit to those churches where the Word is not central exposes you to false teachings. These places, akin to dens of thieves, misleadingly suggest that your financial offerings to deceitful prophets dictate the extent of the LORD God's assistance!

11. It has been divinely disclosed to me to share the genuine Word of God with you, prompting me to write this book.

12. In a dream, I was approached by a multitude of people lamenting their hunger, sharing that they had been offered food they distrusted by some individuals. Among this crowd, I recognized a woman with whom I regularly engage in Bible study and prayer. She, too, voiced her concerns about the inadequacy of this "food." Initially, I interpreted this warning as a sign of a looming physical famine and began to pray for clarity. After consulting with another Bible teacher, the Holy Spirit clarified through him that the dream pointed not to a physical but a spiritual famine—the lack of the true Word of God. I admit, I am not righteous or sin-free, as **Romans 3:10-11** acknowledges. Yet, with fear and trembling, I strive for salvation through God's grace, knowing that the

Word is my guide to salvation, not the miracles or prophecies offered by others. As **2 Peter 1:20** emphasizes, "Above all, you must understand that no prophecy of Scripture came about by the prophet's own interpretation."

13. My goal through this book is to share the authentic Word of God with you. The more I teach or learn, the more I have a deep reservoir of the Word in me. – The Word of God is a deep Water!

14. My aim is to strengthen the Body of Christ, leading to the salvation of the faithful. Engaging with Scripture is the foundational step in enhancing your faith, fostering holiness, and promoting unity among believers.

15. My desire is to pass on "the knowledge" — specifically, the knowledge of God — to you, not for my own glorification but to magnify the presence of God's Word within me for the benefit of the saints.

16. I am thankful for you, recognizing you as a child of God, as long as you persist in adhering to His Word diligently and reverently.

17. I embarked on my first literary venture in Ghana while teaching at the Ada Teacher Training College, my alma mater. I am grateful to Mr. J.K Sagoe, the then Principal, who supported my aspiration to author a book upon recognizing the need for one: "A Handbook on Religious and Moral Education" (2001). His endorsement was invaluable, especially since the course on Religious & Moral Education was relatively novel in schools at the time, and there was a scarcity of resources on the subject. This book, marking my initial foray into authorship, served as a vital supplementary text for religious and moral education in educational institutions.

18. The years since my first publication in 2001 have spanned a significant hiatus, a period rich with life's lessons, maturity, and numerous challenges that have shaped my journey up to this point.

19. Currently, in 2022, in the United States, where the majority of my latest work has been completed, I am profoundly thankful to Rev. Prof. Peter Pryce, Ph.D., for his invaluable mentorship on various critical and sensitive topics, alongside our enlightening conversations focused on the Holy Bible

20. Since 2001, there has been a big gap from my initial book but this gap is filled with life experiences and maturity coupled with many adversities until now.

21. I must also express my heartfelt appreciation for the sacrifices, love, and support from my family: my wife, Rose Ashton Kpodzo, and my son, Sedem Kwami Kpodzo, along with Rev.Kosi Theodore Ani, for their direct involvement and contributions. Sedem,

your meticulous proofreading and insightful comments on the manuscript have been invaluable, shaping my viewpoints on various aspects of this book.

22. Rev. Prof. Peter Pryce, Ph.D., and my son Sedem have been instrumental in making this book not only scripturally sound but also accessible and engaging. Their consistent advice, comments, and suggestions, which I believe were divinely inspired, helped me find a balanced perspective and identify the most fitting Scriptures for my topics.

23. Their guidance illuminated that the Gospel of the LORD Jesus Christ is a challenge only to those who lack the Word of God in their hearts, minds, souls, and bodies.

> **Proverbs 24:9 (KJV)** The thought of foolishness *is* sin: and the scorner *is* an abomination to men.
>
> **Ecclesiastes 7:25 (KJV)** I applied mine heart to know, and to search, and to seek out wisdom, and the reason *of things*, and to know the wickedness of folly, even of foolishness *and* madness:
>
> **1 Corinthians 1:18 (KJV)** For the preaching of the cross is to them that perish foolishness; but unto us which are saved it is the power of God.
>
> **1 Corinthians 1:19 (KJV)** For it is written, I will destroy the wisdom of the wise, and will bring to nothing the understanding of the prudent.
>
> **1 Corinthians 1:20 (KJV)** Where *is* the wise? where *is* the scribe? where *is* the disputer of this world? hath not God made foolish the wisdom of this world?
>
> **1 Corinthians 1:21 (KJV)** For after that in the wisdom of God the world by wisdom knew not God, it pleased God by the foolishness of preaching to save them that believe.

I pray that this book serves not as a cause for offense but as a valuable instrument for imparting the Gospel of Christ Jesus. It is my hope that it acts as a comprehensive guide, accurately delineating the Word of truth to offer not offense but correction and guidance for your soul and spirit. May Jesus Christ accompany your spirit, endowing you with wisdom and understanding. Blessings to all of you!

**Mr. Charles E. Kpodzo**
BA Sociology and Religion,
M.Ed. Instructional Technology and
Information Systems Maryland, USA

# DEDICATION

This book is dedicated to my beloved parents, Mr. Emmanuel Yao Kpodzo and Mrs. Emily Yobla Kpodzo, nee Woyome, who are fondly remembered. To my dear Rose, and to my children, whose support and encouragement have been pivotal in bringing this project to completion.

The contributions of my immediate family members are no less significant than those of my deceased relatives. Indeed, without the successful groundwork laid by those who came before us, those present would have had no foundation to build upon. Thus, I hold each contribution in equal esteem and am deeply thankful to the LORD God Almighty for enabling everyone to make their unique and collective contributions to the life I lead today.

Reflecting on the genesis of this book, it becomes clear that the seeds were sown early on, spurred by the cherished memories of my mother devoutly reading the Holy Bible to me in my childhood, igniting my passion for the Scriptures from a tender age.

**2 Timothy 1:1 (KJV)** Paul, an apostle of Jesus Christ by the will of God, according to the promise of life which is in Christ Jesus,

**2 Timothy 1:2 (KJV)** To Timothy, *my* dearly beloved son: Grace, mercy, *and* peace, from God the Father and Christ Jesus our Lord.

**2 Timothy 1:3 (KJV)** I thank God, whom I serve from *my* forefathers with pure conscience, that without ceasing I have remembrance of thee in my prayers night and day;

**2 Timothy 1:4 (KJV)** Greatly desiring to see thee, being mindful of thy tears, that I may be filled with joy;

**2 Timothy 1:5 (KJV)** When I call to remembrance the unfeigned faith that is in thee, which dwelt first in thy grandmother Lois, and thy mother Eunice; and I am persuaded that in thee also.

**2 Timothy 1:6 (KJV)** Wherefore I put thee in remembrance that thou stir up the gift of God, which is in thee by the putting on of my hands.

**2 Timothy 1:7 (KJV)** For God hath not given us the spirit of fear; but of power, and of love, and of a sound mind.

**2 Timothy 1:8 (KJV)** Be not thou therefore ashamed of the testimony of our Lord, nor of me his prisoner: but be thou partaker of the afflictions of the gospel according to the power of God;

Echoing the legacy of Grandmother Lois and Mother Eunice, Mrs. E. Y. Kpodzo succeeded in imparting the Spirit and Light of the testimony of our Lord and Savior Jesus Christ to me. Today, after many years, I am a testament to her faithfulness, safeguarded by the Word of God.

Mrs. E. Y. Kpodzo fulfilled the divine mandate given to every devoted mother: to teach the Word of God to their children. She faithfully carried out the Lord's work without falter. A vivid memory that stands out to me is of a night returning from the hospital. We found ourselves on a dark, intimidating path. As a child, I was terrified of the night's darkness, but my mother reassured me, urging me not to fear. She promised that prayer would protect us, and as she began to recite **Psalm 23**, she encouraged me to follow her words. Together, we recited these verses, finding our way through the darkness with faith as our guide.

i. **Psalm 23:1 (KJV)** A Psalm of David. The LORD *is* my shepherd; I shall not want.

ii. **Psalm 23:2 (KJV)** He maketh me to lie down in green pastures: he leadeth me beside the still waters.

iii. **Psalm 23:3 (KJV)** He restoreth my soul: he leadeth me in the paths of righteousness for his name's sake.

iv. **Psalm 23:4 (KJV)** Yea, though I walk through the valley of the shadow of death, I will fear no evil: for thou *art* with me; thy rod and thy staff they comfort me.

v. **Psalm 23:5 (KJV)** Thou preparest a table before me in the presence of mine enemies: thou anointest my head with oil; my cup runneth over.

vi. **Psalm 23:6 (KJV)** Surely goodness and mercy shall follow me all the days of my life: and I will dwell in the house of the LORD for ever.

Following my mother's guidance, I found that my fear swiftly dissipated, and I no longer dwelled on the potential dangers that might lurk within the shadows of those dark paths. For this act of faith and countless others, may the Good LORD hold her in eternal remembrance!

**Proverbs 31:1 (KJV)** The words of king Lemuel, the prophecy that his mother taught him.

**Proverbs 31:2 (KJV)** What, my son? and what, the son of my womb? and what, the son of my vows?

**Proverbs 31:3 (KJV)** Give not thy strength unto women, nor thy ways to that which destroyeth kings.

Encouraged by my mother, I began attending the weekly meetings of the Christian Youth Builders (**C.Y.B.**) alongside my older siblings, leading to my early membership in the group—a rare exception to the usual age requirements. Initially, my brothers were resistant to my mother's insistence, often trying to dissuade me from joining them, believing I didn't belong there at that time. Despite their reluctance, and although both of my parents served as church elders, with my father also being a preacher, it was my mother who truly mentored me. She demonstrated through her actions the importance of a Christian's daily commitment to engaging with the Word of God.

My mother's dedication to reading the Bible was particularly memorable, even more so than my father's, who often read in preparation for his sermons. My mother, a trader by profession, saw reading the Word of God not just as a duty but as a calling, setting an example that remains worth following for mothers everywhere today.

I firmly believe that my upbringing in the Holy Scriptures, guided by my parents, was not mere coincidence but divinely ordained. Their influence has led me to walk in the footsteps of those remembered with fondness and reverence, such as my dear parents.

**Ephesians 1:3 (KJV)** Blessed *be* the God and Father of our Lord Jesus Christ, who hath blessed us with all spiritual blessings in heavenly *places* in Christ:

**Ephesians 1:4 (KJV)** According as he hath chosen us in him before the foundation of the world, that we should be holy and without blame before him in love:

**Ephesians 1:5 (KJV)** Having predestinated us unto the adoption of children by Jesus Christ to himself, according to the good pleasure of his will,

**Ephesians 1:6 (KJV)** To the praise of the glory of his grace, wherein he hath made us accepted in the beloved.

This book stands as a vibrant tribute to the memory of my parents, Mr. Emmanuel Yao Kpodzo and Mrs. Emily Yobla Kpodzo, nee Woyome, whose legacies continue to inspire.

# ABOUT THE AUTHOR

Charles Kpodzo,
BA Sociology and Religion,
M.Ed. Instructional Technology and Information Systems

Mr. Charles Kpodzo is a distinguished individual known for his commitment to education, instructional technology and community service. Holding a Bachelor of Arts in Sociology and Religion, as well as a Master of Education with specialization in Instructional Technology and Information Systems from Strayer University in Washington, DC., he has amassed over 18 years of experience as Instructional Technology Consultant.

Throughout his career, Mr. Kpodzo has shown a deep dedication to education and instructional methodologies, His undergraduate studies laid the foundation for his first significant accomplishment- a handbook on Religious and Moral Education. He has also been an esteem educator for more than 28 years.

In 2007, Mr. Kpodzo assumed the role of President and Chief Executive Officer at Starlinx Group of Companies, under his leadership, the company has successfully addressed safety concerns through collaborative efforts, notably partnering with Tajintech Inc in 2010. His passion for problem-solving, especially in the realm of driver safety and wellness programs.

Mr. Kpodzo has played a pivotal role in organized commercial and non-commercial Driving Consultancy Fora and Seminars, showcasing his expertise in Instructional Management. His contributions have been widely recognized and acknowledged, particularly in collaborative initiatives within the Driver Education, Transportation and Counselling Services sectors in Maryland, Virginia, and Washington, DC., as well as with various State Agencies.

Currently serving as President and Chief Executive Officer of Starlinx Group LLC in the United States of America (USA), Mr. Kpodzo oversees the performance measurement, strategic planning process development, marketing systems and data analysis. His strategic vision and planning process aim to optimize resources for emerging instructional technologies and enhance safety standards.

In addition to his professional accomplishment, Mr. Kpodzo remains dedicated to his faith and community. A devoted Christian and also the director of Christian Sunday Podcast who teaches the Bible to edify the body of Christ and to advance God's kingdom. With a career spanning nearly three decades, Mr. Kpodzo consistently demonstrates his ability to assess individuals and community needs through teaching and learning. He is a Teacher of the Word of God first, and a teacher by profession. He believed that, any gift of God must first be used to His Glory. He wants to fulfil his calling and purpose of God in his life in the service of God and humanity.

# Table of Contents

# FOREWORD

Pastor Charles Edem Kpodzo and I first met in a church and in several years after that, we have collaborated in several topics relating to the Holy Bible, to doctrines, to church functionality, to church management, and to Pastoral Education and Training in the Word of God.

That would be a broad summary to characterize out varied interactions over the years. From the beginning of our relationship, Pastor Charles Kpodzo has been very keen on identifying what was wrong in church leadership, church doctrines, and church administration, with the hope of doing what was right by the Word of God:

> **1 Corinthians 14:29 (KJV)** Let the prophets speak two or three, and let the other judge.

> **Proverbs 29:17 (KJV)** Correct thy son, and he shall give thee rest; yea, he shall give delight unto thy soul.

> **1 Corinthians 14:12 (KJV)** Even so ye, forasmuch as ye are zealous of spiritual *gifts*, seek that ye may excel to the edifying of the church.

> **1 Corinthians 14:26 (KJV)** How is it then, brethren? when ye come together, every one of you hath a psalm, hath a doctrine, hath a tongue, hath a revelation, hath an interpretation. Let all things be done unto edifying.

> **2 Corinthians 12:19 (KJV)** Again, think ye that we excuse ourselves unto you? we speak before God in Christ: but *we do* all things, dearly beloved, for your edifying.

> **Ephesians 4:12 (KJV)** For the perfecting of the saints, for the work of the ministry, for the edifying of the body of Christ:

> **Ephesians 4:29 (KJV)** Let no corrupt communication proceed out of your mouth, but that which is good to the use of edifying, that it may minister grace unto the hearers.

> **1 Timothy 1:4 (KJV)** Neither give heed to fables and endless genealogies, which minister questions, rather than godly edifying which is in faith: *so do*.

One of the spiritual experiences that have characterized my relationship with Pastor Charles Kpodzo is the way Holy Spirit has been confirming things that I have said to him right from the early days of our relationship:

1. When I told Pastor Charles Kpodzo that a Prophet that we both knew was a false Prophet, the LORD God confirmed that message to him in several dreams that I never knew of and which he himself did not tell me at the time.

2. When I told Pastor Charles Kpodzo that we are living in the days of a strong famine of the Word of God, Holy Spirit revealed the same message to him in his dream.

3. When I explained the Word of God to Pastor Charles Kpodzo in our consultation hour, Holy Spirit confirmed to him in his dreams, that same Word that I had given to him earlier.

4. When Pastor Charles Kpodzo asked me how many books I was buying for him, thinking that they were just 2 book, and I told him that it was a surprise and did not tell him the number of books, Holy Spirit revealed the exact number of the 12 books that I had bought for him and even the invoice of the purchased books, and when he asked me whether I was buying 12 books for him, because he said that he saw it in his dream I myself was shocked to learn that what I was hiding from him, Holy Spirit already revealed it to him in a dream!

5. About 3 years, the LORD God had shown me a vision in a dream of a beautifully furnished studio where I sat and taught the Word of God and did Bible Q and A with audiences around the world. Now Pastor Charles Kpodzo did not know anything about this vision because

   I never told him, yet he came one day and told me how the LORD has shown him to make ready a studio for the same work of the LORD!

One of the priceless blessings that the LORD Holy Spirit has blessed the relationship and spiritual collaboration between Pastor Charles Kpodzo and myself with, is called "Understanding".

Understanding of the Word of God is your Ticket to Heaven and if the LORD God does not give you understanding, then there is no way you can reach Heaven!

**Deuteronomy 29:4 (KJV)** Yet the LORD hath not given you an heart to perceive, and eyes to see, and ears to hear, unto this day.

**Proverbs 4:7 (KJV)** Wisdom *is* the principal thing; *therefore* get wisdom: and with all thy getting get understanding.

**Matthew 13:10 (KJV)** And the disciples came, and said unto him, Why speakest thou unto them in parables?

**Matthew 13:11 (KJV)** He answered and said unto them, Because it is given unto you to know the mysteries of the kingdom of heaven, but to them it is not given.

**Matthew 13:12 (KJV)** For whosoever hath, to him shall be given, and he shall have more abundance: but whosoever hath not, from him shall be taken away even that he hath.

**Matthew 13:13 (KJV)** Therefore speak I to them in parables: because they seeing see not; and hearing they hear not, neither do they understand.

**Matthew 13:14 (KJV)** And in them is fulfilled the prophecy of Esaias, which saith, By hearing ye shall hear, and shall not understand; and seeing ye shall see, and shall not perceive:

**Matthew 13:15 (KJV)** For this people's heart is waxed gross, and *their* ears are dull of hearing, and their eyes they have closed; lest at any time they should see with *their* eyes, and hear with *their* ears, and should understand with *their* heart, and should be converted, and I should heal them.

**Matthew 13:16 (KJV)** But blessed *are* your eyes, for they see: and your ears, for they hear.

**Matthew 13:17 (KJV)** For verily I say unto you, That many prophets and righteous *men* have desired to see *those things* which ye see, and have not seen *them*; and to hear *those things* which ye hear, and have not heard *them*.

Therefore, it is one thing to teach and to show a Man of God or a Pastor the Word of God, but it is entirely left to the LORD God Almighty to have mercy on that Pastor to give him understanding in the Word of God!

**Psalm 127:1 (KJV)** A Song of degrees for Solomon. Except the LORD build the house, they labour in vain that build it: except the LORD keep the city, the watchman waketh *but* in vain.

**Psalm 119:169 (KJV)** TAU. Let my cry come near before thee, O LORD: give me understanding according to thy word.

**Daniel 9:21 (KJV)** Yea, whiles I *was* speaking in prayer, even the man Gabriel, whom I had seen in the vision at the beginning, being caused to fly swiftly, touched me about the time of the evening oblation.

**Daniel 9:22 (KJV)** And he informed *me*, and talked with me, and said, O Daniel, I am now come forth to give thee skill and understanding.

**Acts 11:18 (KJV)** When they heard these things, they held their peace, and glorified God, saying, Then hath God also to the Gentiles granted repentance unto life.

**2 Timothy 2:7 (KJV)** Consider what I say; and the Lord give thee understanding in all things.

Hence, for this understanding, I remain eternally thankful unto the God of Heaven, that God has not let my work in the LORD to become fruitless, but has truly given understanding to Pastor

Charles Kpodzo in the Doctrines of the LORD Jesus Christ such that, what he did not know nor understand for 50 years of his life, he has now come to understand it and even preached it to others with confidence, no man despising him, but instead, all men and women to whom he has shared his new spiritual understanding of the Word of God, they have all received his teachings with amazement and gladness.

> **1 Timothy 4:12 (KJV)** Let no man despise thy youth; but be thou an example of the believers, in word, in conversation, in charity, in spirit, in faith, in purity.

> **Titus 2:15 (KJV)** These things speak, and exhort, and rebuke with all authority. Let no man despise thee.

Be that as it may, my only prayer is that in all things, let the Name of the LORD God be glorified, and may the LORD God bless a greater collaboration for both our Ministries, to the effectual teaching of the Gospel of the LORD Jesus Christ, for the saving of precious souls, and for edification of the Body of Christ:

If Pastor Charles Kpodzo has written to you in a book, so that your eyes may be open to the spiritual realities of the Gospel of the LORD Jesus Christ, it is because that is the right way: to write Holy Scriptures to teach the Word of the LORD Jesus Christ:

> **Acts 15:19 (KJV)** Wherefore my sentence is, that we trouble not them, which from among the Gentiles are turned to God:

> **Acts 15:20 (KJV)** But that we write unto them, that they abstain from pollutions of idols, and *from* fornication, and *from* things strangled, and *from* blood.

> **Acts 15:25 (KJV)** It seemed good unto us, being assembled with one accord, to send chosen men unto you with our beloved Barnabas and Paul,

> **Acts 15:26 (KJV)** Men that have hazarded their lives for the name of our Lord Jesus Christ.

> **Acts 15:27 (KJV)** We have sent therefore Judas and Silas, who shall also tell *you* the same things by mouth.

> **Acts 15:28 (KJV)** For it seemed good to the Holy Ghost, and to us, to lay upon you no greater burden than these necessary things;

> **Acts 16:4 (KJV)** And as they went through the cities, they delivered them the decrees for to keep, that were ordained of the apostles and elders which were at Jerusalem.

> **Acts 16:5 (KJV)** And so were the churches established in the faith, and increased in number daily.

> **Revelation 1:11 (KJV)** Saying, I am Alpha and Omega, the first and the last: and, What thou seest, write in a book, and send *it* unto the seven churches which are in

Asia; unto Ephesus, and unto Smyrna, and unto Pergamos, and unto Thyatira, and unto Sardis, and unto Philadelphia, and unto Laodicea.

In the spirit of understanding and unity, I would like to address those who follow the Christian faith. It is my hope that through reading this book, you may find enlightenment and spiritual growth, gaining deeper understanding in knowledge of our faith in Jesus Christ.

I implore those who may have strayed from the teaching of love and kindness, veering towards actions that contradict the true meaning of Christianity, to reflect upon their actions. It is my aspiration that this book provides clarity and guidance, helping all believers draw nearer to the truth of the gospel of our Lord and Savior Jesus.

Let us all strive to embody the teachings of Christianity, acknowledging the significance of gratitude and respect towards those who help us along our spiritual journey. By showing gratitude towards mentors, pastors or any guide in our lives is essential, as it encourages a spirit of thankfulness and humility.

In this light, I emphasize the importance of treating those who dedicated their lives to spreading the gospel message with the respect and support they deserve. Let us uphold the teaching of fairness and just compensation, as in Exodus 21:19 and 2 Corinthians 8:12-15, acknowledging the value of their efforts in bringing you closer to God.

**Exodus 21:19 (KJV)** If he rise again, and walk abroad upon his staff, then shall he that smote *him* be quit: only he shall pay *for* the loss of his time, and shall cause *him* to be thoroughly healed.

**Jeremiah 22:13 (KJV)** Woe unto him that buildeth his house by unrighteousness, and his chambers by wrong; *that* useth his neighbour's service without wages, and giveth him not for his work;

**2 Corinthians 8:12 (KJV)** For if there befirsta willing mind, *it is* accepted according to that a man hath, *and* not according to that he hath not.

**2 Corinthians 8:13 (KJV)** For *I mean* not that other men be eased, and ye burdened:

**2 Corinthians 8:14 (KJV)** But by an equality, *that* now at this time your abundance *may be a supply* for their want, that their abundance also may be *a supply* for your want: that there may be equality:

**2 Corinthians 8:15 (KJV)** As it is written, He that *had gathered* much had nothing over; and he that *had gathered* little had no lack.

If you know that this book has blessed you spiritually, then send a respectable gift of appreciation to Mr. Charles Kpodzo. By donating in one of his numerous projects of teaching the word of God: www.christiansunday.com

By Rev. Prof. Peter Pryce.

# PREFACE

In the tapestry of my life, woven with threads of faith and trials, my Christian journey commenced under the nurturing guidance of my beloved parents, Mr. and Mrs. E. Y. Kpodzo, esteemed Church Elders in the Evangelical Presbyterian Church. Their devout stewardship provided me with an invaluable foundation in Christianity, leading to my baptism and confirmation within this cherished community.

As a boy, I was imbued with a spirited zeal for the Lord's work, joining the ranks of the Christian Youth Builders (C.Y.B.). My involvement was marked by fervent participation in church activities, where I proudly represented my group in Bible Quizzes and Sword Bible Study Drill Competitions, a testament to my budding faith and dedication.

Yet, as the chapters of my life unfolded into early adulthood, I found myself adrift in a sea of worldly distractions, becoming a mere spectator in the house of God. My attendance waned, and the sacred scripture no longer held the central place in my daily life it once did.

Despite these wanderings, the grace of God—a beacon of kindness, mercy, and unwavering faithfulness—shepherded me through the wilderness of life's myriad challenges.

A crucible of sorrow catalyzed my reawakening to Christ's path: the successive loss of three beloved brothers—Marlon in August 2010, William in September, and Daniel in November—each departure a tempest rending my heart. This sorrowful period was not my first acquaintance with grief; the loss of Robert Kpodzo in 1990, a cherished sibling and my mother's dearest, heralded a decade of familial suffering, culminating in my mother's passing in 1995.

In this narrative of loss, I emerged as the sole surviving son, a testament, I believe, to divine preservation. Just as Moses was sequestered in the land of Midian, spared from Pharaoh's decree, so too was I shepherded to the sanctuary of America, shielded from spiritual desolation.

This preface to "Christianity Lost in Translation" is not merely an account of my journey but a homage to the resilience of faith through the trials and tribulations of life. It is a testament to the transformative power of divine grace, guiding a wayward son back to the sanctuary of His love and purpose.

> **Exodus 2:15 (KJV)** Now when Pharaoh heard this thing, he sought to slay Moses. But Moses fled from the face of Pharaoh, and dwelt in the land of Midian: and he sat down by a well.

**Psalm 83:1 (KJV)** A Song *or* Psalm of Asaph. Keep not thou silence, O God: hold not thy peace, and be not still, O God.

**Psalm 83:2 (KJV)** For, lo, thine enemies make a tumult: and they that hate thee have lifted up the head.

**Psalm 83:3 (KJV)** They have taken crafty counsel against thy people, and consulted against thy hidden ones.

**Isaiah 26:20 (KJV)** Come, my people, enter thou into thy chambers, and shut thy doors about thee: hide thyself as it were for a little moment, until the indignation be overpast.

**Isaiah 26:21 (KJV)** For, behold, the LORD cometh out of his place to punish the inhabitants of the earth for their iniquity: the earth also shall disclose her blood, and shall no more cover her slain.

The LORD God Almighty masterfully orchestrated the preservation of Jacob's lineage through a divinely guided plan involving Joseph, Jacob's son. Despite being sold into slavery by his brothers, Joseph's journey to Egypt was a strategic divine intervention. Rising to become Pharaoh's trusted advisor, Joseph's foresight in storing grain preempted the survival of Egypt and neighboring regions during a severe famine. Unbeknownst to his brothers, their quest for sustenance in Egypt was met by Joseph's God-guided provision. This act wasn't just about saving Joseph but was pivotal in ensuring the continuity of Jacob's descendants, fulfilling God's covenant with Abraham, Isaac, and Jacob, and setting the groundwork for Israel's future exodus. It showcases God's sovereign power to repurpose calamity into a vehicle for His blessings and purposes.

**Genesis 45:7 (KJV)** And God sent me before you to preserve you a posterity in the earth, and to save your lives by a great deliverance.

**Genesis 45:8 (KJV)** So now *it was* not you *that* sent me hither, but God: and he hath made me a father to Pharaoh, and lord of all his house, and a ruler throughout all the land of Egypt.

**Genesis 46:1 (KJV)** And Israel took his journey with all that he had, and came to Beer-sheba, and offered sacrifices unto the God of his father Isaac.

**Genesis 46:2 (KJV)** And God spake unto Israel in the visions of the night, and said, Jacob, Jacob. And he said, Here *am* I.

**Genesis 46:3 (KJV)** And he said, I *am* God, the God of thy father: fear not to go down into Egypt; for I will there make of thee a great nation:

**Genesis 46:4 (KJV)** I will go down with thee into Egypt; and I will also surely bring thee up *again*: and Joseph shall put his hand upon thine eyes.

Similarly, the LORD God shielded me from spiritual turmoil by leading me to refuge in America, where in the fullness of time, the world will recognize His work. I am deeply grateful to God Almighty for the path we have undertaken together. I seek His guidance and inspiration to fulfill His mission, in alignment with the truth and the teachings of the Holy Scriptures.

> **Matthew 28:18 (KJV)** And Jesus came and spake unto them, saying, All power is given unto me in heaven and in earth.

> **Matthew 28:19 (KJV)** Go ye therefore, and teach all nations, baptizing them in the name of the Father, and of the Son, and of the Holy Ghost:

> **Matthew 28:20 (KJV)** Teaching them to observe all things whatsoever I have commanded you: and, lo, I am with you alway, *even* unto the end of the world. Amen.

I am concerned that numerous individuals are drifting from the truth found in the Scriptures, misled by deceitful individuals influenced by darkness, who misuse the pulpit and distort the Scriptures to deceive many within the body of Christ through misinterpretation, deceit, and outright falsehoods. Let us return to the teachings and will of Christ, embracing His path once more!

> **Amos 8:11 (KJV)** Behold, the days come, saith the Lord GOD, that I will send a famine in the land, not a famine of bread, nor a thirst for water, but of hearing the words of the LORD:

> **2 Timothy 4:2 (KJV)** Preach the word; be instant in season, out of season; reprove, rebuke, exhort with all longsuffering and doctrine.

> **2 Timothy 4:3 (KJV)** For the time will come when they will not endure sound doctrine; but after their own lusts shall they heap to themselves teachers, having itching ears;

> **2 Timothy 4:4 (KJV)** And they shall turn away *their* ears from the truth, and shall be turned unto fables.

> **2 Timothy 4:5 (KJV)** But watch thou in all things, endure afflictions, do the work of an evangelist, make full proof of thy ministry.

How much can a person endure? The impact of these losses was profound, leaving everyone around me filled with fear, myself included. During this period of uncertainty, my father reached out to ensure I was managing. At the conclusion of our conversation, he imparted a reminder that resonated deeply: to remain steadfast in prayer.

This advice propelled me into a state of introspection, pondering my own mortality with the question, "Am I next?" Fear gripped me and I suddenly remembered one thing that I learned during my days in one of those Sword Bible Drills competitions surfaced, offering a glimmer of guidance through the darkness.

**Matthew 10:28 (KJV)** And fear not them which kill the body, but are not able to kill the soul: but rather fear him which is able to destroy both soul and body in hell.

Despite the overwhelming challenges, I resisted succumbing to despair or selfpity. Instead, I upheld an optimistic outlook and steadfast faith in God. My source of encouragement and direction was the Word of God, which I recalled from the Holy Bible:

**1 Samuel 30:6 (KJV)** And David was greatly distressed; for the people spake of stoning him, because the soul of all the people was grieved, every man for his sons and for his daughters: but David encouraged himself in the LORD his God.

Initially, I felt compelled to return to church attendance, which I promptly acted upon. However, it's crucial to clarify that merely attending church did not bring about my salvation. It was, instead, the Word of God that rescued me from my anguish, fear, and the looming shadow of death!

**Psalm 18:48 (KJV)** He delivereth me from mine enemies: yea, thou liftest me up above those that rise up against me: thou hast delivered me from the violent man.

**Psalm 34:19 (KJV)** Many *are* the afflictions of the righteous: but the LORD delivereth him out of them all.

**Psalm 97:10 (KJV)** Ye that love the LORD, hate evil: he preserveth the souls of his saints; he delivereth them out of the hand of the wicked.

**Proverbs 10:2 (KJV)** Treasures of wickedness profit nothing: but righteousness delivereth from death.

**Proverbs 11:4 (KJV)** "Riches profit not in the day of wrath: but righteousness delivereth from death."

**Psalm 107:20 (KJV)** He sent his word, and healed them, and delivered *them* from their destructions.

**John 8:32 (KJV)** And ye shall know the truth, and the truth shall make you free.

**John 8:36 (KJV)** If the Son therefore shall make you free, ye shall be free indeed.

I am deeply inspired to write this book on how Christians have lost their way in search of the truth by trusting fellow Christians, men and women, instead of trusting the Word of God:

**Psalm 119:42 (KJV)** So shall I have wherewith to answer him that reproacheth me: for I trust in thy word.

**Ephesians 1:13 (KJV)** In whom ye also *trusted*, after that ye heard the word of truth, the gospel of your salvation: in whom also after that ye believed, ye were sealed with that holy Spirit of promise,

In writing this second book, I have brought to bear my personal experience as a Christian in different churches as well as my professional and educational background to guide me to show how we have watered down the essence of being a Christian. Knowing full well now that, the **Word of God is our counsel and a deep water!**

ALSO, BY THE SAME AUTHOR

Charles Kpodzo **also authored:**

A Handbook on Religious and Moral Education, (2001)

BA Sociology, and Religion, M.Ed. Instructional Technology

- Currently in the works and coming out soon, **The Mighty Equalizer!**

# INTRODUCTION

## HOW TO UNDERSTAND THE TITLE OF THE BOOK

=====================

## FIAYI Ewe symbol of authority

========================

Deciphering the Meaning Behind the Book Title: "Christianity Lost in Translation – A Critical Look at Christianity" delves into:

1.  The term "Christianity" is not just a label; it signifies a profound religious tradition rooted in the teachings and life of Yeshua the Christ, known as Jesus Christ. This term encompasses the extensive array of doctrines and ethical teachings he introduced, shaping the faith and its practices.

    **John 7:16 (KJV)** Jesus answered them, and said, My doctrine is not mine, but his that sent me.

    **John 7:17 (KJV)** If any man will do his will, he shall know of the doctrine, whether it be of God, or *whether* I speak of myself.

    **Acts 26:28 (KJV)** Then Agrippa said unto Paul, Almost thou persuadest me to be a Christian.

    **1 Peter 4:16 (KJV)** Yet if *any man suffer* as a Christian, let him not be ashamed; but let him glorify God on this behalf.

2.  By stating that "Christianity is lost," we are echoing a truth already disclosed by the Lord Jesus Christ: no church in existence today fully aligns with the divine expectations set by God Almighty!

    **Revelation 1:10 (KJV)** I was in the Spirit on the Lord's day, and heard behind me a great voice, as of a trumpet,

**Revelation 1:11 (KJV)** Saying, I am Alpha and Omega, the first and the last: and, What thou seest, write in a book, and send it unto the seven churches which are in Asia; unto Ephesus, and unto Smyrna, and unto Pergamos, and unto Thyatira, and unto Sardis, and unto Philadelphia, and unto Laodicea.

**Revelation 3:2 (KJV)** Be watchful, and strengthen the things which remain, that are ready to die: for I have not found thy works perfect before God.

3. "Christianity" is considered lost also due to the revelation from the Lord God Almighty that every church across the globe today is marred by corruption and is metaphorically described as being unclean and overwhelmed with detestable practices, akin to being filled with filth and vomit.

**Isaiah 28:5 (KJV)** In that day shall the LORD of hosts be for a crown of glory, and for a diadem of beauty, unto the residue of his people,

**Isaiah 28:6 (KJV)** And for a spirit of judgment to him that sitteth in judgment, and for strength to them that turn the battle to the gate.

**Isaiah 28:7 (KJV)** But they also have erred through wine, and through strong drink are out of the way; the priest and the prophet have erred through strong drink, they are swallowed up of wine, they are out of the way through strong drink; they err in vision, they stumble in judgment.

**Isaiah 28:8 (KJV)** For all tables are full of vomit and filthiness, so that there is no place clean.

4. In the book's title, "Translation" symbolizes "Teaching"—it represents the crucial ministry of accurately conveying God's Word to nurture and build up the Body of Christ towards the salvation of believers. To translate, in this context, means to transfer the divine knowledge from one source to the recipient, where "knowledge" specifically refers to the understanding of God. Unfortunately, many preachers dilute or skew this knowledge to suit their audience, often interpreting significant biblical texts based on personal biases or motivations rather than faithful accuracy.

5. The emphasis on teaching and translating God's Word in this book is paramount because it is identified as the sole method, the exclusive path, and the unique spiritual cleanser capable of eradicating the vast array of sins and moral decay—such as corruption, deceit, falsehood, slander, gossip, sexual immorality, and betrayal—that pervade places of worship. This process of teaching and translating the Word of God is highlighted as the only effective means to purify the spiritual filthiness that afflicts churches worldwide.

**Isaiah 28:9 (KJV)** Whom shall he teach knowledge? and whom shall he make to understand doctrine? *them that are* weaned from the milk, *and* drawn from the breasts.

**Isaiah 28:10 (KJV)** For precept *must be* upon precept, precept upon precept; line upon line, line upon line; here a little, *and* there a little:

**Isaiah 28:11 (KJV)** For with stammering lips and another tongue will he speak to this people.

**Isaiah 28:12 (KJV)** To whom he said, This *is* the rest *wherewith* ye may cause the weary to rest; and this *is* the refreshing: yet they would not hear.

**Isaiah 28:13 (KJV)** But the word of the LORD was unto them precept upon precept, precept upon precept; line upon line, line upon line; here a little, *and* there a little; that they might go, and fall backward, and be broken, and snared, and taken.

**Isaiah 28:14 (KJV)** Wherefore hear the word of the LORD, ye scornful men, that rule this people which *is* in Jerusalem.

**Matthew 21:13 (KJV)** And said unto them, It is written, My house shall be called the house of prayer; but ye have made it a den of thieves.

**Mark 11:17 (KJV)** And he taught, saying unto them, Is it not written, My house shall be called of all nations the house of prayer? but ye have made it a den of thieves.

**Luke 19:45 (KJV)** And he went into the temple, and began to cast out them that sold therein, and them that bought;

**Luke 19:46 (KJV)** Saying unto them, It is written, My house is the house of prayer: but ye have made it a den of thieves.

6.  The question arises once more: Why does this book concentrate so intently on teaching and translation? The Word of God is likened to a vast ocean, rich and profound, embodying the counsel of God that demands precise and unadulterated teaching. It is through the Word of God, often referred to as the "offence of the cross," that true instruction occurs. This term captures the inherent challenge and confrontational nature of God's message, which, when faithfully conveyed, teaches and transforms.

    **Galatians 5:11** And I, brethren, if I yet preach circumcision, why do I yet suffer persecution? Then is the **offence of the cross ceased.**

7.  The exclusive mandate given by the Lord Jesus Christ to every authentic minister and man of God is the teaching of the Word of God. This directive stands as the singular, divinely-appointed task for those truly serving under the banner of Christ. It underscores the importance and centrality of disseminating God's teachings accurately and faithfully as the primary responsibility entrusted to genuine servants of the Christian faith.

    **Matthew 28:18 (KJV)** And Jesus came and spake unto them, saying, All power is given unto me in heaven and in earth.

**Matthew 28:19 (KJV)** Go ye therefore, and teach all nations, baptizing them in the name of the Father, and of the Son, and of the Holy Ghost:

**Matthew 28:20 (KJV)** Teaching them to observe all things whatsoever I have commanded you: and, lo, I am with you alway, *even* unto the end of the world. Amen.

8. The book's title explicitly signals our intent to scrutinize Christianity with a critical eye. This approach involves identifying, rebuking, and condemning sin within society, not based on personal opinions or thoughts, but through the lens of God's Word. This method aligns with the directive given by the Lord Jesus Christ, commanding us to use the scriptures as our guide for discernment and correction, thereby holding ourselves and others accountable to divine standards.

> **Leviticus 19:17 (KJV)** Thou shalt not hate thy brother in thine heart: thou shalt in any wise rebuke thy neighbour, and not suffer sin upon him.

> **1 Corinthians 14:29 (KJV)** Let the prophets speak two or three, and let the other judge.

> **1 Timothy 5:20 (KJV)** Them that sin rebuke before all, that others also may fear.

> **2 Timothy 4:2 (KJV)** Preach the word; be instant in season, out of season; reprove, rebuke, exhort with all longsuffering and doctrine.

> **Titus 1:13 (KJV)** This witness is true. Wherefore rebuke them sharply, that they may be sound in the faith;

> **Titus 2:15 (KJV)** These things speak, and exhort, and rebuke with all authority. Let no man despise thee.

> **Revelation 3:19 (KJV)** As many as I love, I rebuke and chasten: be zealous therefore, and repent.

# OPEN DIALOGUE

## FOR TODAY'S CHURCHES

## AND FOLLOWERS OF CHRIST

In this book, our aim is to foster an honest conversation among contemporary churches and disciples of Christ. Our goal is to examine Christianity through the lens of a believer, offering a new perspective on the teaching, interpretation, reception, and application of Christian doctrine, with the ultimate aim of returning to the core teachings of Christ.

The essence of Christianity has been compromised. Modern churches have eroded the very cornerstone of Christianity, which is the Truth as taught by the Lord Jesus Christ. What was once a physical foundation laid out in the Old Testament has transitioned into the spiritual foundation established by Jesus Christ in the New Testament.

> **Ezra 3:10 (KJV)** And when the builders laid the foundation of the temple of the LORD, they set the priests in their apparel with trumpets, and the Levites the sons of Asaph with cymbals, to praise the LORD, after the ordinance of David king of Israel.

> **Ezra 3:11 (KJV)** And they sang together by course in praising and giving thanks unto the LORD; because *he is* good, for his mercy *endureth* for ever toward Israel. And all the people shouted with a great shout, when they praised the LORD, because the foundation of the house of the LORD was laid.

> **1 Corinthians 3:9 (KJV)** For we are labourers together with God: ye are God's husbandry, *ye are* God's building.

> **1 Corinthians 3:10 (KJV)** According to the grace of God which is given unto me, as a wise masterbuilder, I have laid the foundation, and another buildeth thereon. But let every man take heed how he buildeth thereupon.

> **1 Corinthians 3:11 (KJV)** For other foundation can no man lay than that is laid, which is Jesus Christ.

Christians have acquiesced to the prevailing world order, surrendering the essence of what it means to follow Christ. In my view, Christianity has permitted the global system to overshadow its fundamental principles. We have entirely missed the mark. Our concessions to worldly religions and systems have fundamentally undermined the integrity of Christianity.

**John 8:12 (KJV)** Then spake Jesus again unto them, saying, I am the light of the world: he that followeth me shall not walk in darkness, but shall have the light of life.

**John 14:17 (KJV)** *Even* the Spirit of truth; whom the world cannot receive, because it seeth him not, neither knoweth him: but ye know him; for he dwelleth with you, and shall be in you.

**John 15:19 (KJV)** If ye were of the world, the world would love his own: but because ye are not of the world, but I have chosen you out of the world, therefore the world hateth you.

**Romans 12:2 (KJV)** And be not conformed to this world: but be ye transformed by the renewing of your mind, that ye may prove what *is* that good, and acceptable, and perfect, will of God.

**1 Corinthians 2:12 (KJV)** Now we have received, not the spirit of the world, but the spirit which is of God; that we might know the things that are freely given to us of God.

**1 John 2:16 (KJV)** For all that *is* in the world, the lust of the flesh, and the lust of the eyes, and the pride of life, is not of the Father, but is of the world.

The manner in which we observe our days of worship, our worship practices, and our religious celebrations have significantly diluted and diminished the Christian faith in contemporary times. I find myself bewildered, and I wonder if you feel the same. Our places of worship have been transformed into venues of entertainment rather than sanctuaries of devotion. The preaching and teaching of the Word have been sidelined, giving way to endeavors that prioritize profit over piety, turning congregants into mere financial resources for these deceptive leaders.

The current generations of Christians seem to have strayed far from their roots. As I delve into the Holy Bible, the disconnect between the teachings therein and the actions of today's Christians is stark. We have veered off the path leading to Christ. The entire Church of Christ is in dire need of purification, to cleanse itself of the falsehoods disseminated by deceitful preachers and those masquerading as servants of Christ Jesus, who have led many astray.

**Isaiah 28:7 (KJV)** But they also have erred through wine, and through strong drink are out of the way; the priest and the prophet have erred through strong drink, they are swallowed up of wine, they are out of the way through strong drink; they err in vision, they stumble *in* judgment.

**Isaiah 28:8 (KJV)** For all tables are full of vomit *and* filthiness, *so that there is* no place *clean*.

**Hosea 9:7 (KJV)** The days of visitation are come, the days of recompence are come; Israel shall know *it*: the prophet *is* a fool, the spiritual man *is* mad, for the multitude of thine iniquity, and the great hatred.

**Romans 16:17 (KJV)** Now I beseech you, brethren, mark them which cause divisions and offences contrary to the doctrine which ye have learned; and avoid them.

**Romans 16:18 (KJV)** For they that are such serve not our Lord Jesus Christ, but their own belly; and by good words and fair speeches deceive the hearts of the simple.

**Romans 16:19 (KJV)** For your obedience is come abroad unto all *men*. I am glad therefore on your behalf: but yet I would have you wise unto that which is good, and simple concerning evil.

**Romans 16:20 (KJV)** And the God of peace shall bruise Satan under your feet shortly. The grace of our Lord Jesus Christ *be* with you. Amen.

This is precisely the caution embedded within the Word of God: to distance ourselves from the charismatic, yet misleading figures who have risen to prominence within the church, leading the faithful astray. These individuals have ascended to the upper ranks of church leadership, commanding loyalty and allegiance not only from their direct followers but also from their emissaries, who, driven by financial gain, lavish them with honorifics like "My Father," "My Daddy," and even "My Lord." This dynamic reveals a troubling deviation from spiritual humility and accountability, as these titles and the reverence they imply place these leaders on pedestals far removed from the foundational teachings of Christ.

**Matthew 23:1 (KJV)** Then spake Jesus to the multitude, and to his disciples,

**Matthew 23:2 (KJV)** Saying, The scribes and the Pharisees sit in Moses' seat:

**Matthew 23:3 (KJV)** All therefore whatsoever they bid you observe, *that* observe and do; but do not ye after their works: for they say, and do not.

**Matthew 23:4 (KJV)** For they bind heavy burdens and grievous to be borne, and lay *them* on men's shoulders; but they *themselves* will not move them with one of their fingers.

**Matthew 23:5 (KJV)** But all their works they do for to be seen of men: they make broad their phylacteries, and enlarge the borders of their garments,

**Matthew 23:6 (KJV)** And love the uppermost rooms at feasts, and the chief seats in the synagogues,

**Matthew 23:7 (KJV)** And greetings in the markets, and to be called of men, Rabbi, Rabbi.

**Matthew 23:8 (KJV)** But be not ye called Rabbi: for one is your Master, *even* Christ; and all ye are brethren.

**Matthew 23:9 (KJV)** And call no *man* your father upon the earth: for one is your Father, which is in heaven.

**Matthew 23:10 (KJV)** Neither be ye called masters: for one is your Master, *even* Christ.

**Matthew 23:11 (KJV)** But he that is greatest among you shall be your servant.

**Matthew 23:12 (KJV)** And whosoever shall exalt himself shall be abased; and he that shall humble himself shall be exalted.

**Matthew 23:13 (KJV)** But woe unto you, scribes and Pharisees, hypocrites! for ye shut up the kingdom of heaven against men: for ye neither go in *yourselves*, neither suffer ye them that are entering to go in.

There is no justification for these religious leaders to disregard these basic principles of the commandments and seek, desire, or insist on being addressed as "Father" other than to assert dominance, sway, and govern the thoughts of their followers and congregations.

**Romans 8:16 (KJV)** The Spirit itself beareth witness with our spirit, that we are the children of God:

The verse in question unequivocally establishes our identity as children of God, with Him as our heavenly Father, leaving no room for confusion or dispute about the relationship of "a father and a child."

Claiming any child of God without a legal or biological basis is essentially a perilous act of impersonating God, as highlighted in **Malachi 2:10,** which questions why we betray our kin by violating the covenant of our ancestors when we all share one Father and Creator.

The concept of someone being my spiritual father raises the question: who then is his spiritual father? Does he assume the role of his own father or, by extension, that of the creator? The notion of spiritual paternity is not novel within Christianity, emphasizing that any such relationship should be Christ-centered. Any deviation serves merely to perpetuate dominance, control, and authority. If a pastor or prophet claims a closer connection to God than others, implying we must always seek them for divine guidance, this approach is fundamentally flawed.

Should we not consider ourselves God's children, then to whom do we belong? The use of Paul's reference to Timothy as "my son" by some preachers to support this flawed perspective overlooks the context of their bond, which was rooted in a personal affection through Christ and the transformative power of the Gospel.

Thus, the Lord God Almighty instructs us, following the teachings of Jesus Christ in **Matthew 23:1-13,** to avoid calling anyone on Earth our father or son, particularly when such titles are claimed by those who do not embody Christlike qualities or adhere to God's Word, much like the scribes and Pharisees whom Jesus rebuked.

However, when both the individual and the son adhere to the Word of God and live according to the righteousness of the Lord Jesus Christ, then a true, genuine, and correct "father-son relationship" that is recognized and approved by Heaven is formed. These are the proper standards for a "father-son relationship." The Scribes and Pharisees failed to meet these criteria, leading to their condemnation by the Lord Jesus Christ. In contrast, Apostle Paul and Timothy exemplified such a relationship, which is documented in the Holy Bible as a lesson and guide for us.

Nevertheless, when both the man and that son obey the Word of God and walk in the Righteousness of the LORD Jesus Christ, then a genuine, correct, and true "father-son relationship" that is acceptable in Heaven has been established! That are the correct criteria of "father-son relationship"! The Scribes and the Pharisees did not qualify to use that "father-son relationship" title so the LORD Jesus Christ condemned them! Apostle Paul and Timothy qualified to use that "father-son relationship" title so it is recorded in the Holy Bible for our admonition and teaching!

> **2 Timothy 3:16 (KJV)** All scripture *is* given by inspiration of God, and *is* profitable for doctrine, for reproof, for correction, for instruction in righteousness:

> **2 Timothy 3:17 (KJV)** That the man of God may be perfect, throughly furnished unto all good works.

Today, many religious leaders expect their colleagues, such as Associate Pastors, to view them as spiritual fathers. These leaders do not regard their associates as equals in ministry but rather as subordinates serving them and their families. Often, this dynamic is justified by the training, mentoring, and ordination provided by these senior figures, demanding loyalty and service in return.

Take, for instance, a scenario I am aware of where a self-proclaimed Prophet who had trained and ordained another pastor publicly declared that, according to a so-called divine message, the Assistant Pastor was obliged to serve him for thirteen years. This claim, lacking any scriptural backing, was false and unjust. It exemplifies a problematic expectation where newly ordained pastors are supposed to pledge their allegiance to their senior pastors or prophets, treating them as a father or even "Daddy" (Papa). This is an incorrect practice.

In personal relationships, it's common to refer to someone close as a brother, sister, son, or daughter, highlighting the depth of the connection. Such references symbolize the bond rather than stating a factual relationship, a concept that is also reflected in the Holy Scriptures.

> **2 Samuel 1:26 (KJV)** I am distressed for thee, my brother Jonathan: very pleasant hast thou been unto me: thy love to me was wonderful, passing the love of women.

David described Jonathan as a brother, not because of biological ties, but through a deep bond of friendship and covenant, illustrating their close relationship and mutual affection.

As Christians, we should emulate our Lord Jesus, approach the Bible with clarity and without baseless interpretations, and avoid actions that could discredit Christianity in the eyes of the world. Our teachings and daily conduct should mirror those of Jesus Christ, ensuring that we embody the principles we advocate to others.

**Matthew 5:19 (KJV)** Whosoever therefore shall break one of these least commandments, and shall teach men so, he shall be called the least in the kingdom of heaven: but whosoever shall do and teach *them*, the same shall be called great in the kingdom of heaven.

As a child of God, to safeguard against straying from the truth, it is crucial to personally study the Word of God, the Holy Bible, from Genesis to Revelation, in accordance with the commandments given to us by the Lord God.

**Proverbs 8:17 (KJV)** I love them that love me; and those that seek me early shall find me.

**2 Timothy 2:15 (KJV)** Study to shew thyself approved unto God, a workman that needeth not to be ashamed, rightly dividing the word of truth.

**2 Peter 3:18 (KJV)** But grow in grace, and in the knowledge of our Lord and Saviour Jesus Christ. To him be glory both now and for ever. Amen.

In this passage, the Lord Jesus communicates that by earnestly seeking Him with sincerity and affection, we are guaranteed to encounter Him. This pursuit of Christ is not merely about feeling love for Him but also involves a dedicated adherence to His commandments and teachings. These guidelines for living a life aligned with His will are detailed within His Gospel, offering a roadmap for those who wish to deepen their relationship with Him through understanding, obedience, and practice.

**Psalm 119:105 (KJV)** NUN. Thy word *is* a lamp unto my feet, and a light unto my path.

**John 14:15 (KJV)** If ye love me, keep my commandments.

**John 14:23 (KJV)** Jesus answered and said unto him, If a man love me, he will keep my words: and my Father will love him, and we will come unto him, and make our abode with him.

**John 14:24 (KJV)** He that loveth me not keepeth not my sayings: and the word which ye hear is not mine, but the Father's which sent me.

The paradox lies in our tendency to rely on Pastors and Prophets to interpret the Bible on our behalf, without taking the initiative to verify the accuracy of the teachings we receive from the pulpit, whether they are truthful or misleading. This lack of diligence in seeking the truth is a direct path to eternal damnation. Indeed, claiming the title of Christian while neglecting to engage with and understand the Word of God is a certain path to eternal judgment.

**Acts 17:11 (KJV)** These were more noble than those in Thessalonica, in that they received the word with all readiness of mind, and searched the scriptures daily, whether those things were so.

**Nehemiah 9:26 (KJV)** Nevertheless they were disobedient, and rebelled against thee, and cast thy law behind their backs, and slew thy prophets which testified against them to turn them to thee, and they wrought great provocations.

**Job 36:12 (KJV)** But if they obey not, they shall perish by the sword, and they shall die without knowledge.

**Proverbs 1:28 (KJV)** Then shall they call upon me, but I will not answer; they shall seek me early, but they shall not find me:

**Proverbs 1:29 (KJV)** For that they hated knowledge, and did not choose the fear of the LORD:

**Proverbs 1:30 (KJV)** They would none of my counsel: they despised all my reproof.

**Hosea 4:6 (KJV)** My people are destroyed for lack of knowledge: because thou hast rejected knowledge, I will also reject thee, that thou shalt be no priest to me: seeing thou hast forgotten the law of thy God, I will also forget thy children.

**2 Timothy 2:15 (KJV)** Study to shew thyself approved unto God, a workman that needeth not to be ashamed, rightly dividing the word of truth.

Therefore, it's essential to actively invest in our spiritual journey. We should diligently study the Holy Bible, engage in heartfelt prayer, worship God sincerely, and practice love towards our neighbors as we do ourselves. This proactive approach is key to nurturing a fulfilling and righteous path forward.

# WHY LOCK THE CHURCH BUILDINGS,

## OPEN THEM FOR WORSHIP!

Have you ever paused to contemplate the rationale behind our places of worship being frequently locked away, secured under locks and chains for the majority of the time? This situation serves as a poignant metaphor for the current state of Christian hearts and minds across the globe, which, it appears, are similarly secured and closed off. In contemporary times, it seems that many Christians have gravitated towards a form of worship that is largely ceremonial in nature.

This invites a deeper reflection on our approach to worship and the accessibility of our sacred spaces. The practice of keeping church buildings locked not only symbolizes a physical barrier but also reflects a broader spiritual and communal disconnect. It raises critical questions about the openness and availability of our faith communities to those in search of spiritual refuge and fellowship.

By advocating for the doors of our churches to remain open, we call for a reevaluation of how we embody the principles of faith, hospitality, and community. Opening the doors of our churches symbolizes an invitation to all, offering a welcoming space for worship, prayer, and connection at any time. This act of openness could foster a more engaged and spiritually vibrant community, encouraging continuous and accessible worship that extends beyond the confines of scheduled services and ceremonies.

The appeal to open our church doors transcends the mere desire for physical entry; it embodies a deeper summons to open our hearts and minds to the expansive teachings of our faith. This challenge compels us to embody the principles of Christianity in a manner that is welcoming, reachable, and mirrors a faith that actively engages with the world around us. This concept finds its roots in the biblical narrative found in the Gospel of John, where Jesus converses with the Samaritan woman at the well.

In this passage, Jesus elucidates that true worship transcends specific physical locations, such as mountains or Jerusalem, suggesting that genuine worship is about spirit and truth rather than bound to any singular sacred space (**John 4:21-24**). This teaching invites us to reconsider the purpose of our worship spaces. While we have constructed buildings to honor God, the essence of worship according to Jesus' teaching is not confined to these structures. Rather, it's about fostering a relationship with God that is vibrant, personal, and unbound by geographical or physical constraints.

Thus, by advocating for our churches to remain open, we are not merely seeking to keep the doors of a building unlocked; we are striving to live in alignment with Jesus' vision of worship that is accessible and inclusive for everyone, anywhere. This approach encourages a faith community that is open in both a literal and metaphorical sense, inviting all to partake in a living, breathing expression of faith that honors God not just in specific locations, but in the everyday actions and spaces of our lives.

> **Isaiah 29:13 (KJV)** Wherefore the Lord said, forasmuch as this people draw near *me* with their mouth, and with their lips do honour me, but have removed their heart far from me, and their fear toward me is taught by the precept of men:

> **Isaiah 29:14 (KJV)** Therefore, behold, I will proceed to do a marvellous work among this people, *even* a marvellous work and a wonder: for the wisdom of their wise *men* shall perish, and the understanding of their prudent *men* shall be hid.

> **Matthew 15:7 (KJV)** *Ye* hypocrites, well did Esaias prophesy of you, saying,

> **Matthew 15:8 (KJV)** This people draweth nigh unto me with their mouth, and honoureth me with *their* lips; but their heart is far from me.

> **Matthew 15:9 (KJV)** But in vain they do worship me, teaching *for* doctrines the commandments of men.

While various religious groups have made efforts to ensure their sacred spaces are accessible for followers to pray and worship at any time, Christian con-gregations often keep their places of assembly locked throughout the week, opening them only for a single day.

> **John 4:21 (KJV)** Jesus saith unto her, Woman, believe me, the hour cometh, when ye shall neither in this mountain, nor yet at Jerusalem, worship the Father.

Despite the teaching in **John 4:21** that worship is not confined to any specific location, this does not diminish the importance of treating our places of worship with reverence. As Christians, there is a call for us to invest more effort and resources into the upkeep and accessibility of our Houses of Christian Assembly.

The practice of allocating an entire building for worship and prayer, yet limiting its use to Sundays and certain special events, appears inconsistent. Worship transcends both time and place, capable of happening anytime and anywhere, even with just one or two people gathered.

> **Matthew 18:20 (KJV)** For where two or three are gathered together in my name, there am I in the midst of them.

We often give mere verbal acknowledgment to crucial aspects of our Christian journey. Fellow believers, the issue of when and how often to open our places of worship should not be a matter of contention. Ideally, there should be a policy of openness, barring instances where the property is inaccessible to us.

Moreover, if we possess the building that serves as our worship space, we should strive to ensure its availability to any worshiper at any time of the day, emulating the practices observed during the Apostolic Age.

> **Acts 5:42 (KJV)** And daily in the temple, and in every house, they ceased not to teach and preach Jesus Christ.

In light of **John 4:21-24**, where Jesus teaches that true worship is not confined to any particular location but is a matter of spirit and truth, it's perplexing to see the varied accessibility of religious spaces. While shrines, mosques, temples, and synagogues often welcome visitors with open doors, many Christian places of worship, such as chapels and cathedrals, remain locked outside of service times. Despite criticisms leveled by some within the Pentecostal and evangelical communities towards the Catholic Church, one commendable aspect is the accessibility of places like the Basilica, which typically remain open to all.

In smaller communities, Roman Catholic churches and their clergy are known for their openness and hospitality. This reality was part of my own experience growing up, where mission schools operated by the church were more accessible than their secular counterparts.

Contrastingly, certain segments of today's church, particularly within the Pentecostal movement, appear to have shifted away from a mission-focused approach that includes caring for the needy. An illustrative example occurred in 2020 in Houston, USA, when a mega-church, despite the severe natural disasters causing widespread homelessness in its vicinity, did not open its doors to provide shelter to those in need. This incident underscores a departure from the church's potential role as a sanctuary and support for the community, especially in times of crisis.

Moreover, the tendency of these churches not to engage in educational initiatives, open their worship spaces to strangers and worshippers beyond Sunday services, or conduct outreach programs without the presence of media for self-promotion, highlights a need for reflection on what it means to live out the teachings of Jesus in the context of **John 4:21-24**. Amidst the distractions and challenges of our time, those who still find solace and connection in the physical church environment should have the opportunity to seek it, reinforcing the church's role as a place of refuge, worship, and community engagement.

> **Matthew 6:3 (KJV)** But when thou doest alms, let not thy left hand know what thy right hand doeth:

> **Matthew 6:4 (KJV)** That thine alms may be in secret: and thy Father which seeth in secret himself shall reward thee openly.

The practice of erecting educational institutions, such as universities, by some churches only to set tuition fees at exorbitant rates, excludes the majority of their own congregants who cannot afford such costs, favoring instead the affluent. This starkly illustrates how the church has drifted from its foundational principle of community.

Moreover, the notion of opening places of worship not as a means to collect tithes and offerings but as an act of community service seems lost. Instead, a significant portion of church resources is channeled towards extravagant expenditures like private jets, opulent residences, luxury vehicles, and lavish decorations for their stages, misleadingly referred to as altars. This misallocation underscores a growing preoccupation with wealth, fame, and materialism within the church, marking a departure from its core mission of serving and uniting the community.

> **1 Peter 3:3 (KJV)** Whose adorning let it not be that outward *adorning* of plaiting the hair, and of wearing of gold, or of putting on of apparel;

> **1 Peter 3:4 (KJV)** But *let it be* the hidden man of the heart, in that which is not corruptible, *even the ornament* of a meek and quiet spirit, which is in the sight of God of great price.

A conversation with a pastor friend revealed an intriguing justification for why churches often remain locked, which I found quite revealing. He explained that the primary concern lies in protecting the valuable items within the building. This rationale subtly suggests a shift in priorities, where the emphasis on material assets within the church premises outweighs the focus on both the act of worship and the worshippers themselves.

This perspective is somewhat at odds with biblical teachings, which emphasize the spiritual over the material. For instance, **Matthew 6:19-21** encourages believers to store up treasures in heaven rather than on earth, highlighting the impermanence of material wealth compared to the enduring nature of spiritual riches. Similarly, the early church, as described in Acts 2:44-47, shared everything they had, prioritizing community and spiritual fellowship over possessions.

The implication that property and valuables take precedence over the church's primary mission of fostering a vibrant community of faith raises questions about our modern-day interpretation of what it means to be a church. It seems we may need to re-evaluate our priorities to ensure they align more closely with the teachings and example of Christ, who valued people over possessions.

> **Acts 20:28 (KJV)** Take heed therefore unto yourselves, and to all the flock, over the which the Holy Ghost hath made you overseers, to feed the church of God, which he hath purchased with his own blood.

The utilization of church buildings presents a striking paradox; despite being prime real estate, they are among the most underused properties, largely due to their limited operational hours. Typically, these buildings open their doors for worship only on Sundays, and promptly close once services conclude. This practice inconveniences worshippers who may need to retrieve personal belongings left behind, often requiring them to wait until the following Sunday or to make special arrangements for access. While some larger churches, equipped with paid staff, might offer limited additional open hours, the issue remains widespread.

The manner in which we regard and use our worship spaces warrants a deeper reflection. Sacred by definition, places of worship are intended for prayer and reverence. Yet, modern Christian practice often sees these spaces hosting a variety of social functions, from birthday celebrations for pastors and their spouses—referred to informally as "first ladies"—to Father's Day and Mother's Day events aimed at soliciting gifts from the congregation. Such activities challenge the traditional view of sanctity and purpose of these spaces, which is at odds with Jesus Christ's example, who is never recorded in the Holy Scriptures as having used a synagogue for personal celebrations or to receive gifts.

This departure from a focus on worship and prayer towards accommodating secular activities within sacred spaces suggests a shift in how reverence for God is expressed in contemporary Christian practice. Other religious traditions maintain a strict dedication of their worship spaces solely for prayer and worship, highlighting a stark contrast in the approach to reverence and sanctity.

Moreover, the broader issue of how Christians attribute events in their lives reflects a misunderstanding of God's sovereignty. The tendency to credit successes to oneself and blame failures or misfortunes on Satan overlooks the omniscience and omnipotence of God. This habit disregards the biblical teaching that God's will is paramount and that He permits both good and bad events for His purposes. The frequent misattribution to Satan not only misrepresents the nature of spiritual warfare but also diminishes the recognition of God's ultimate authority over all aspects of life, challenging us to reconsider our understanding and acknowledgment of God's omnipresent role in our lives.

> **Proverbs 15:3 (KJV)** The eyes of the LORD are in every place, beholding the evil and the good.

This underscores the demonstration of God's dominion over both benevolence and malevolence. It serves as a reminder of the importance of moderating the emphasis we place on Satan when discussing the trials, we encounter in life.

Often, prayer becomes a tool employed by many Christians solely during times of need, a means to petition God for solutions. Upon receiving the desired outcome, the habit of attributing success to personal efforts emerges, with phrases like "I did this and that" overshadowing the acknowledgment of God's intervention. Such an attitude fails to honor God with gratitude, a neglect that constitutes ingratitude, which the Lord God will ultimately address.

This is the testament of God's power over good and evil. This is why we must be careful how much reverence we give to Satan in our conversations and testimonies about our life's challenges.

# FASTING

Fasting serves as a personal act of devotion, where individuals choose to abstain from food and drink as a form of spiritual sacrifice. It's often practiced by many Christians as a way to deepen their spiritual discipline. However, it's crucial to understand the motivation behind fasting. Rather than fasting simply because it is demanded by a church leader or because it is a widespread practice within one's religious community, the decision to fast should be a personal one. The essence of fasting, as highlighted in the Bible, is to engage in worship that is genuine and rooted in truth. Fasting, influenced by directives from religious leaders without personal conviction, may not yield the spiritual benefits one seeks.

In the context of biblical teachings, fasting was indeed a requirement under the Old Testament laws. Yet, with the death and resurrection of Jesus Christ, the emphasis shifted. While Christians living under the grace of the New Testament are not explicitly commanded to fast, the practice is nonetheless encouraged as a means to foster spiritual growth. It's important to approach fasting with the right heart and intentions, aiming for a sincere connection with God. When done with honesty and guided by the Holy Spirit, fasting can be a powerful tool for accelerating one's spiritual journey.

> **Matthew 9:14 (KJV)** Then came to him the disciples of John, saying, Why do we and the Pharisees fast oft, but thy disciples fast not?

> **Matthew 9:15 (KJV)** And Jesus said unto them, Can the children of the bridechamber mourn, as long as the bridegroom is with them? but the days will come, when the bridegroom shall be taken from them, and then shall they fast.

> **Mark 2:20 (KJV)** But the days will come, when the bridegroom shall be taken away from them, and then shall they fast in those days.

> **Luke 5:35 (KJV)** But the days will come, when the bridegroom shall be taken away from them, and then shall they fast in those days.

**Matthew 9:14-15** underscores fasting as a spiritual practice, intertwining prayer with personal sacrifice to foster spiritual strength and combat sin. The true essence of fasting lies in its initiation and conclusion based on one's own spiritual quest, rather than following the directives of others. Such an approach ensures that the sacrifice of fasting aligns with the individual's spiritual intentions.

Jesus Christ's sacrifice has already provided atonement for our sins, offering us a path to redemption through repentance and embracing the sacrifice made on our behalf. The act of fasting, when undertaken with a clear understanding of its spiritual significance, offers profound benefits. It aligns us with the truth of our purpose in fasting, enhancing our spiritual well-being.

Apostle Paul, in his epistles, advocates for a broader understanding of abstention, suggesting that beyond refraining from food and drink, we should also consider abstaining from physical indulgences such as sexual activities and the consumption of alcohol. However, it's crucial to recognize that Paul's guidance comes as counsel rather than a mandate, highlighting the importance of personal conviction and the voluntary nature of such sacrifices in our spiritual journey.

> **1 Corinthians 7:5 (KJV)** Defraud ye not one the other, except *it be* with consent for a time, that ye may give yourselves to fasting and prayer; and come together again, that Satan tempt you not for your incontinency.

> **1 Corinthians 7:6 (KJV)** But I speak this by permission, *and* not of commandment.

Therefore, my fellow believers, let us not blindly follow practices without understanding their impact on our spiritual growth, particularly when it comes to fasting. As we embark on this spiritual discipline, let us heed the guidance of our Lord Jesus, who provides clear instructions on how to fast with a heart aligned towards God. Recall the words of Jesus in Matthew 6:16-18, where He instructs us not to fast with a somber demeanor for the sake of appearances, but to fast in a manner that is not obvious to others, for our Father who sees what is done in secret will reward us. This teaching underscores the importance of fasting as a deeply personal act of devotion, not for the validation of others, but as a sincere gesture of our faith and desire for spiritual nourishment. Let our fasting be a testament to our commitment to seek God's presence and guidance in our lives, embodying the principles taught by Jesus and fostering a deeper, more intimate relationship with our Creator.

> **Matthew 6:16 (KJV)** Moreover when ye fast, be not, as the hypocrites, of a sad countenance: for they disfigure their faces, that they may appear unto men to fast. Verily I say unto you, They have their reward.

> **Matthew 6:17 (KJV)** But thou, when thou fastest, anoint thine head, and wash thy face;

> **Matthew 6:18 (KJV)** That thou appear not unto men to fast, but unto thy Father which is in secret: and thy Father, which seeth in secret, shall reward thee openly.

Consider the scenario where, during a church service, it's announced that the congregation is to embark on a fasting period of seven or forty days. One might question, "Based on whose authority or decision is this mandate given?" Faith, by its very nature, is deeply personal. Thus, if you find yourself coerced into fasting due to a decision made by the church board—a decision perhaps made without your input—or if you're directed to do so by church leadership, such as a Pastor, Teacher, Prophet, Evangelist, Bishop, or Apostle, this approach misses the mark. It strays from biblical teachings and the essence of what fasting should represent. Leveraging the Word of God to serve hidden agendas under the guise of spiritual discipline is a grave misstep. Fasting is intended to be a voluntary, spiritual, and personal commitment. Engaging in this sacred act ought to stem from individual conviction and a genuine desire to deepen one's spiritual connection, rather than from external pressures or mandates.

**Romans 1:18 (KJV)** For the wrath of God is revealed from heaven against all ungodliness and unrighteousness of men, who hold the truth in unrighteousness;

# THE DOCTRINE OF LOVING ONE ANOTHER

One of the core teachings of Jesus is the commandment to love one another, a principle that, unfortunately, seems challenging for many within the Christian community. It's not uncommon to observe discord and animosity among church members, between leaders, and even in the broader Christian fellowship, with some individuals paradoxically invoking prayers for the downfall of their adversaries while simultaneously seeking to experience God's love in their lives.

This dichotomy presents a profound spiritual challenge. Consider the profound act of extending love and prayers towards those who wish us harm or actively seek our downfall. Embracing this level of forgiveness and unconditional love mirrors the journey Jesus undertook. Bearing the cross was no easy feat for Christ; it symbolized a path of immense suffering, leading to His crucifixion, resurrection, and ultimately, offering us the gift of salvation. This act of supreme sacrifice and love serves as a powerful reminder of the depth of love and forgiveness we are called to embody in our own lives, even in the face of persecution or hostility.

> **Matthew 5:44 (KJV)** But I say unto you, Love your enemies, bless them that curse you, do good to them that hate you, and pray for them which despitefully use you, and persecute you;

> **Mark 8:34 (KJV)** And when he had called the people *unto him* with his disciples also, he said unto them, Whosoever will come after me, let him deny himself, and take up his cross, and follow me.

Some individuals within the Christian community, encompassing both leaders and followers, find reasons to withhold love from certain people, despite the clear teachings of Jesus Christ on love. They anchor their stance on specific interpretations of the Bible, asserting that they are divinely mandated, even to the extent of praying for the demise of others. They often cite passages such as **Exodus 22:18** and **Luke 19:27** to support their claims. This perspective seeks to legitimize their actions through scripture, suggesting a misalignment with the broader, foundational message of love and forgiveness that is central to the teachings of Jesus.

> **Exodus 22:18 (KJV)** Thou shalt not suffer a witch to live.

> **Luke 19:27 (KJV)** But those mine enemies, which would not that I should reign over them, bring hither, and slay *them* before me.

Fellow believers, can we truly reconcile the nature of the Lord God with the notion of contradicting His own word, thereby justifying our misunderstandings of scripture? How can we align the commandment "Thou shalt not kill" with the idea that God might instruct us to do the opposite and harm our adversaries? This raises a profound question: would a God who is known for His consistency and clarity ever promote such a contradictory teaching, especially considering that creating confusion is not in His nature?

> **1 Corinthians 14:33 (KJV)** For God is not *the author* of confusion, but of peace, as in all churches of the saints.

From the discussion above, it becomes apparent that the issue at hand stems from a lack of understanding among certain Christians, Pastors, and Prophets who advocate for prayers against their enemies' lives. The question then arises: How do we address this gap in spiritual knowledge?

The answer lies in providing comprehensive education on the true teachings of the Bible, thereby enabling believers, church leaders, and spiritual guides to attain a more accurate interpretation.

Consider the commandment, "Thou shalt not suffer a witch to live." It's intriguing to note that the term "witch" is mentioned only twice throughout the entirety of the Bible, and "witchcraft" is referenced just three times. This fact alone invites a deeper examination of the context and meaning behind these mentions, underscoring the importance of a nuanced understanding of scripture.

> **Exodus 22:18 (KJV)** Thou shalt not suffer a witch to live.

> **Deuteronomy 18:10 (KJV)** There shall not be found among you *any one* that maketh his son or his daughter to pass through the fire, *or* that useth divination, *or* an observer of times, or an enchanter, or a witch,

> 1. **Samuel 15:23 (KJV)** For rebellion *is as* the sin of witchcraft, and stubbornness *is as* iniquity and idolatry. Because thou hast rejected the word of the LORD, he hath also rejected thee from *being* king.

> 2. **Chronicles 33:6 (KJV)** And he caused his children to pass through the fire in the valley of the son of Hinnom: also he observed times, and used enchantments, and used witchcraft, and dealt with a familiar spirit, and with wizards: he wrought much evil in the sight of the LORD, to provoke him to anger.

> **Galatians 5:20 (KJV)** Idolatry, witchcraft, hatred, variance, emulations, wrath, strife, seditions, heresies,

Did you know that the Bible does not provide explicit guidance on identifying a witch? This absence of instruction leads us to an important reflection. Given that the scripture does not delve deeply into the topic of witches, and considering that individuals accused of witchcraft do not typically announce their practices openly, it becomes clear that making such accusations could be misguided. Instead of focusing on identifying and condemning supposed witches, Christians are called to a higher purpose.

As believers, our approach should not be to seek the harm of those we suspect or label as enemies, including those accused of witchcraft. The Bible teaches us that vengeance is the Lord's domain, not ours. This principle, coupled with the commandment "Thou shalt not kill," underscores a vital truth: we are not to take judgment or retribution into our own hands.

In light of this, Christians are encouraged to seek a more compassionate and God-centered response. We should pray for God to work in the hearts of those we perceive as adversaries, asking Him to foster peace and reconciliation. Our prayers should also invite God to reveal His glory and wisdom in His own timing. By focusing on transformation and the unveiling of God's glory, we align ourselves with the teachings of Christ, who calls us to love our enemies and pray for those who persecute us. This approach not only adheres to the biblical commandments but also opens the way for God's transformative power to manifest in the lives of all individuals, leading us closer to the essence of Christian living.

> **Deuteronomy 32:35 (KJV)** To me *belongeth* vengeance, and recompence; their foot shall slide in *due* time: for the day of their calamity *is* at hand, and the things that shall come upon them make haste.

> **Deuteronomy 32:41 (KJV)** If I whet my glittering sword, and mine hand take hold on judgment; I will render vengeance to mine enemies, and will reward them that hate me.

> **Psalm 94:1 (KJV)** O LORD God, to whom vengeance belongeth; O God, to whom vengeance belongeth, shew thyself.

> **Luke 21:22 (KJV)** For these be the days of vengeance, that all things which are written may be fulfilled.

> **Hebrews 10:30 (KJV)** For we know him that hath said, Vengeance *belongeth* unto me, I will recompense, saith the Lord. And again, The Lord shall judge his people.

Thirdly, one must ponder the profound moral and spiritual implications of praying for the demise of others. Engaging in such prayers directly conflicts with the teachings of Romans **12:17-19** which explicitly admonishes believers not to repay evil for evil, but to live peaceably with all. The scripture further entrusts vengeance to God, stating, "Vengeance is mine; I will repay, saith the Lord." This passage underscores a fundamental Christian principle: the call to respond to wrongdoing with righteousness, leaving judgment to the divine.

By praying for someone's death, a believer steps into a territory that is reserved for God alone, thereby assuming a role that is neither granted nor endorsed by biblical teachings. Such actions not only contravene the explicit command to love our neighbors but also challenge the essence of divine justice, which teaches us that redemption and transformation are possible for all souls.

In light of this, it becomes clear that praying for the harm or death of another is incongruent with the life of sanctity and forgiveness to which Christians are called. This practice not only harbors the sin of harboring malice but also distances the believer from the path of grace and forgiveness outlined in the gospel. The invitation extended by **Romans 12:17-19** is to cultivate a heart of compassion, to overcome evil with good, and to commit oneself to the pursuit of peace and reconciliation, embodying the love and mercy at the heart of Christian doctrine.

> **Romans 12:17 (KJV)** Recompense to no man evil for evil. Provide things honest in the sight of all men.

> **Romans 12:18 (KJV)** If it be possible, as much as lieth in you, live peaceably with all men.

> **Romans 12:19 (KJV)** Dearly beloved, avenge not yourselves, but *rather* give place unto wrath: for it is written, Vengeance *is* mine; I will repay, saith the Lord.

Fourthly, addressing the adherence to **Exodus 22:18** and **Luke 19:27** while maintaining one's path towards salvation involves a significant shift in perspective. Instead of personally acting against those accused of witchcraft or praying for the demise of perceived enemies, the Christian response should be rooted in prayer for divine intervention in a manner that aligns with God's will.

The prayerful appeal to God should be reframed as: "Lord, let not Your enemies prevail; may Your justice be done through the power of Your word." This approach entrusts judgment entirely to God, recognizing His sovereignty and the divine prerogative to address wrongdoing. It emphasizes the believer's role as one of intercession rather than retribution, seeking God's righteous judgment rather than personal vengeance.

Such a stance not only ensures compliance with biblical mandates but also places the believer on a path consistent with Christian values of forgiveness, mercy, and trust in God's ultimate authority over justice. This method of prayer acknowledges God's capacity to transform hearts and situations, leaving the outcome to His omniscient and compassionate judgment, thus maintaining the integrity of one's spiritual journey towards eternity with Him.

> i. **Exodus 22:18 (KJV)** Thou shalt not suffer a witch to live.

> ii. **Luke 19:27 (KJV)** But those mine enemies, which would not that I should reign over them, bring hither, and slay them before me.

> iii. **Revelation 2:16 (KJV)** Repent; or else I will come unto thee quickly, and will fight against them with the sword of my mouth.

The Almighty Lord has assured us that He regards our adversaries as His own, reinforcing the message that, as His faithful followers, we should not diverge from His teachings by invoking harm upon those we suspect of malevolence, such as witches. This practice starkly contrasts with the guidance provided by the Scriptures, particularly the commandment against taking life, underscoring the importance of adhering to divine instructions over personal judgments.

In our quest to live in accordance with God's Word, it is imperative to renounce actions and intentions that contradict the essence of His teachings. The pathway to addressing our concerns about those who might wish us harm is not through prayers for their demise but through seeking God's intervention in a manner that aligns with His will and righteousness.

**Psalm 35:1-28** serves as a model prayer, advocating not for personal retribution but for divine justice and protection. It exemplifies how to call upon God to be our defender against those who seek to cause us harm, entrusting Him to deal justly with our adversaries. This approach keeps our hearts and actions in harmony with the spirit of God's commandments, fostering a life that reflects His love, mercy, and justice.

> **Psalm 35:1 (KJV)** *A Psalm* of David. Plead *my cause*, O LORD, with them that strive with me: fight against them that fight against me.

> **Psalm 35:2 (KJV)** Take hold of shield and buckler, and stand up for mine help.

> **Psalm 35:3 (KJV)** Draw out also the spear, and stop *the way* against them that persecute me: say unto my soul, I *am* thy salvation.

> **Psalm 35:4 (KJV)** Let them be confounded and put to shame that seek after my soul: let them be turned back and brought to confusion that devise my hurt.

> **Psalm 35:5 (KJV)** Let them be as chaff before the wind: and let the angel of the LORD chase *them*.

> **Psalm 35:6 (KJV)** Let their way be dark and slippery: and let the angel of the LORD persecute them.

Dear fellow Christian, it is not easy, but this love is the second most important commandment that makes all other commandments easy to follow. Apart from loving the Lord; your God with all your heart, soul, mind, and strength, along with cherishing your neighbor as yourself, represents a profound responsibility that we, as believers, must embrace with deep reverence and earnestness.

> **Mark 12:30 (KJV)** And thou shalt love the Lord thy God with all thy heart, and with all thy soul, and with all thy mind, and with all thy strength: this *is* the first commandment.

> **Mark 12:31 (KJV)** And the second *is* like, *namely* this, Thou shalt love thy neighbour as thyself. There is none other commandment greater than these.

In contemporary times, it's disheartening to observe Christians becoming adversaries to their fellow believers, despite God's clear instruction to not only love our neighbors but also to extend prayers for our enemies.

**Proverbs 16:7 (KJV)** When a man's ways please the LORD, he maketh even his enemies to be at peace with him.

If you encounter someone, even if they claim to be a prophet, instructing you to pray for the demise of your adversaries, respond by emphasizing that you believe in a God who has the power to transform the hearts of your enemies and that vengeance belongs solely to Him. Expressing love for your neighbor which includes friends, classmates, tribespeople, countrymen, and fellow believers means refraining from praying for their harm, contrary to what some leaders might advocate today. Such actions betray the essence of Christian teachings and include harmful behaviors that are unfortunately present in many congregations, such as:

**Spreading rumors about others.**
**Making false accusations against someone (Exodus 20:16). Engaging in deceitful dealings.**
**Lying (1 Peter 3:10).**
**Holding onto resentment (Ephesians 4:26).**
**Feeling jealous.**
**Speaking negatively about others (Ephesians 4:29).**
**Stealing.**
**Coveting what others have.**
**Inflicting harm.**

These behaviors, sadly, are not uncommon among Christians, sometimes even more prevalent within the church than outside it. Often, these issues are more intense among church leaders, fueled by guidance from those who should be shepherding their flock towards righteousness. Instead of fostering unity and love, some pastors and self-proclaimed prophets create divisions, advising caution against friends and family, inciting discord in marriages, and promoting a departure from humility.

Today's church community is too often characterized by pride, greed, selfish ambition, corruption, division, and a pursuit of materialism, far removed from the humble and loving lifestyle called for by Christianity. This shift away from the core values of faith highlights a need for a return to genuine, compassionate, and selfless Christian living, as originally taught by Christ.

**1 John 2:15 (KJV)** Love not the world, neither the things *that are* in the world. If any man love the world, the love of the Father is not in him.

**1 John 2:16 (KJV)** For all that *is* in the world, the lust of the flesh, and the lust of the eyes, and the pride of life, is not of the Father, but is of the world.

**1 John 2:17 (KJV)** And the world passeth away, and the lust thereof: but he that doeth the will of God abideth for ever.

For many within the Christian community, displays of opulence have become a hallmark of their lifestyle. Wealth, financial success, and possessions are frequently heralded as signs of divine favor and prosperity. This perspective is not only prevalent among congregants but is also often reinforced by the messages delivered from the pulpit.

Leaders themselves, adorned in luxurious attire and accessories that likely come from the contributions of their congregations, exemplify this trend. The topic of "tithes and offerings" opens up a broader discussion, yet it's clear that the prevailing interpretation of what constitutes a righteous and prosperous life in the eyes of God diverges significantly from traditional Christian values in many modern churches.

> **1 Timothy 2:9 (KJV)** In like manner also, that women adorn themselves in modest apparel, with shamefacedness and sobriety; not with broided hair, or gold, or pearls, or costly array;

In contemporary church settings, a notable trend has emerged where attire and outward appearances are often chosen to impress or attract, particularly among women who may dress elaborately in hopes of catching the attention of affluent and successful suitors. The desire for a lavish church wedding has become a common aspiration, fueling a competitive atmosphere. This competition not only influences the way individuals present themselves but also drives some men to seek partners beyond the church community. The emphasis on fashion, luxury vehicles, and material aspirations reflects a broader shift towards worldly values within the church environment.

> **1 Corinthians 12:23 (KJV)** And those members of the body, which we think to be less honourable, upon these we bestow more abundant honour; and our uncomely parts have more abundant comeliness.

> **1 Peter 3:3 (KJV)** Whose adorning let it not be that outward adorning of plaiting the hair, and of wearing of gold, or of putting on of apparel;

> **1 Peter 3:4 (KJV)** But let it be the hidden man of the heart, in that which is not corruptible, even the ornament of a meek and quiet spirit, which is in the sight of God of great price.

# RELIGION AND POLITICS

The interplay between religion and government is a complex and nuanced issue, one that has been part of human society since time immemorial. Drawing on scriptural references, we can see that the coexistence of religion and government is not only possible but has been a reality throughout history. Before the advent of Christ, governments existed as entities separate from religious institutions, yet they often intersected in various ways. During the life of Jesus Christ, the Roman Empire governed the land, demonstrating that civil authority operated alongside religious life. The Gospels, particularly in passages like **Matthew 22:21**, where Jesus says, **"Render therefore unto Caesar the things which are Caesar's; and unto God the things that are God's,"** illustrate the distinction and coexistence between the domains of government and religion. This teaching underscores the principle that while the spiritual and temporal realms have their own distinct roles and responsibilities, they are both part of the broader tapestry of human society.

After the death and resurrection of Jesus, the early Christian community navigated the complexities of practicing their faith within a political framework that was often indifferent or even hostile to their beliefs. **Acts 5:29** offers a poignant example, where Peter and the other apostles assert, "We ought to obey God rather than men," signifying the early Christians' commitment to their faith, even in the face of governmental authority. This tension between obeying God and respecting governmental authority underscores the nuanced relationship between religion and government—a relationship that continues to evolve and manifest in various forms throughout history.

Thus, the scriptural narrative provides a foundation for understanding the coexistence of religion and government as a multifaceted relationship. It suggests that while religion and government can operate independently, acknowledging their separate spheres of influence, they also interact in ways that shape the moral, ethical, and social fabric of society. This historical and scriptural perspective invites ongoing reflection on how these two pillars of society can contribute to the common good, respecting the autonomy of each while seeking ways to collaborate for the welfare and flourishing of all.

> **Romans 13:1 (KJV)** Let every soul be subject unto the higher powers. For there is no power but of God: the powers that be are ordained of God.

Hence, it is imperative for Christians to navigate a path of coexistence with the prevailing government authorities. Yet, Scripture does not advocate for religious leaders, such as pastors and prophets, to integrate with political entities in an official capacity on behalf of the church, to formally endorse political figures or parties under the church's banner, or to engage in political campaigning within the sacred spaces of worship.

The intertwining of governmental and religious spheres, particularly within Christianity, has significantly undermined the core principles and beliefs that Christians hold dear. The distinction between the secular world and the ecclesiastical realm has become increasingly indistinct, leading to a conflation of religious and political identities.

The notion of a clear separation between the church (representing Christian values) and the state (symbolizing secular governance) has been eroded. While governments exercise worldly authority, the Christian community is called to live as though it is not fully aligned with worldly systems. Unfortunately, the allure and benefits of political engagement have led some church leaders to embrace secular powers too closely, causing them to stray from their spiritual mission.

It is crucial to underscore the role that Christians are meant to play in fostering a society that is just and compassionate for everyone, drawing inspiration from biblical figures like Esther and Daniel, who influenced governmental policies for the betterment of the Jewish people. Nonetheless, to authentically execute its prophetic duty of providing guidance and rectifying errors within society and government, the church is required to uphold a distinct separation from political ties and engagements. This separation enables the church to offer unbiased moral and ethical guidance, thereby contributing positively to the governance of society while preserving its sacred calling.

> **John 17:14 (KJV)** I have given them thy word; and the world hath hated them, because they are not of the world, even as I am not of the world.
>
> **John 17:15 (KJV)** I pray not that thou shouldest take them out of the world, but that thou shouldest keep them from the evil.
>
> **John 17:16 (KJV)** They are not of the world, even as I am not of the world.
>
> **John 17:17 (KJV)** Sanctify them through thy truth: thy word is truth.

Among the myriad virtues exhibited by Queen Esther, there is much we can draw upon and embody in our modern world, which is not without its own challenges and evils. Esther's obedience to her uncle Mordecai is noteworthy. Her faith was firmly placed in the God of Abraham, Isaac, and Jacob. Holding a position of significant influence as Queen did not deter her from engaging in fasting and prayer to seek divine intervention. This example serves as a powerful reminder that, regardless of one's role in government—be it a Minister, Judge, Member of Parliament, Ambassador, or even a President—embracing humility and seeking guidance through prayer is both possible and commendable.

Above all, Esther's legacy is defined by her courageous decision to embrace truth and righteousness, even when faced with the potential cost of her own life. She leveraged her position to advocate for and assist the marginalized within her society—the poor, the needy, widows, foreigners, and the fatherless. Her actions underscore the profound impact that one individual, driven by virtue and a commitment to justice, can have on their community and beyond, serving as an inspiring model for leaders and individuals alike in pursuing the welfare of all, especially the most vulnerable.

> **Esther 4:13 (KJV)** Then Mordecai commanded to answer Esther, Think not with thyself that thou shalt escape in the king's house, more than all the Jews.

> **Esther 4:14 (KJV)** For if thou altogether holdest thy peace at this time, *then* shall there enlargement and deliverance arise to the Jews from another place; but thou and thy father's house shall be destroyed: and who knoweth whether thou art come to the kingdom for *such* a time as this?

> **Esther 4:15 (KJV)** Then Esther bade *them* return Mordecai *this answer,*

> **Esther 4:16 (KJV)** Go, gather together all the Jews that are present in Shushan, and fast ye for me, and neither eat nor drink three days, night or day: I also and my maidens will fast likewise; and so will I go in unto the king, which *is* not according to the law: and if I perish, I perish.

> **Esther 4:17 (KJV)** So Mordecai went his way, and did according to all that Esther had commanded him.

Consider Daniel, another devout servant of God, who navigated the treacherous waters of political office. Like Esther, Daniel was deeply committed to principles of truth and righteousness, qualities that set him apart and, regrettably, made him the target of envy and hostility from his peers in government. Despite the allure of wealth, power, and status, Daniel chose a different path. He remained steadfast in his devotion to the God of Abraham, Isaac, and Jacob. His decision to live a life aligned with divine principles provoked such resentment among his colleagues that they conspired to end his life.

Imagine yourself in a similar position within the government. Would you have the courage to stand firm in truth and righteousness, especially when faced with opposition from your peers, who might be engaged in unethical activities? How would you respond if they plotted against you, seeking to remove you because your integrity exposes their misconduct? Would you, like Daniel, remain faithful to God and the teachings of Jesus Christ, even when doing so puts you at great risk?

Daniel's story, particularly in **Daniel 6:1**, where King Darius appointed him because of his exceptional qualities, illustrates the profound impact that living by one's convictions can have, not just personally but also within the broader societal and political landscape. It challenges us to consider the depth of our commitment to our principles and our faith, especially in environments where such a stance is neither popular nor safe.

> **Daniel 6:1 (KJV)** It pleased Darius to set over the kingdom an hundred and twenty princes, which should be over the whole kingdom;

**Daniel 6:2 (KJV)** And over these three presidents; of whom Daniel *was* first: that the princes might give accounts unto them, and the king should have no damage.

**Daniel 6:3 (KJV)** Then this Daniel was preferred above the presidents and princes, because an excellent spirit *was* in him; and the king thought to set him over the whole realm.

**Daniel 6:4 (KJV)** Then the presidents and princes sought to find occasion against Daniel concerning the kingdom; but they could find none occasion nor fault; forasmuch as he *was* faithful, neither was there any error or fault found in him.

**Daniel 6:5 (KJV)** Then said these men, We shall not find any occasion against this Daniel, except we find *it* against him concerning the law of his God.

**Daniel 6:6 (KJV)** Then these presidents and princes assembled together to the king, and said thus unto him, King Darius, live for ever.

**Daniel 6:7 (KJV)** All the presidents of the kingdom, the governors, and the princes, the counsellers, and the captains, have consulted together to establish a royal statute, and to make a firm decree, that whosoever shall ask a petition of any God or man for thirty days, save of thee, O king, he shall be cast into the den of lions.

**Daniel 6:8 (KJV)** Now, O king, establish the decree, and sign the writing, that it be not changed, according to the law of the Medes and Persians, which altereth not.

**Daniel 6:9 (KJV)** Wherefore king Darius signed the writing and the decree.

**Daniel 6:10 (KJV)** Now when Daniel knew that the writing was signed, he went into his house; and his windows being open in his chamber toward Jerusalem, he kneeled upon his knees three times a day, and prayed, and gave thanks before his God, as he did aforetime.

**Daniel 6:11 (KJV)** Then these men assembled, and found Daniel praying and making supplication before his God.

**Daniel 6:12 (KJV)** Then they came near, and spake before the king concerning the king's decree; Hast thou not signed a decree, that every man that shall ask *a petition* of any God or man within thirty days, save of thee, O king, shall be cast into the den of lions? The king answered and said, The thing *is* true, according to the law of the Medes and Persians, which altereth not.

**Daniel 6:13 (KJV)** Then answered they and said before the king, That Daniel, which *is* of the children of the captivity of Judah, regardeth not thee, O king, nor the decree that thou hast signed, but maketh his petition three times a day.

**Daniel 6:14 (KJV)** Then the king, when he heard *these* words, was sore displeased with himself, and set *his* heart on Daniel to deliver him: and he laboured till the going down of the sun to deliver him.

Today's Christians often struggle to heed the biblical call to distinguish between spiritual commitments and worldly entanglements, leading to a troubling convergence of religious faith and secular politics. In the United States, a notable example can be observed among certain groups identifying as Evangelical Political Activists. These groups, somewhat misleadingly named, frequently pledge their and their followers' allegiance to conservative Republican candidates or the party itself, overlooking instances where the candidates' policies starkly contrast with biblical teachings and the essence of Christ's gospel.

They assert that their support is rooted in values they claim are consistent with biblical principles and those championed by the politicians in question. Yet, one must critically ask: What specific values are being referenced? The act of whole heartedly endorsing a political party or candidate without discernment does not reflect the example set by Christ. This tendency is not confined to one region but is a phenomenon observed across the global Christian community.

While it is entirely acceptable for Christians to hold political views and even to engage in politics themselves, blindly aligning with the political zeitgeist contradicts the call to be a distinct and transformative presence in the world.

Such unquestioning allegiance to the prevailing political order not only poses a risk but also represents a profound departure from the teachings and example of Jesus Christ and the early church. Christians are encouraged to navigate the political landscape with wisdom and discernment, ensuring their actions and affiliations genuinely reflect their commitment to Christ's teachings and example.

> **Titus 1:12 (KJV)** One of themselves, *even* a prophet of their own, said, The Cretians *are* alway liars, evil beasts, slow bellies.
>
> **Titus 1:13 (KJV)** This witness is true. Wherefore rebuke them sharply, that they may be sound in the faith;
>
> **1 Timothy 5:20 (KJV)** Them that sin rebuke before all, that others also may fear.

Therefore, Christians should not bury the hatchet in their honest views based on the Word of God. The desire of some Church leaders to be seen in arms and gloves with a particular government or political administration is contrary to the teachings of our LORD Jesus Christ.

# THE PRACTICE OF WORSHIP

Worship represents the tangible manifestation of one's spiritual journey, embodying a believer's reaction to their focal point of reverence. It stands as the ultimate demonstration of an individual's commitment and reverence, articulated through both verbal and non-verbal expressions.

For Christians, the practice of worship encompasses more than just adoration, praise, and symbolic representation; it serves as a foundational element of their faith. The purpose of worship extends beyond mere ritual, aiming to align all of creation with the divine will and order of God. This transformative process seeks to bring every aspect of existence into a harmonious relationship with the Divine, reflecting the profound impact of worship on both the worshipper and the world around them.

> **John 4:24 (KJV)** God *is* a Spirit: and they that worship him must worship *him* in spirit and in truth.

Therefore, the structure and execution of worship rituals are deeply liturgical, serving as outward expressions of inner faith and conviction. Yet, it's essential to recognize that the perspective on worship has evolved beyond the confines of Old Testament practices, which were governed by the Law. In those times, worship was restricted to specific occasions, locations, and required the presence of priests, an altar, and a sacrificial lamb. Today's understanding of worship extends beyond these parameters, embracing a broader and more inclusive interpretation that reflects the spiritual journey and relationship with the Divine in contemporary life:

> **John 4:20 (KJV)** Our fathers worshipped in this mountain; and ye say, that in Jerusalem is the place where men ought to worship.

> **John 4:21 (KJV)** Jesus saith unto her, Woman, believe me, the hour cometh, when ye shall neither in this mountain, nor yet at Jerusalem, worship the Father.

Hence, gathering at a designated holy site is not always a prerequisite for worship or the execution of religious acts. Nonetheless, conducting worship rituals with ceremonial reverence, where possible, adds a layer of dignity and solemnity to the practice:

> **Hebrews 10:10 (KJV)** By the which will we are sanctified through the offering of the body of Jesus Christ once *for all*.

In the New Testament era, following the sacrificial death of our Lord Jesus Christ for the redemption of our sins, a profound transformation occurred. Through His crucifixion and the outpouring of His blood, Jesus became the ultimate Priest, Altar, and Sacrifice. This act of selfless love stands unparalleled, marking a new covenant between God and humanity.

True worship of God is not a transactional affair, seeking material benefits, rewards, or protection in return. Rather, it is the inherent responsibility and privilege of humanity, as God's creation, to engage in worship. Genuine worship encompasses every aspect of our lives, reflecting our devotion and reverence through our actions and words. This embodies the essence of true worship:

> **Colossians 3:17 (KJV)** And whatsoever ye do in word or deed, *do* all in the name of the Lord Jesus, giving thanks to God and the Father by him.

As followers of Christ, we are invited to understand that our obligation to show gratitude and reverence to God transcends the physical boundaries of a church edifice. Acknowledging God's hand in every facet of our lives, through simple gestures of thanks and praise, is a profound act of worship. It celebrates the blessings of life and divine safeguarding. Worship, in its truest form, is embodied in our everyday actions—whether through acts of kindness and generosity, the renunciation of worldly desires, or the pursuit of holiness and mutual love. These expressions of faith and devotion, woven into the fabric of our daily lives, hold greater significance and are more pleasing to God than attending church services only on Sundays. This perspective invites us to live out our faith in tangible, impactful ways, making every moment an opportunity to worship and honor God.

> **Zechariah 8:16 (KJV)** These *are* the things that ye shall do; Speak ye every man the truth to his neighbour; execute the judgment of truth and peace in your gates:
>
> **Zechariah 8:17 (KJV)** And let none of you imagine evil in your hearts against his neighbour; and love no false oath: for all these *are things* that I hate, saith the LORD.

Visit any Christian church outside of service times, and you'll likely notice a shared characteristic: the doors are locked, awaiting the next scheduled service, typically on Sunday. This observation underscores a broader issue — a limited understanding of worship as merely an act of reverence that's confined to specific times and places. This phenomenon has led to the emergence of "oneday Christians," individuals whose spiritual engagement is largely restricted to church attendance. Furthermore, there's a tendency among some to elevate their spiritual leaders to a pedestal, prioritizing their reverence for priests or pastors above their devotion to God Almighty. In such instances, God is often referred to as the "God of their Pastor," indicating a misplaced focus that views the divine through the lens of church leadership rather than a personal relationship with God. This raises questions about why spiritual leaders don't more actively discourage this shift in focus and guide their congregations back to a more direct and personal connection with God:

> **Jeremiah 23:15 (KJV)** Therefore thus saith the LORD of hosts concerning the prophets; Behold, I will feed them with wormwood, and make them drink the water of gall: for from the prophets of Jerusalem is profaneness gone forth into all the land.
>
> **Hosea 9:7 (KJV)** The days of visitation are come, the days of recompence are come; Israel shall know *it*: the prophet *is* a fool, the spiritual man *is* mad, for the multitude of thine iniquity, and the great hatred.

The explanation for this phenomenon is straightforward: these leaders are positioned and revered as deities themselves. Congregation members refer to them as "Father" or "Papa," not in reference to the Heavenly Father we recognize as God Almighty, but to their church leaders whom they idolize and worship daily, including Sundays. Concern arises when followers attribute all positive outcomes to the blessings of the "Man of God" (Pastor/Prophet), while any adversity is blamed on Satan, effectively removing God from the picture and focusing instead on human figures and their followers, who may lack genuine faith.

Authentic worship should spring from the heart, inspired by the Holy Spirit, rather than being directed towards the earthly "gods" represented by church leaders or the specific doctrines and practices they promote. True devotion is a personal journey guided by a direct relationship with God, independent of intermediary figures or institutions:

> **Matthew 15:9 (KJV)** But in vain they do worship me, teaching *for* doctrines the commandments of men.

> **Mark 7:7 (KJV)** Howbeit in vain do they worship me, teaching *for* doctrines the commandments of men.

> **Colossians 2:22 (KJV)** Which all are to perish with the using;) after the commandments and doctrines of men?

The Church of Christ ought to be centered on Christ and led by the teachings of the Gospel. As followers of Christ, it is crucial for us to recognize that the responsibility for upholding the truth rests solely with us; there is no one else to fault. God has endowed each of us with the capacity for discernment:

> **Proverbs 1:7 (KJV)** The fear of the LORD *is* the beginning of knowledge: *but* fools despise wisdom and instruction.

As a follower of Christ, armed with knowledge of His teachings and actions, you are safeguarded against being led astray towards ruin. Familiarity with the Word of God, combined with an understanding of the principles Jesus Christ embodied, serves as a crucial tool for recognizing and avoiding false teachings and practices. This knowledge empowers you to steer clear of deception:

> **Hebrews 13:15 (KJV)** By him therefore let us offer the sacrifice of praise to God continually, that is, the fruit of *our* lips giving thanks to his name.

> **1 Timothy 6:11 (KJV)** But thou, O man of God, flee these things; and follow after righteousness, godliness, faith, love, patience, meekness.

# CHRISTIAN DEVOTION AND WORSHIP

In the context of contemporary Christianity, the approach to worship often leaves much to be desired. For many believers and their spiritual leaders, including pastors and prophets, worship is confined to Sundays. This once-aweek pilgrimage to a place they designate as a church suggests a limited understanding of worship, as if authentic communion with God is restricted to a specific location and time. This perspective overlooks the essence of true worship, which is a continuous, daily relationship with God, not limited to the walls of any building:

> **Matthew 16:18 (KJV)** And I say also unto thee, That thou art Peter, and upon this rock I will build my church; and the gates of hell shall not prevail against it.

> **Acts 7:48 (KJV)** Howbeit the most High dwelleth not in temples made with hands; as saith the prophet,

> **Acts 17:24 (KJV)** God that made the world and all things therein, seeing that he is Lord of heaven and earth, dwelleth not in temples made with hands;

> **Acts 17:25 (KJV)** Neither is worshipped with men's hands, as though he needed anything, seeing he giveth to all life, and breath, and all things;

The Holy Bible explicitly defines the nature of worship. Worshiping God is not confined to a single day but is an ongoing engagement with the Divine in our everyday lives. Sunday worship aligns with the Biblical designation of the day of rest.

> **Genesis 1:5 (KJV)** And God called the light Day, and the darkness he called Night. And the evening and the morning were the first day.

> **Genesis 2:1 (KJV)** Thus the heavens and the earth were finished, and all the host of them.

> **Genesis 2:2 (KJV)** And on the seventh day God ended his work which he had made; and he rested on the seventh day from all his work which he had made.

> **Genesis 2:3 (KJV)** And God blessed the seventh day, and sanctified it: because that in it he had rested from all his work which God created and made.

The seventh day holds the unique distinction of being sanctified, marking the day the Lord our God chose to rest. The Sabbath commences at sundown on the eve of the seventh day, which could be Saturday or Sunday, depending on one's interpretation. God, who discerns the intentions of every heart, will in His timing, bestow rewards upon those who engage in genuine worship.

> **1 Timothy 2:1 (KJV)** I exhort therefore, that, first of all, supplications, prayers, intercessions, *and* giving of thanks, be made for all men;
>
> **1 Timothy 2:2 (KJV)** For kings, and *for* all that are in authority; that we may lead a quiet and peaceable life in all godliness and honesty.
>
> **1 Timothy 2:3 (KJV)** For this *is* good and acceptable in the sight of God our Saviour;

Prayer, as a vital expression of worship, encompasses a broad spectrum of intentions and settings, as highlighted by Apostle Paul in his guidance to Timothy. This comprehensive approach to worship includes:

1. **Intercessory Prayer:** Paul emphasizes the importance of praying for everyone, including those who oppose us. This includes urging us to pray for people no matter their attitude towards us, championing their welfare and spiritual direction.

2. **Praying for Leaders:** The instruction extends to praying for those in authority, regardless of their moral standing, to foster an environment where peace, godliness, and dignity prevail, even amidst challenging leadership.

3. **Universal Worship:** The encouragement to pray "anywhere and everywhere," signifies the boundless nature of worship, where physical location does not constrain one's ability to connect with the Divine.

4. **Modesty and Focus:** Paul advises women to approach God with modesty in appearance and demeanor, prioritizing the spiritual over the material or the superficial, to maintain the sanctity of worship.

5. **Humility in Worship:** The call to worship God with humility and submission acknowledges the sacrifice of Jesus Christ for our salvation, emphasizing worship as a response to His redemptive act.

Worship, therefore, is not just an act but a state of being, reflecting an ongoing devotion rather than a sporadic or transactional engagement with God. It challenges Christians to assess their depth of devotion: Is worship a constant in your life, or is it reserved for moments of need?

Unfortunately, many Christians exhibit a lack of devotion, treating worship more as a means to an end than a genuine expression of faith. This attitude often translates into worship motivated by personal desires rather than an unconditional reverence for God.

True worship, as outlined in the scriptures, transcends the transactional, offering protection and guidance not because we have explicitly asked for it but as a natural extension of our relationship with God. It means engaging in daily worship, not merely on Sundays or special occasions, and not worshiping with the sole intention of receiving something in return, like a spouse, child, or financial blessing.

Worship should be an unconditional act of gratitude towards God, acknowledging His provision and care in our lives without our prompting. It's about recognizing that God is already attending to our needs and that our worship is a way to thank Him for His perpetual generosity and love.

> **Romans 12:1 (KJV)** I beseech you therefore, brethren, by the mercies of God, that ye present your bodies a living sacrifice, holy, acceptable unto God, *which is* your reasonable service.

> **Romans 12:2 (KJV)** And be not conformed to this world: but be ye transformed by the renewing of your mind, that ye may prove what is that good, and acceptable, and perfect, will of God.

# GUIDELINES FOR

## LIVING A LIFE OF HOLINESS AND RIGHTEOUSNESS IN AUTHENTIC WORSHIP OF GOD

1. Humans possess a keen awareness of their inherent imperfection and propensity towards sin, acknowledging the profound gap between their flawed human nature and the divine standard of purity and righteousness.

   **Romans 3:23 (KJV)** For all have sinned, and come short of the glory of God;

   **Romans 5:12 (KJV)** Wherefore, as by one man sin entered into the world, and death by sin; and so death passed upon all men, for that all have sinned:

2. To approach the divine, it is necessary to sanctify our undeserving nature, requiring a period of preparation before worship. This involves striving for a life of holiness and righteousness, seeking the favor, grace, and forgiveness of God.

3. Immersing oneself in the Scripture, allowing it to dwell in your heart, and living according to its teachings (embodying righteousness) signifies that Christ Jesus (the Son of God) resides within you. And if the Son dwells within you, then so does God Himself.

   **John 15:3 (KJV)** Now ye are clean through the word which I have spoken unto you.

   **John 17:23 (KJV)** I in them, and thou in me, that they may be made perfect in one; and that the world may know that thou hast sent me, and hast loved them, as thou hast loved me.

4. In their efforts to bridge the gap between their inherent sinfulness and the divine standard, humans engage in a process of self-sanctification. This involves actively pursuing a life of righteousness, thereby elevating themselves to a state deemed acceptable in the eyes of God. Through this conscientious effort to live according to moral and spiritual principles, individuals seek to cleanse their nature and align more closely with divine expectations.

   **John 17:17 (KJV)** Sanctify them through thy truth: thy word is truth.

5. This process entails a thorough purification of one's being, aiming to render individuals worthy of standing before the divine presence. Through acts of repentance, prayer, and adherence to spiritual disciplines, believers work to cleanse their hearts and minds, removing impurities that hinder their relationship with the divine. This purification is

not merely external but reaches deep into the soul, preparing it to receive and reflect the grace of God with humility and gratitude.

> **Hebrews 9:13 (KJV)** For if the blood of bulls and of goats, and the ashes of an heifer sprinkling the unclean, sanctifieth to the purifying of the flesh:

> **Hebrews 9:14 (KJV)** How much more shall the blood of Christ, who through the eternal Spirit offered himself without spot to God, purge your conscience from dead works to serve the living God?

6. Demonstrating obedience to the Word of God represents the highest form of love that a person can show towards God.

> **John 14:21 (KJV)** He that hath my commandments, and keepeth them, he it is that loveth me: and he that loveth me shall be loved of my Father, and I will love him, and will manifest myself to him.

> **John 14:24 (KJV)** He that loveth me not keepeth not my sayings: and the word which ye hear is not mine, but the Father's which sent me.

7. Fostering an environment within ourselves that allows the Holy Spirit to operate effectively is essential for the revelation of Jesus Christ to us. This involves cultivating a heart and mind open to divine guidance, engaging in prayer, meditation, and the study of Scripture, and living a life that aligns with God's commandments. By doing so, we create the spiritual conditions necessary for the Holy Spirit to work within us, unveiling the nature, teachings, and salvation offered through Jesus Christ in a deeply personal and transformative manner.

> **1 Samuel 3:21 (KJV)** And the LORD appeared again in Shiloh: for the LORD revealed himself to Samuel in Shiloh by the word of the LORD.

> **John 14:26 (KJV)** But the Comforter, *which is* the Holy Ghost, whom the Father will send in my name, he shall teach you all things, and bring all things to your remembrance, whatsoever I have said unto you.

> **John 15:26 (KJV)** But when the Comforter is come, whom I will send unto you from the Father, *even* the Spirit of truth, which proceedeth from the Father, he shall testify of me:

> **John 16:13 (KJV)** Howbeit when he, the Spirit of truth, is come, he will guide you into all truth: for he shall not speak of himself; but whatsoever he shall hear, *that* shall he speak: and he will shew you things to come.

Renouncing all worldly and sinful desires that conflict with the principles of the Body of Christ is a crucial step towards receiving a genuine revelation of God. This entails a deliberate and conscious effort to detach from behaviors, thoughts, and habits that stand in opposition to spiritual growth and purity. By purifying our lives of actions and desires deemed unworthy within the Christian faith, we create space in our hearts and minds for the truth and light of God to enter. This process of spiritual cleansing not only aligns us more closely with the will of God but also prepares us to fully embrace and understand the divine revelations that God wishes to impart upon us, leading to a deeper, more meaningful relationship with the Divine.

> **Matthew 19:21 (KJV)** Jesus said unto him, If thou wilt be perfect, go *and* sell that thou hast, and give to the poor, and thou shalt have treasure in heaven: and come *and* follow me.

> **Galatians 5:16 (KJV)** *This* I say then, Walk in the Spirit, and ye shall not fulfil the lust of the flesh.

> **1 John 2:16 (KJV)** For all that *is* in the world, the lust of the flesh, and the lust of the eyes, and the pride of life, is not of the Father, but is of the world.

8. Adopting a modest appearance in the presence of God involves eschewing extravagant, expensive clothing and ostentatious jewelry that reflect arrogance or a preoccupation with material wealth. This principle emphasizes the importance of humility and simplicity in how we present ourselves during worship and in our daily lives, prioritizing spiritual integrity over worldly display. By choosing attire that reflects modesty and restraint, believers demonstrate a respect for the sacredness of their relationship with God, acknowledging that true value and beauty stem from one's character and devotion rather than external adornments. This approach fosters an environment of equality and focuses attention on the heart and spirit, aligning with biblical teachings that caution against letting outward appearances overshadow the inner essence of faith and holiness.

> **Philippians 4:5 (KJV)** Let your moderation be known unto all men. The Lord *is* at hand.

> **Philippians 4:6 (KJV)** Be careful for nothing; but in everything by prayer and supplication with thanksgiving let your requests be made known unto God.

9. The act of confessing our sins is a pivotal practice in the Christian faith, involving the acknowledgment and verbalization of our wrongdoings before God. This process is not merely about admitting fault but is a profound exercise in humility, repentance, and the sincere desire to turn away from sin. Through confession, we communicate directly with God about our transgressions, seeking forgiveness and the strength to change our ways. This act strengthens our relationship with the Divine by fostering transparency, accountability, and a deeper awareness of our need for God's grace and mercy in our lives.

**Daniel 9:20 (KJV)** And whiles I *was* speaking, and praying, and confessing my sin and the sin of my people Israel, and presenting my supplication before the LORD my God for the holy mountain of my God;

**Daniel 9:21 (KJV)** Yea, whiles I *was* speaking in prayer, even the man Gabriel, whom I had seen in the vision at the beginning, being caused to fly swiftly, touched me about the time of the evening oblation.

**Matthew 3:5 (KJV)** Then went out to him Jerusalem, and all Judaea, and all the region round about Jordan,

**Matthew 3:6 (KJV)** And were baptized of him in Jordan, confessing their sins.

10. Cultivating a constant attitude of gratitude is fundamental to the Christian ethos. This directive encourages believers to maintain a perpetual state of thankfulness towards God for His endless blessings, grace, and provision, regardless of life's circumstances. Embracing thankfulness not only acknowledges God's sovereignty and goodness but also fosters a positive outlook, enriching our spiritual journey and deepening our relationship with the Divine. This practice of ongoing gratitude transforms our perspective, enabling us to see God's hand in every aspect of our lives and strengthening our faith through both trials and triumphs.

> **Psalm 7:17 (KJV)** I will praise the LORD according to his righteousness: and will sing praise to the name of the LORD most high.

> **Colossians 3:15 (KJV)** And let the peace of God rule in your hearts, to the which also ye are called in one body; and be ye thankful.

# 25 QUESTIONS TO IDENTIFY A PLACE OF WORSHIP THAT LACKS A BIBLE AND CHRIST-CENTERED FOCUS

1. Are you aware of any religious leader or church that frequently criticizes other religious groups or leaders to their followers, while also claiming superiority as the true or genuine choice?

   **Discover for yourself**

   **John 8:7 (KJV)** So when they continued asking him, he lifted up himself, and said unto them, He that is without sin among you, let him first cast a stone at her.

   **Ecclesiastes 7:20 (KJV)** For *there is* not a just man upon earth, that doeth good, and sinneth not.

   **Matthew 19:16 (KJV)** And, behold, one came and said unto him, Good Master, what good thing shall I do, that I may have eternal life?

   **Matthew 19:17 (KJV)** And he said unto him, Why callest thou me good? *there is* none good but one, *that is*, God: but if thou wilt enter into life, keep the commandments.

   **Matthew 19:18 (KJV)** He saith unto him, Which? Jesus said, Thou shalt do no murder, Thou shalt not commit adultery, Thou shalt not steal, Thou shalt not bear false witness,

   **Matthew 19:19 (KJV)** Honour thy father and *thy* mother: and, Thou shalt love thy neighbour as thyself.

   **Matthew 19:20 (KJV)** The young man saith unto him, All these things have I kept from my youth up: what lack I yet?

   **Matthew 19:21 (KJV)** Jesus said unto him, If thou wilt be perfect, go *and* sell that thou hast, and give to the poor, and thou shalt have treasure in heaven: and come *and* follow me.

2. Are you aware of any religious leader or church that often asserts they have direct communication with God and conveys God's messages personally to you or others?

**Please refer to the scripture below on your own:**

   **1 Peter 4:10 (KJV)** As every man hath received the gift, *even so* minister the same one to another, as good stewards of the manifold grace of God.

**1 Peter 4:11 (KJV)** If any man speak, *let him speak* as the oracles of God; if any man minister, *let him do it* as of the ability which God giveth: that God in all things may be glorified through Jesus Christ, to whom be praise and dominion for ever and ever. Amen.

Are you familiar with any religious leader or church that frequently offers prophecies about individuals, focusing only on past events rather than predicting future occurrences?

**Examine the following scripture for your spiritual enrichment:**

**Ezekiel 13:6 (KJV)** They have seen vanity and lying divination, saying, The LORD saith: and the LORD hath not sent them: and they have made *others* to hope that they would confirm the word.

3. Are you aware of any religious leader or church that frequently encourages you or someone you know to make a financial "seed offering" at the altar (the area around the podium) as a sacrifice to God, suggesting it will earn God's favor or result in answered prayers, essentially treating it like a monetary transaction?

**Explore on your own:**

**Micah 3:9 (KJV)** Hear this, I pray you, ye heads of the house of Jacob, and princes of the house of Israel, that abhor judgment, and pervert all equity.

**Micah 3:10 (KJV)** They build up Zion with blood, and Jerusalem with iniquity.

**Micah 3:11 (KJV)** The heads thereof judge for reward, and the priests thereof teach for hire, and the prophets thereof divine for money: yet will they lean upon the LORD, and say, *Is* not the LORD among us? none evil can come upon us.

**Zephaniah 1:18 (KJV)** Neither their silver nor their gold shall be able to deliver them in the days of the LORDS'S wrath: but the whole land shall be devoured by the fire of his jealousy: for he shall make even a speedy riddance of all them that dwell in the land.

**Micah 7:2 (KJV)** The good *man* is perished out of the earth: and *there is* none upright among men: they all lie in wait for blood; they hunt every man his brother with a net.

**Micah 7:3 (KJV)** That they may do evil with both hands earnestly, the prince asketh, and the judge *asketh* for a reward; and the great *man*, he uttereth his mischievous desire: so they wrap it up.

**Micah 7:4 (KJV)** The best of them *is* as a brier: the most upright *is sharper* than a thorn hedge: the day of thy watchmen *and* thy visitation cometh; now shall be their perplexity.

**John 3:16 (KJV)** For God so loved the world, that he gave his only begotten Son, that whosoever believeth in him should not perish, but have everlasting life.

**John 3:17 (KJV)** For God sent not his Son into the world to condemn the world; but that the world through him might be saved.

**John 3:19 (KJV)** And this is the condemnation, that light is come into the world, and men loved darkness rather than light, because their deeds were evil.

4. Are you aware of any religious leader or church that teaches regardless of the sins you have committed or continue to commit, you will still enter Heaven as long as you have not denied Jesus as your Lord and Savior (adhering to the belief of "once saved, always saved")?

## Examine the following scripture for your spiritual enrichment

**Matthew 8:11 (KJV)** And I say unto you, That many shall come from the east and west, and shall sit down with Abraham, and Isaac, and Jacob, in the kingdom of heaven.

**Matthew 8:12 (KJV)** But the children of the kingdom shall be cast out into outer darkness: there shall be weeping and gnashing of teeth.

**John 8:10 (KJV)** When Jesus had lifted up himself, and saw none but the woman, he said unto her, Woman, where are those thine accusers? hath no man condemned thee?

**John 8:11 (KJV)** She said, No man, Lord. And Jesus said unto her, Neither do I condemn thee: go, and sin no more.

**1 Peter 4:17 (KJV)** For the time *is come* that judgment must begin at the house of God: and if *it* first *begin* at us, what shall the end *be* of them that obey not the gospel of God?

**1 Peter 4:18 (KJV)** And if the righteous scarcely be saved, where shall the ungodly and the sinner appear?

5. Are you familiar with any religious leader or church that regularly encourages you or their congregation to engage in extensive fasting, using catchy but hollow phrases like "fasting time is blessing time" as a lure, while pretending to lead prayer and fasting sessions, but in reality conducting daily prophetic services with the ulterior motive of soliciting or extracting offerings from participants?

## Examine the scriptures on your own, as the Bereans did:

**Matthew 6:16 (KJV)** Moreover when ye fast, be not, as the hypocrites, of a sad countenance: for they disfigure their faces, that they may appear unto men to fast. Verily I say unto you, They have their reward.

**Matthew 6:17 (KJV)** But thou, when thou fastest, anoint thine head, and wash thy face;

**Matthew 6:18 (KJV)** That thou appear not unto men to fast, but unto thy Father which is in secret: and thy Father, which seeth in secret, shall reward thee openly.

6. Are you aware of any religious leader or church that criticizes individuals for not paying tithes, asserting their right to collect tithes, even though they, along with their spouses and children, do not pay tithes themselves?

**Examine the scriptures on your own, as the Bereans did:**

**Matthew 17:24 (KJV)** And when they were come to Capernaum, they that received tribute *money* came to Peter, and said, Doth not your master pay tribute?

**Matthew 17:25 (KJV)** He saith, Yes. And when he was come into the house, Jesus prevented him, saying, What thinkest thou, Simon? of whom do the kings of the earth take custom or tribute? of their own children, or of strangers?

**Matthew 17:26 (KJV)** Peter saith unto him, Of strangers. Jesus saith unto him, Then are the children free.

**Acts 20:35 (KJV)** I have shewed you all things, how that so labouring ye ought to support the weak, and to remember the words of the Lord Jesus, how he said, It is more blessed to give than to receive.

7. Do you know of any church or religious leader who claims the church as their personal or family property, leading to decisions like appointing their son as a pastor regardless of his qualifications or interest, overlooking those who have been foundational to the church's development? Can ownership of a church truly be shared between a human and Jesus Christ?

**Examine the scriptures on your own, as the Bereans did**

**Matthew 16:18 (KJV)** And I say also unto thee, That thou art Peter, and upon this rock I will build my church; and the gates of hell shall not prevail against it.

**Romans 16:16 (KJV)** Salute one another with an holy kiss. The churches of Christ salute you.

8. Are you aware of any religious leader or church that prohibits the entry of deceased individuals into their place of worship?

**Examine the scriptures on your own, as the Bereans did:**

**Ecclesiastes 7:2 (KJV)** *It is* better to go to the house of mourning, than to go to the house of feasting: for that *is* the end of all men; and the living will lay *it* to his heart.

**Ecclesiastes 7:3 (KJV)** Sorrow *is* better than laughter: for by the sadness of the countenance the heart is made better.

**Ecclesiastes 7:4 (KJV)** The heart of the wise *is* in the house of mourning; but the heart of fools *is* in the house of mirth.

**Matthew 5:4 (KJV)** Blessed *are* they that mourn: for they shall be comforted.

**Luke 7:11 (KJV)** And it came to pass the day after, that he went into a city called Nain; and many of his disciples went with him, and much people.

**Luke 7:12 (KJV)** Now when he came nigh to the gate of the city, behold, there was a dead man carried out, the only son of his mother, and she was a widow: and much people of the city was with her.

**Luke 7:13 (KJV)** And when the Lord saw her, he had compassion on her, and said unto her, Weep not.

**Luke 7:14 (KJV)** And he came and touched the bier: and they that bare *him* stood still. And he said, Young man, I say unto thee, Arise.

**Luke 7:15 (KJV)** And he that was dead sat up, and began to speak. And he delivered him to his mother.

**Luke 7:16 (KJV)** And there came a fear on all: and they glorified God, saying, That a great prophet is risen up among us; and, That God hath visited his people.

9. Are you familiar with any churches or religious leaders who profess to be sinless and frequently engage in condemning others?

**Review the following scriptures carefully on your own, in the manner of the Bereans, as described in Acts 17:11.**

**1 Kings 8:46 (KJV)** If they sin against thee, (for *there is* no man that sinneth not,) and thou be angry with them, and deliver them to the enemy, so that they carry them away captives unto the land of the enemy, far or near;

**Romans 3:23 (KJV)** For all have sinned, and come short of the glory of God;

**Romans 5:12 (KJV)** Wherefore, as by one man sin entered into the world, and death by sin; and so death passed upon all men, for that all have sinned:

10. Are you aware of any churches or religious figures who predominantly instruct from the Old Testament, emphasizing legalistic doctrines over New Testament grace, thereby imposing undue burdens on their listeners?

**Review the following scriptures carefully on your own, in the manner of the Bereans, as described in Acts 17:11.**

**Jeremiah 31:31 (KJV)** Behold, the days come, saith the LORD, that I will make a new covenant with the house of Israel, and with the house of Judah:

**Jeremiah 31:32 (KJV)** Not according to the covenant that I made with their fathers in the day *that* I took them by the hand to bring them out of the land of Egypt; which my covenant they brake, although I was an husband unto them, saith the LORD:

**Matthew 9:16 (KJV)** No man putteth a piece of new cloth unto an old garment, for that which is put in to fill it up taketh from the garment, and the rent is made worse.

**Matthew 9:17 (KJV)** Neither do men put new wine into old bottles: else the bottles break, and the wine runneth out, and the bottles perish: but they put new wine into new bottles, and both are preserved.

**Romans 3:20 (KJV)** Therefore by the deeds of the law there shall no flesh be justified in his sight: for by the law *is* the knowledge of sin.

**Romans 8:13 (KJV)** For if ye live after the flesh, ye shall die: but if ye through the Spirit do mortify the deeds of the body, ye shall live.

**Hebrews 8:6 (KJV)** But now hath he obtained a more excellent ministry, by how much also he is the mediator of a better covenant, which was established upon better promises.

**Hebrews 8:7 (KJV)** For if that first *covenant* had been faultless, then should no place have been sought for the second.

**Hebrews 8:8 (KJV)** For finding fault with them, he saith, Behold, the days come, saith the Lord, when I will make a new covenant with the house of Israel and with the house of Judah:

**Hebrews 8:9 (KJV)** Not according to the covenant that I made with their fathers in the day when I took them by the hand to lead them out of the land of Egypt; because they continued not in my covenant, and I regarded them not, saith the Lord.

**Hebrews 8:10 (KJV)** For this *is* the covenant that I will make with the house of Israel after those days, saith the Lord; I will put my laws into their mind, and write them in their hearts: and I will be to them a God, and they shall be to me a people:

**Hebrews 8:11 (KJV)** And they shall not teach every man his neighbour, and every man his brother, saying, Know the Lord: for all shall know me, from the least to the greatest.

**Hebrews 8:12 (KJV)** For I will be merciful to their unrighteousness, and their sins and their iniquities will I remember no more.

**Hebrews 8:13 (KJV)** In that he saith, A new *covenant*, he hath made the first old. Now that which decayeth and waxeth old *is* ready to vanish away.

**Hebrews 10:9 (KJV)** Then said he, Lo, I come to do thy will, O God. He taketh away the first, that he may establish the second.

11. Have you encountered any churches or spiritual leaders who consistently express a preference or encourage their followers to refer to them as "father" (Papa or Daddy)?

**I encourage you to explore this matter on your own from the Holy Scriptures:**

**Malachi 2:10 (KJV)** Have we not all one father? hath not one God created us? why do we deal treacherously every man against his brother, by profaning the covenant of our fathers?

**Matthew 23:9 (KJV)** And call no *man* your father upon the earth: for one is your Father, which is in heaven.

**Matthew 23:10 (KJV)** Neither be ye called masters: for one is your Master, *even* Christ.

**Romans 8:16 (KJV)** The Spirit itself beareth witness with our spirit, that we are the children of God:

12. Are you aware of any churches or religious leaders who habitually guide their congregations in prayers specifically aimed at the demise of their adversaries during every church gathering?

**I encourage you to explore this matter on your own from the Holy Scriptures:**

**Leviticus 19:17 (KJV)** Thou shalt not hate thy brother in thine heart: thou shalt in any wise rebuke thy neighbour, and not suffer sin upon him.

**Luke 9:51 (KJV)** And it came to pass, when the time was come that he should be received up, he stedfastly set his face to go to Jerusalem,

**Luke 9:52 (KJV)** And sent messengers before his face: and they went, and entered into a village of the Samaritans, to make ready for him.

**Luke 9:53 (KJV)** And they did not receive him, because his face was as though he would go to Jerusalem.

**Luke 9:54 (KJV)** And when his disciples James and John saw *this*, they said, Lord, wilt thou that we command fire to come down from heaven, and consume them, even as Elias did?

**Luke 9:56 (KJV)** For the Son of man is not come to destroy men's lives, but to save *them*. And they went to another village.

**Romans 12:19 (KJV)** Dearly beloved, avenge not yourselves, but *rather* give place unto wrath: for it is written, Vengeance *is* mine; I will repay, saith the Lord.

13. Are you familiar with any churches or spiritual leaders who frequently focus their sermons on demons, witches, wizards, evil spirits, and attribute all misfortunes to the workings of Satan?

**Read for yourself:**

> **Matthew 28:18 (KJV)** And Jesus came and spake unto them, saying, All power is given unto me in heaven and in earth.

> **Matthew 28:19 (KJV)** Go ye therefore, and teach all nations, baptizing them in the name of the Father, and of the Son, and of the Holy Ghost:

> **Matthew 28:20 (KJV)** Teaching them to observe all things whatsoever I have commanded you: and, lo, I am with you alway, *even* unto the end of the world. Amen.

14. Do you know of any churches or spiritual leaders who regularly link prosperity or material gains to being signs of God's favor or as advantages of being a child of God?

**I encourage you to explore this on your own:**

> **Ephesians 1:3 (KJV)** Blessed *be* the God and Father of our Lord Jesus Christ, who hath blessed us with all spiritual blessings in heavenly *places* in Christ:

> **Ephesians 1:4 (KJV)** According as he hath chosen us in him before the foundation of the world, that we should be holy and without blame before him in love:

> **Ephesians 1:5 (KJV)** Having predestinated us unto the adoption of children by Jesus Christ to himself, according to the good pleasure of his will,

> **Ephesians 1:6 (KJV)** To the praise of the glory of his grace, wherein he hath made us accepted in the beloved.

15. Are you familiar with any churches or religious leaders who persistently assert that redemption is unattainable even after genuine repentance and acceptance of Christ?

**Read for yourself:**

> **Galatians 3:13 (KJV)** Christ hath redeemed us from the curse of the law, being made a curse for us: for it is written, Cursed *is* every one that hangeth on a tree:

> **1 Peter 1:18 (KJV)** Forasmuch as ye know that ye were not redeemed with corruptible things, *as* silver and gold, from your vain conversation *received* by tradition from your fathers;

> **Revelation 5:9 (KJV)** And they sung a new song, saying, Thou art worthy to take the book, and to open the seals thereof: for thou wast slain, and hast redeemed us to God by thy blood out of every kindred, and tongue, and people, and nation;

**Revelation 14:3 (KJV)** And they sung as it were a new song before the throne, and before the four beasts, and the elders: and no man could learn that song but the hundred *and* forty *and* four thousand, which were redeemed from the earth.

**Revelation 14:4 (KJV)** These are they which were not defiled with women; for they are virgins. These are they which follow the Lamb whithersoever he goeth. These were redeemed from among men, *being* the firstfruits unto God and to the Lamb.

16. Are you aware of any churches or spiritual figures who frequently boast about their financial success and consistently view the display of material wealth as an indication of their spiritual authority?

**Please investigate this matter personally through the lens of the scriptures:**

**1 Timothy 6:3 (KJV)** If any man teach otherwise, and consent not to wholesome words, *even* the words of our Lord Jesus Christ, and to the doctrine which is according to godliness;

**1 Timothy 6:4 (KJV)** He is proud, knowing nothing, but doting about questions and strifes of words, whereof cometh envy, strife, railings, evil surmisings,

**1 Timothy 6:5 (KJV)** Perverse disputings of men of corrupt minds, and destitute of the truth, supposing that gain is godliness: from such withdraw thyself.

**1 Timothy 6:6 (KJV)** But godliness with contentment is great gain.

**1 Timothy 6:7 (KJV)** For we brought nothing into *this* world, *and it is* certain we can carry nothing out.

**1 Timothy 6:8 (KJV)** And having food and raiment let us be therewith content.

**1 Timothy 6:9 (KJV)** But they that will be rich fall into temptation and a snare, and *into* many foolish and hurtful lusts, which drown men in destruction and perdition.

**1 Timothy 6:10 (KJV)** For the love of money is the root of all evil: which while some coveted after, they have erred from the faith, and pierced themselves through with many sorrows.

**1 Timothy 6:11 (KJV)** But thou, O man of God, flee these things; and follow after righteousness, godliness, faith, love, patience, meekness.

17. Are you familiar with any churches or religious leaders who adorn their church stage, inaccurately referred to as an altar, with vibrant psychedelic lights and gold decorations reminiscent of those found in a discotheque?

**I encourage you to personally delve into this issue by examining it through the perspective of scripture:**

**Isaiah 30:22 (KJV)** Ye shall defile also the covering of thy graven images of silver, and the ornament of thy molten images of gold: thou shalt cast them away as a menstruous cloth; thou shalt say unto it, Get thee hence.

**Ezekiel 7:20 (KJV)** As for the beauty of his ornament, he set it in majesty: but they made the images of their abominations *and* of their detestable things therein: therefore have I set it far from them.

**1 Peter 3:3 (KJV)** Whose adorning let it not be that outward *adorning* of plaiting the hair, and of wearing of gold, or of putting on of apparel;

**1 Peter 3:4 (KJV)** But *let it be* the hidden man of the heart, in that which is not corruptible, *even the ornament* of a meek and quiet spirit, which is in the sight of God of great price.

18. Are you aware of any churches or spiritual leaders who habitually call upon God's wrath and curses against individuals who offer criticism towards them?

**I urge you to explore this topic on your own by scrutinizing it through the lens of biblical teachings.**

**Leviticus 19:17 (KJV)** Thou shalt not hate thy brother in thine heart: thou shalt in any wise rebuke thy neighbour, and not suffer sin upon him.

**Matthew 5:44 (KJV)** But I say unto you, Love your enemies, bless them that curse you, do good to them that hate you, and pray for them which despitefully use you, and persecute you;

**Luke 6:28 (KJV)** Bless them that curse you, and pray for them which despitefully use you.

**Romans 12:14 (KJV)** Bless them which persecute you: bless, and curse not.

19. Are you familiar with any churches or religious figures who engage in rituals under the guise of divine practice during or after services, such as incense burning or conducting prayers to spirits of the deceased in cemeteries?

**Explore on your own to deepen your understanding in the Lord:**

**1 Samuel 28:7 (KJV)** Then said Saul unto his servants, Seek me a woman that hath a familiar spirit, that I may go to her, and inquire of her. And his servants said to him, Behold, *there is* a woman that hath a familiar spirit at En-dor.

**1 Samuel 28:8 (KJV)** And Saul disguised himself, and put on other raiment, and he went, and two men with him, and they came to the woman by night: and he said, I pray thee, divine unto me by the familiar spirit, and bring me *him* up, whom I shall name unto thee.

**1 Samuel 28:9 (KJV)** And the woman said unto him, Behold, thou knowest what Saul hath done, how he hath cut off those that have familiar spirits, and the wizards, out of the land: wherefore then layest thou a snare for my life, to cause me to die?

**1 Samuel 28:10 (KJV)** And Saul sware to her by the LORD, saying, *As* the LORD liveth, there shall no punishment happen to thee for this thing.

**1 Samuel 28:11 (KJV)** Then said the woman, Whom shall I bring up unto thee? And he said, Bring me up Samuel.

**1 Samuel 28:12 (KJV)** And when the woman saw Samuel, she cried with a loud voice: and the woman spake to Saul, saying, Why hast thou deceived me? for thou *art* Saul.

**1 Samuel 28:13 (KJV)** And the king said unto her, Be not afraid: for what sawest thou? And the woman said unto Saul, I saw gods ascending out of the earth.

**1 Samuel 28:14 (KJV)** And he said unto her, What form *is* he of? And she said, An old man cometh up; and he *is* covered with a mantle. And Saul perceived that it *was* Samuel, and he stooped with *his* face to the ground, and bowed himself.

**1 Samuel 28:15 (KJV)** And Samuel said to Saul, Why hast thou disquieted me, to bring me up? And Saul answered, I am sore distressed; for the Philistines make war against me, and God is departed from me, and answereth me no more, neither by prophets, nor by dreams: therefore I have called thee, that thou mayest make known unto me what I shall do.

**1 Samuel 28:16 (KJV)** Then said Samuel, Wherefore then dost thou ask of me, seeing the LORD is departed from thee, and is become thine enemy?

20. Are you aware of any churches or religious leaders who maintain close relationships with influential and wealthy individuals in society, often acknowledging them during sermons and citing the rich and famous as exemplars of their congregation?

**Explore on your own to deepen your understanding in the Lord:**

**James 2:1 (KJV)** My brethren, have not the faith of our Lord Jesus Christ, *the Lord* of glory, with respect of persons.

**James 2:2 (KJV)** For if there come unto your assembly a man with a gold ring, in goodly apparel, and there come in also a poor man in vile raiment;

**James 2:3 (KJV)** And ye have respect to him that weareth the gay clothing, and say unto him, Sit thou here in a good place; and say to the poor, Stand thou there, or sit here under my footstool:

**James 2:4 (KJV)** Are ye not then partial in yourselves, and are become judges of evil thoughts?

**James 2:5 (KJV)** Hearken, my beloved brethren, Hath not God chosen the poor of this world rich in faith, and heirs of the kingdom which he hath promised to them that love him?

**James 2:6 (KJV)** But ye have despised the poor. Do not rich men oppress you, and draw you before the judgment seats?

**James 2:7 (KJV)** Do not they blaspheme that worthy name by the which ye are called?

**James 5:1 (KJV)** Go to now, *ye* rich men, weep and howl for your miseries that shall come upon *you.*

**James 5:2 (KJV)** Your riches are corrupted, and your garments are motheaten.

**James 5:3 (KJV)** Your gold and silver is cankered; and the rust of them shall be a witness against you, and shall eat your flesh as it were fire. Ye have heaped treasure together for the last days.

**James 5:4 (KJV)** Behold, the hire of the labourers who have reaped down your fields, which is of you kept back by fraud, crieth: and the cries of them which have reaped are entered into the ears of the Lord of sabaoth.

**James 5:5 (KJV)** Ye have lived in pleasure on the earth, and been wanton; ye have nourished your hearts, as in a day of slaughter.

**James 5:6 (KJV)** Ye have condemned *and* killed the just; *and* he doth not resist you.

21. Are you familiar with any churches or spiritual leaders who show indifference or even condone premarital sexual relationships among their church members?

**Explore on your own to deepen your understanding in the Lord:**

**1 Corinthians 6:15 (KJV)** Know ye not that your bodies are the members of Christ? shall I then take the members of Christ, and make *them* the members of an harlot? God forbid.

**1 Corinthians 6:16 (KJV)** What? know ye not that he which is joined to an harlot is one body? for two, saith he, shall be one flesh.

**1 Corinthians 6:17 (KJV)** But he that is joined unto the Lord is one spirit.

**1 Corinthians 6:18 (KJV)** Flee fornication. Every sin that a man doeth is without the body; but he that committeth fornication sinneth against his own body.

**1 Corinthians 6:19 (KJV)** What? know ye not that your body is the temple of the Holy Ghost *which is* in you, which ye have of God, and ye are not your own?

**1 Corinthians 6:20 (KJV)** For ye are bought with a price: therefore glorify God in your body, and in your spirit, which are God's.

22. Are you aware of any churches or religious figures who frequently assert their superiority in power over other churches or pastors?

**Explore on your own to deepen your understanding in the Lord:**

**Matthew 18:1 (KJV)** At the same time came the disciples unto Jesus, saying, Who is the greatest in the kingdom of heaven?

**Matthew 18:2 (KJV)** And Jesus called a little child unto him, and set him in the midst of them,

**Matthew 18:3 (KJV)** And said, Verily I say unto you, Except ye be converted, and become as little children, ye shall not enter into the kingdom of heaven.

**Matthew 18:4 (KJV)** Whosoever therefore shall humble himself as this little child, the same is greatest in the kingdom of heaven.

**Mark 9:33 (KJV)** And he came to Capernaum: and being in the house he asked them, What was it that ye disputed among yourselves by the way?

**Mark 9:34 (KJV)** But they held their peace: for by the way they had disputed among themselves, who *should be* the greatest.

**Mark 9:35 (KJV)** And he sat down, and called the twelve, and saith unto them, If any man desire to be first, *the same* shall be last of all, and servant of all.

23. Are you familiar with any churches or religious leaders who regularly exhibit disdain towards their congregation, positioning themselves as authoritarian figures over the members? This behavior could include mocking the congregants for their occupations (deeming them as lesser professions), the vehicles they drive, and pressuring them to pursue more prestigious careers. Additionally, have you encountered instances where such figures have disrespectfully scattered Holy Communion elements on the floor, prompting members to scramble and collect them?

**Explore on your own to deepen your understanding in the Lord:**

**Matthew 23:1 (KJV)** Then spake Jesus to the multitude, and to his disciples,

**Matthew 23:2 (KJV)** Saying, The scribes and the Pharisees sit in Moses' seat:

**Matthew 23:3 (KJV)** All therefore whatsoever they bid you observe, *that* observe and do; but do not ye after their works: for they say, and do not.

**Matthew 23:4 (KJV)** For they bind heavy burdens and grievous to be borne, and lay *them* on men's shoulders; but they *themselves* will not move them with one of their fingers.

**Matthew 23:5 (KJV)** But all their works they do for to be seen of men: they make broad their phylacteries, and enlarge the borders of their garments,

**Matthew 23:6 (KJV)** And love the uppermost rooms at feasts, and the chief seats in the synagogues,

**Matthew 23:7 (KJV)** And greetings in the markets, and to be called of men, Rabbi, Rabbi.

**Matthew 23:8 (KJV)** But be not ye called Rabbi: for one is your Master, *even* Christ; and all ye are brethren.

**Matthew 23:9 (KJV)** And call no *man* your father upon the earth: for one is your Father, which is in heaven.

**Matthew 23:10 (KJV)** Neither be ye called masters: for one is your Master, *even* Christ.

**Matthew 23:11 (KJV)** But he that is greatest among you shall be your servant.

**Matthew 23:12 (KJV)** And whosoever shall exalt himself shall be abased; and he that shall humble himself shall be exalted.

24. Are you aware of any churches or spiritual leaders who consistently position themselves as the sole source of spiritual guidance for their members, to the extent of advising on everyday decisions? This could range from determining the spiritually auspicious time to book a flight, to personal choices like selecting a spouse, deciding the timing of travel, or even the location of purchasing a home.

**Explore on your own to deepen your understanding in the Lord:**

**Psalm 37:23 (KJV)** The steps of a *good* man are ordered by the LORD: and he delighteth in his way.

**2 Timothy 2:19 (KJV)** Nevertheless the foundation of God standeth sure, having this seal, The Lord knoweth them that are his. And, Let every one that nameth the name of Christ depart from iniquity.

**1 Peter 3:12 (KJV)** For the eyes of the Lord *are* over the righteous, and his ears *are open* unto their prayers: but the face of the Lord *is* against them that do evil.

25. Are you familiar with any churches or religious leaders who frequently suggest that your friends and family members are the root of your troubles, thus fostering discord and animosity?

**Explore on your own to deepen your understanding in the Lord:**

**Proverbs 6:12 (KJV)** A naughty person, a wicked man, walketh with a froward mouth.

**Proverbs 6:13 (KJV)** He winketh with his eyes, he speaketh with his feet, he teacheth with his fingers;

**Proverbs 6:14 (KJV)** Frowardness *is* in his heart, he deviseth mischief continually; he soweth discord.

**Proverbs 6:15 (KJV)** Therefore shall his calamity come suddenly; suddenly shall he be broken without remedy.

**Proverbs 16:7 (KJV)** When a man's ways please the LORD, he maketh even his enemies to be at peace with him.

# PRAYER AS A
# FORM OF WORSHIP

Prayer is an act of invocation, supplication, or intercession of the Holy Spirit, in order to activate our presence before God Almighty. This belief in the presence of the Spirit of God is what actually establishes the communication chain for a dialogue with our God. When we pray, we must understand that we are seeking the presence of the Supreme Being.

> **1 Thessalonians 5:16-18** Rejoice evermore. Pray without ceasing. In everything give thanks; for this is the will of God in Christ Jesus concerning you.

Pray always in secret as your first resort:

> **Matthew 6:5 (KJV)** And when thou prayest, thou shalt not be as the hypocrites *are*: for they love to pray standing in the synagogues and in the corners of the streets, that they may be seen of men. Verily I say unto you, They have their reward

> **Matthew 6:6 (KJV)** But when thou prayest, enter into thy closest, and when thou hast shut thy door, pray to the Father which is in secret; and thy Father which seeth in secret shall reward thee openly.

26. Start your day with thanks and Praise GOD in truth.

27. Tell God why you want to thank HIM:

    • Pour out your heart out in truth.

    • Express your love to him.

    • Assure yourself in confirmation of his love for you.

    • Ask forgiveness of sin (because of your sinful nature)

    • Pray for your enemies and leave the rest to God.

28. Ask God for rebirth and his continued presence in your life.

29. Praise and Glorify God Almighty first in your prayer:

    • acknowledge that God is in Heaven

    • acknowledge that God is Holy

    • speak words that show that you believe and are expecting the Kingdom of God and the will of God to be established on the Earth even as it is already established in Heaven

30. Pray fervently with a pure heart and in truth:

- Ask your petition and your petition should not be worldly carnal physical things, but the right amount of the Word of God.

- Ask for forgiveness for sins that we have committed: in our thoughts, in our words/speech, and in our deeds/actions while remembering to forgive those who have hurt us.

- Petition God Almighty to order your steps in His Word so that you do not fall.

31. Do not repeat yourself in long complaints and demands:

**Mathew 12:50 (KJV)** But when you pray, use not vain repetitions; as the heathen do; for they think that they shall be heard for their much speaking.

## THE LORD'S PRAYER IS YOUR MODEL
## THAT JESUS TAUGHT US!

**Matthew 6:6 (KJV)** But thou, when thou prayest, enter into thy closet, and when thou hast shut thy door, pray to thy Father which is in secret; and thy Father which seeth in secret shall reward thee openly.

**Matthew 6:7 (KJV)** But when ye pray, use not vain repetitions, as the heathen *do*: for they think that they shall be heard for their much speaking.

**Matthew 6:8 (KJV)** Be not ye therefore like unto them: for your Father knoweth what things ye have need of, before ye ask him.

**Matthew 6:10 (KJV)** Thy kingdom come. Thy will be done in earth, as *it is* in heaven.

**Matthew 6:11 (KJV)** Give us this day our daily bread.

**Matthew 6:12 (KJV)** And forgive us our debts, as we forgive our debtors.

**Matthew 6:13 (KJV)** And lead us not into temptation, but deliver us from evil: For thine is the kingdom, and the power, and the glory, for ever. Amen.

The LORD Jesus Christ be with your spirit. The LORD Jesus Christ give you understanding.

# OPTIMAL TIMES FOR WORSHIP – UNDERSTANDING SACRED MOMENTS

Worshipping God should not be based on schedules or occasions but should be part of our daily living, and spontaneous. In other religions including Christianity, worship is set for certain times of the day, certain days in the week, and certain weeks in the month are more suitable for worship than other times. This is presumably a relic of the Old Testament whereas in the New Testament, every day is worship day:

> **Exodus 23:17 (KJV)** Three times in the year all thy males shall appear before the Lord GOD.

> **Deuteronomy 16:16 (KJV)** Three times in a year shall all thy males appear before the LORD thy God in the place which he shall choose; in the feast of unleavened bread, and in the feast of weeks, and in the feast of tabernacles: and they shall not appear before the LORD empty:

> **Matthew 22:37 (KJV)** Jesus said unto him, Thou shalt love the Lord thy God with all thy heart, and with all thy soul, and with all thy mind.

> **Mark 12:28 (KJV)** And one of the scribes came, and having heard them reasoning together, and perceiving that he had answered them well, asked him, Which is the first commandment of all?

> **Mark 12:29 (KJV)** And Jesus answered him, The first of all the commandments *is*, Hear, O Israel; The Lord our God is one Lord:

> **Mark 12:30 (KJV)** And thou shalt love the Lord thy God with all thy heart, and with all thy soul, and with all thy mind, and with all thy strength: this *is* the first commandment.

> **Mark 12:31 (KJV)** And the second *is* like, *namely* this, Thou shalt love thy neighbour as thyself. There is none other commandment greater than these.

There are holy days, ordinary days, and days or periods that are set aside for special worship and recognition. For example, in Christianity, Sunday is a worship day for the majority. While some, on their part, worship on Saturday, which they call the Sabbath Day even though the spiritual alignment of the days and months in the Holy Bible are lost, to the extent that what we call Saturday today does not correspond to the real and correct Sabbath Day in Genesis and Exodus!

Christians have also made it a religious tradition to celebrate the Birth of Jesus Christ every 25th of December in the year, which in fact could not be farther from the Truth because the LORD Jesus

Christ was NOT born on 25th December! Brethren, there is nothing wrong with setting aside a day to remember the birth of our Lord and Master Jesus Christ but it is important to know the truth behind every single "religious tradition" in order to ensure that whatever you are practicing is biblically sound. Tell me a child of God, all that goes on during Christmas celebration how they edify you or the body of Christ.

> **Mark 7:13 (KJV)** Making the word of God of none effect through your tradition, which ye have delivered: and many such like things do ye.

> **Jeremiah 10:2 (KJV)** Thus saith the LORD, Learn not the way of the heathen, and be not dismayed at the signs of heaven; for the heathen are dismayed at them.

> **Jeremiah 10:3 (KJV)** For the customs of the people are vain: for one cutteth a tree out of the forest, the work of the hands of the workman, with the axe.

> **Jeremiah 10:4 (KJV)** They deck it with silver and with gold; they fasten it with nails and with hammers, that it move not.

> **Colossians 2:8 (KJV)** Beware lest any man spoil you through philosophy and vain deceit, after the tradition of men, after the rudiments of the world, and not after Christ.

Easter is a bold celebration of Christ's victory over Death and the Resurrection that brings restoration of our relationship with God through the Grace and Sacrifice of our Lord Jesus Christ to Godward. Yet, Easter is also a pagan religious ceremony!

> **Romans 6:8 (KJV)** Now if we be dead with Christ, we believe that we shall also live with him:

> **Romans 6:9 (KJV)** Knowing that Christ being raised from the dead dieth no more; death hath no more dominion over him.

> **Deuteronomy 12:31 (KJV)** Thou shalt not do so unto the LORD thy God: for every abomination to the LORD, which he hateth, have they done unto their gods; for even their sons and their daughters they have burnt in the fire to their gods.

The Death and Resurrection of Jesus Christ have removed the stigma of sin and bought us Salvation. Therefore, we must always be joyful with praise and worship not only on special days, but also on all days. Some of these days and the special times are becoming less significant today than what it was supposed to mean about fifty years ago. All of today's religious observances have become worldly, commercialized, non-sacrosanct, and money-driven events for both believers and non-believers of Christ Jesus.

Do we worship for rewards from God such as protection, good health, or prosperity in our human endeavors? The Grace of God was already with humankind before we were even born hence, it is not our prayers that will bring them down to us. The Grace of God was revealed to us through the Death and Resurrection of our Lord and Savior Jesus Christ:

> **2 Timothy 1:8 (KJV)** Be not thou therefore ashamed of the testimony of our Lord, nor of me his prisoner: but be thou partaker of the afflictions of the gospel according to the power of God;

> **2 Timothy 1:9 (KJV)** Who hath saved us, and called *us* with an holy calling, not according to our works, but according to his own purpose and grace, which was given us in Christ Jesus before the world began,

> **2 Timothy 1:10 (KJV)** But is now made manifest by the appearing of our Saviour Jesus Christ, who hath abolished death, and hath brought life and immortality to light through the gospel:

> **2 Timothy 1:11 (KJV)** Whereunto I am appointed a preacher, and an apostle, and a teacher of the Gentiles.

Undeservingly, God has always taken care of our needs and we must be joyful and thankful to God through worship and praise. Do not only pray because you need something from God and do not wait until Sunday to worship and praise God. All we have to do as humankind is to thank God wherever we are for his goodness and mercy.

Most Christians condition giving and worship to a seed of token that one can sow and then reap. Our nature of appreciativeness toward God's plan for our lives is the barrier that we have created between us and our Father in Heaven. Not until we change our understanding of what constitutes genuine worship, the barricade that we by our own doing have mounted will continue to increase and widen the gap between us and God's master plan for our lives. Genuine worship stems from the heart without any wrath or animosity but trust in God to fulfill His plan and promise in HIS chosen hour.

# SALVATION

When we talk about Salvation as promised in the Scriptures, it is not an automatic inheritance:

**John 3:36 (KJV)** He that believeth on the Son hath everlasting life: and he that believeth not the Son shall not see life; but the wrath of God abideth on him.

Therefore, those who go about telling people that it is automatic Salvation or guaranteed inheritance from Heaven must rethink their approach in this faulty delivery of the Gospel of Christ. To obey Jesus Christ (Son of God), we must go after our Salvation with fear and trembling. As a practical matter, you must:

1.  Love God Almighty

2.  Love your neighbor as yourself

3.  Forgive those who offended you

4.  Ask God to forgive you and your enemies

5.  Understand that Jesus Christ is the Messiah and accept that Jesus Christ has the power to forgive sin

6.  Repent from your sins

7.  You must be authentic and faithful to the LORD

**Philippians 2:12 (KJV)** Wherefore, my beloved, as ye have always obeyed, not as in my presence only, but now much more in my absence, work out your own salvation with fear and trembling.

**Philippians 2:13 (KJV)** For it is God which worketh in you both to will and to do of *his* good pleasure.

Even the disciples of Jesus were not given the impression that their salvation was a done deal. They were instructed to continue to work hard towards it. Let us see what the Bible said in:

**John 8:31 (KJV)** Then said Jesus to those Jews which believed on him, If ye continue in my word, *then* are ye my disciples indeed;

**Romans 11:22 (KJV)** Behold therefore the goodness and severity of God: on them which fell, severity; but toward thee, goodness, if thou continue in *his* goodness: otherwise thou also shalt be cut off.

**Colossians 1:23 (KJV)** If ye continue in the faith grounded and settled, and *be* not moved away from the hope of the gospel, which ye have heard, *and* which was preached to every creature which is under heaven; whereof I Paul am made a minister;

**1 Timothy 2:15 (KJV)** Notwithstanding she shall be saved in childbearing, if they continue in faith and charity and holiness with sobriety.

**1 John 2:24 (KJV)** Let that therefore abide in you, which ye have heard from the beginning. If that which ye have heard from the beginning shall remain in you, ye also shall continue in the Son, and in the Father.

Looking at the foregoing discussion, it is clear that we are only saved if we work towards it by continuing to obey the Word of God. To be saved as a child does not give any Christian an automatic entry to Heaven, neither does it assure any attainment of Salvation. Do not say that a child is an innocent human being because God Almighty assures us that both babies, even unborn babies, and adults are devils even from the womb!

**Psalm 58:3 (KJV)** The wicked are estranged from the womb: they go astray as soon as they be born, speaking lies.

**Isaiah 48:8 (KJV)** Yea, thou heardest not; yea, thou knewest not; yea, from that time *that* thine ear was not opened: for I knew that thou wouldest deal very treacherously, and wast called a transgressor from the womb.

Therefore, if Salvation requires the person to repent of his or her sins, forsake them altogether, and live in righteousness, then when did the little baby or child accomplish all those three processes in order to qualify for the Salvation?

This teaching of "once saved always saved" is a disincentive to our struggle for the Salvation promised by God. We all were once condemned for our sins but were saved by God with a condition.

**1 Peter 4:17 (KJV)** For the time *is come* that judgment must begin at the house of God: and if *it* first *begin* at us, what shall the end *be* of them that obey not the gospel of God?

The scripture is saying that even those of us in the House of God, (Christians) will be judged first before others. Thus, there is an expectation of good deeds and a life of holiness, so that if you know that Jesus Christ is your personal Savior and LORD, it does not exempt you from the judgment of God:

**Romans 14:10 (KJV)** But why dost thou judge thy brother? or why dost thou set at nought thy brother? for we shall all stand before the judgment seat of Christ.

**1 John 3:2 (KJV)** Beloved, now are we the sons of God, and it doth not yet appear what we shall be: but we know that, when he shall appear, we shall be like him; for we shall see him as he is.

**1 John 3:3 (KJV)** And every man that hath this hope in him purifieth himself, even as he is pure.

**1 John 3:4 (KJV)** Whosoever committeth sin transgresseth also the law: for sin is the transgression of the law.

**1 John 3:5 (KJV)** And ye know that he was manifested to take away our sins; and in him is no sin.

**1 John 5:18 (KJV)** We know that whosoever is born of God sinneth not; but he that is begotten of God keepeth himself, and that wicked one toucheth him not.

To be a child of God, we must try to exemplify God as Holy Spirit has taught us. To make Heaven as a believer is not a one-day wonder. That is why the Scripture told us that we must continue to work hard with fear and trembling towards our Salvation. There is a reward for good behavior such as following the right path in all your dealings. There are no rewards for living a deceitful life and expect that because you have been saved once so you are forever save irrespective of your current lifestyle and sins:

**Ezekiel 33:12 (KJV)** Therefore, thou son of man, say unto the children of thy people, The righteousness of the righteous shall not deliver him in the day of his transgression: as for the wickedness of the wicked, he shall not fall thereby in the day that he turneth from his wickedness; neither shall the righteous be able to live for his *righteousness* in the day that he sinneth.

**James 1:12 (KJV)** Blessed *is* the man that endureth temptation: for when he is tried, he shall receive the crown of life, which the Lord hath promised to them that love him.

**2 Timothy 4:6 (KJV)** For I am now ready to be offered, and the time of my departure is at hand.

**2 Timothy 4:7 (KJV)** I have fought a good fight, I have finished *my* course, I have kept the faith:

**2 Timothy 4:8 (KJV)** Henceforth there is laid up for me a crown of righteousness, which the Lord, the righteous judge, shall give me at that day: and not to me only, but unto all them also that love his appearing.

**Revelation 2:10 (KJV)** Fear none of those things which thou shalt suffer: behold, the devil shall cast *some* of you into prison, that ye may be tried; and ye shall have tribulation ten days: be thou faithful unto death, and I will give thee a crown of life.

There are many people that have gone astray (backslidden) from the day that they were saved and became a child of God. The assumption and false teaching that "once saved forever saved" negates the expectation of following the footsteps of Christ and obeying HIS commandments.

God is willing to forgive us if we repent from our evil ways wholeheartedly without reservation. However, to think that you have been saved years ago so you can go on living unworthy life, die in sin, and go on to inherit the Kingdom of God, it amounts to a dangerous false doctrine of the promise of Salvation:

> **1 John 1:8 (KJV)** If we say that we have no sin, we deceive ourselves, and the truth is not in us.

> **1 John 1:9 (KJV)** If we confess our sins, he is faithful and just to forgive us *our* sins, and to cleanse us from all unrighteousness.

> **1 John 1:10 (KJV)** If we say that we have not sinned, we make him a liar, and his word is not in us.

If you are saved, then you have to turn away from sin and live a life worthy of Christ Jesus as your LORD and Savior:

> **1 Peter 3:15 (KJV)** But sanctify the Lord God in your hearts: and *be* ready always to *give* an answer to every man that asketh you a reason of the hope that is in you with meekness and fear:

> **1 Peter 3:16 (KJV)** Having a good conscience; that, whereas they speak evil of you, as of evildoers, they may be ashamed that falsely accuse your good conversation in Christ.

> **1 Peter 3:17 (KJV)** For *it is* better, if the will of God be so, that ye suffer for well doing, than for evil doing.

> **1 Peter 3:18 (KJV)** For Christ also hath once suffered for sins, the just for the unjust, that he might bring us to God, being put to death in the flesh, but quickened by the Spirit:

God is willing and just to forgive us for our transgressions if only we truthfully repent and commit to him, even as we see in **1 John 1:8-10**. God is merciful and HIS Grace in us is sufficient for our Salvation in Christ. The promise of God that God sent his Only Son to die for our sins and if we believe in him as our personal LORD and Savior, and obey His Word, then we shall inherit the Kingdom of God is true then and it is true also now.

To believe in Jesus Christ as our LORD means that we must obey HIS commandments and live a life worthy of HIS name. Jesus Chris gave us some of the prescriptions, as follows:

- You must not kill
- You must not commit adultery
- You must honour your father and mother
- You must love your neighbour as yourself.

In view of what Our Lord Jesus told this man in **Mathew 19: 16-21** as to what he needed to do in order to inherit the Kingdom of God. In this context of the scripture, Jesus acknowledged that nobody is good or perfect except him. This means we are capable of sin, but for his promise of salvation, there is redemption after repentance of sin.

Also in, we have further evidence that this doctrine of "one saved always saved" is a very evil doctrine!

> **Matthew 24:13 (KJV)** But he that shall endure unto the end, the same shall be saved.

It means that there will be challenges in maintaining your holiness and abstaining from sin and all temptations around us. In *1 Peter 4:18 "Even the righteous are scarcely saved"* The scripture acknowledges that there is more to be done by the individual in order to make Heaven and never an automatic thing as some evil Pastors teach:

> **Hebrews 10:26 (KJV)** For if we sin wilfully after that we have received the knowledge of the truth, there remaineth no more sacrifice for sins,

> **Hebrews 10:27 (KJV)** But a certain fearful looking for of judgment and fiery indignation, which shall devour the adversaries.

> **Hebrews 10:28 (KJV)** He that despised Moses' law died without mercy under two or three witnesses:

> **Hebrews 10:29 (KJV)** Of how much sorer punishment, suppose ye, shall he be thought worthy, who hath trodden under foot the Son of God, and hath counted the blood of the covenant, wherewith he was sanctified, an unholy thing, and hath done despite unto the Spirit of grace?

> **Hebrews 10:30 (KJV)** For we know him that hath said, Vengeance *belongeth* unto me, I will recompense, saith the Lord. And again, The Lord shall judge his people.

> **Hebrews 10:31 (KJV)** *It is* a fearful thing to fall into the hands of the living God.

There is no absolution for those people who deliberately continue to live in sin with this false impression that they are saved no matter how many times they sin against God:

> **Jude 4 (KJV)** For there are certain men crept in unawares, who were before of old ordained to this condemnation, ungodly men, turning the grace of our God into lasciviousness, and denying the only Lord God, and our Lord Jesus Christ.

> **Jude 5 (KJV)** I will therefore put you in remembrance, though ye once knew this, how that the Lord, having saved the people out of the land of Egypt, afterward destroyed them that believed not.

There are many Scriptures that contradict these false doctrinal teachings about Salvation. We the followers of Christ must follow all his teachings and obey his commandments:

**Titus 2:11 (KJV)** For the grace of God that bringeth salvation hath appeared to all men,

**Titus 2:12 (KJV)** Teaching us that, denying ungodliness and worldly lusts, we should live soberly, righteously, and godly, in this present world;

**Titus 2:13 (KJV)** Looking for that blessed hope, and the glorious appearing of the great God and our Saviour Jesus Christ;

**Titus 2:14 (KJV)** Who gave himself for us, that he might redeem us from all iniquity, and purify unto himself a peculiar people, zealous of good works.

**Titus 2:15 (KJV)** These things speak, and exhort, and rebuke with all authority. Let no man despise thee.

For the Grace of God brings Salvation to men. This Grace does not come cheap without work. The work is hard and difficult like working out, living on a good diet to gain good health, or detoxifying yourself. Thus, the instruction to good and faithful living such as avoiding the things that are evil and ungodly that the world presents.

This world presents pleasures, which can lead to unrighteous living. Therefore, followers of Christ must be smart to descend from those pleasures around us that can easily deceive us into sinful behavior. Today's Christians lack devotion to GOD. We have compromised a lot of ground on which the Christian faith was built in the beginning.

A case in point, all Christian celebrations have lost their significance. They were mostly established on false doctrines using the desire of believers to lure them into recognizing the idols of the world.

For example, the commercialization of Christmas on December 25th is characterized by sinful feasting and drunkenness, adultery, fornication, and all worldly pleasures that we were instructed against.

Our devotion to God is questionable since we only come to God or go to church to worship when we like and as we please. Some people have forgotten how God Almighty protect them whether they ask Him or not. Thanking God for living should not be a once a week activity, a monthly thing, or a yearly affair during December (end of year gathering in the chapel):

**Kings 8:61 (KJV)** Let your heart therefore be perfect with the LORD our God, to walk in his statutes, and to keep his commandments, as at this day.

Therefore, aside worshipping on Sunday at a church service, do not stop worshipping or living a holy life on Tuesday, Wednesday, Thursday, Friday or Saturday throughout the year:

**Romans 12:11 (KJV)** Not slothful in business; fervent in spirit; serving the Lord;

Let us say that you have this friend of yours who only calls or comes to see you only when he needs your help and vanishes thereafter only to reappear when things are hard for him again. How will you characterize this relationship? Is this friend devoted, is it a friend with benefit, or is this friend only abusing you and the friendship?

Our relationship with God should not be transactional. It is a continuous devotion to HIS will and power:

> **John 8:11 (KJV)** She said, No man, Lord. And Jesus said unto her, Neither do I condemn thee: go, and sin no more.

In John 8:11: Jesus told the woman who was caught in an adulterous lifestyle, to GO AND SIN NO MORE. This is an instruction to a saved soul by our Lord Jesus Christ. Any disobedience to this explicit instruction by any believer (woman) or Pastor can cause a believer's name to be blotted out of the Lamb's Book of Life:

> **Exodus 32:32 (KJV)** Yet now, if thou wilt forgive their sin; and if not, blot me, I pray thee, out of thy book which thou hast written.

> **Exodus 32:33 (KJV)** And the LORD said unto Moses, Whosoever hath sinned against me, him will I blot out of my book.

> **Deuteronomy 9:14 (KJV)** Let me alone, that I may destroy them, and blot out their name from under heaven: and I will make of thee a nation mightier and greater than they.

> **Deuteronomy 29:20 (KJV)** The LORD will not spare him, but then the anger of the LORD and his jealousy shall smoke against that man, and all the curses that are written in this book shall lie upon him, and the LORD shall blot out his name from under heaven.

> **Revelation 3:5 (KJV)** He that overcometh, the same shall be clothed in white raiment; and I will not blot out his name out of the book of life, but I will confess his name before my Father, and before his angels.

The church of today is ignoring **John 8:11 (KJV)** and thus, we have seen some strange things and lawlessness in the House of God:

> **Mark 16:15 (KJV)** And he said unto them, Go ye into all the world, and preach the gospel to every creature.

> **Mark 16:16 (KJV)** He that believeth and is baptized shall be saved; but he that believeth not shall be damned.

> **Mark 16:17 (KJV)** And these signs shall follow them that believe; In my name shall they cast out devils; they shall speak with new tongues;

> **Mark 16:18 (KJV)** They shall take up serpents; and if they drink any deadly thing, it shall not hurt them; they shall lay hands on the sick, and they shall recover.

**Mark 16:15-18 (KJV)** requires believers to believe and be baptized by Holy Ghost. Baptism is a sign of repentance and confession that shows that Christ dwells in us. Therefore, going back into sin after Jesus Christ has forgiven you all your sins is tantamount to rejecting him:

> **Hebrews 6:4 (KJV)** For *it is* impossible for those who were once enlightened, and have tasted of the heavenly gift, and were made partakers of the Holy Ghost,

> **Hebrews 6:5 (KJV)** And have tasted the good word of God, and the powers of the world to come,

> **Hebrews 6:6 (KJV)** If they shall fall away, to renew them again unto repentance; seeing they crucify to themselves the Son of God afresh, and put *him* to an open shame.

When you are baptized into Christ Jesus after becoming saved, it means that you had asked for forgiveness and cleansing from sin, which is possible through believing in our Lord Jesus Christ:

> **John 5:24 (KJV)** Verily, verily, I say unto you, He that heareth my word, and believeth on him that sent me, hath everlasting life, and shall not come into condemnation; but is passed from death unto life.

Specifically, therefore, dear child of God, if any church or Pastor teaches you any doctrines that do not agree with the Holy Scripture, please run away from them very quickly. The Holy Bible tells us that many who use to do exploits for God will be rejected on the last day because of their iniquities. Brethren, Jesus Christ assured us that there would be Prophets and miracle workers in Hell!

> **Matthew 7:18 (KJV)** A good tree cannot bring forth evil fruit, neither *can* a corrupt tree bring forth good fruit.

> **Matthew 7:19 (KJV)** Every tree that bringeth not forth good fruit is hewn down, and cast into the fire.

> **Matthew 7:20 (KJV)** Wherefore by their fruits ye shall know them.

> **Matthew 7:21 (KJV)** Not every one that saith unto me, Lord, Lord, shall enter into the kingdom of heaven; but he that doeth the will of my Father which is in heaven.

> **Matthew 7:22 (KJV)** Many will say to me in that day, Lord, Lord, have we not prophesied in thy name? and in thy name have cast out devils? and in thy name done many wonderful works?

> **Matthew 7:23 (KJV)** And then will I profess unto them, I never knew you: depart from me, ye that work iniquity.

Here is the will of the Father (not your father or Papa) but your Father in Heaven, and the will is to obey HIS commandments and teachings. Therefore, be wise and do not be misled by all those who say that they are Christians and Pastors. This is why we the followers of Christ must ask ourselves some of the probing questions in our relationships with our churches, and in our relationships with all those who call themselves Pastors:

# WHAT IS CHRISTIANITY?

Christianity can be likened to an educational journey, where the Bible serves as the essential textbook. It's through studying and comprehending its teachings that one can 'graduate' from this spiritual school, leading to the ultimate reward of entering Heaven!

**Ezekiel 34:16 (KJV)** I will seek that which was lost, and bring again that which was driven away, and will bind up *that which was* broken, and will strengthen that which was sick: but I will destroy the fat and the strong; I will feed them with judgment.

**Matthew 18:11 (KJV)** For the Son of man is come to save that which was lost.

**Luke 19:10 (KJV)** For the Son of man is come to seek and to save that which was lost.

**Timothy 2:15 (KJV)** Study to shew thyself approved unto God, a workman that needeth not to be ashamed, rightly dividing the word of truth.

Christianity is described as an earthly institution that equips its followers for their eventual passage to Heaven. Success in this divine curriculum doesn't hinge on raw emotion or indistinct displays of unfounded faith. Instead, it demands the engagement of one's intellect and analytical skills, as underscored in **2 Timothy 2:15**, which calls for diligent study to rightly divide the word of truth.

Thus, the foundational text of Christianity, often referred to as the Gospel of Jesus Christ or simply the Bible, emphasizes the importance of serving God not with fleeting feelings but with a thoughtful and discerning mind. This approach is further validated by numerous scriptures that guide our understanding and practice of faith:

**Romans 1:9 (KJV)** For God is my witness, whom I serve with my spirit in the gospel of his Son, that without ceasing I make mention of you always in my prayers;

**Romans 7:25 (KJV)** I thank God through Jesus Christ our Lord. So then with the mind I myself serve the law of God; but with the flesh the law of sin.

Next, we will explore additional evidence reinforcing the concept that Christianity is akin to an educational institution, with the Bible serving as the primary textbook.

1. The singular and most profound interaction between God and humanity is designed to instruct us in God's ways, positioning God primarily as a Teacher to mankind.

   **John 6:45 (KJV)** It is written in the prophets, And they shall be all taught of God. Every man therefore that hath heard, and hath learned of the Father, cometh unto me.

**1 Thessalonians 4:9 (KJV)** But as touching brotherly love ye need not that I write unto you: for ye yourselves are taught of God to love one another.

2. Christianity is known as the School of Heaven on Earth, where the core curriculum revolves around "The Knowledge of God," embodied in the Holy Bible. This fundamental focus on understanding God's word is the primary responsibility of every minister, regardless of their title— be it Apostle, Prophet, Evangelist, Pastor, or Teacher.

**Deuteronomy 4:5 (KJV)** Behold, I have taught you statutes and judgments, even as the LORD my God commanded me, that ye should do so in the land whither ye go to possess it.

**Deuteronomy 4:6 (KJV)** Keep therefore and do *them*; for this *is* your wisdom and your understanding in the sight of the nations, which shall hear all these statutes, and say, Surely this great nation *is* a wise and understanding people.

**Deuteronomy 31:22 (KJV)** Moses therefore wrote this song the same day, and taught it the children of Israel.

**2 Chronicles 30:22 (KJV)** And Hezekiah spake comfortably unto all the Levites that taught the good knowledge of the LORD: and they did eat throughout the feast seven days, offering peace offerings, and making confession to the LORD God of their fathers.

**2 Chronicles 35:3 (KJV)** And said unto the Levites that taught all Israel, which were holy unto the LORD, Put the holy ark in the house which Solomon the son of David king of Israel did build; *it shall* not *be* a burden upon *your* shoulders: serve now the LORD your God, and his people Israel,

**Nehemiah 8:9 (KJV)** And Nehemiah, which *is* the Tirshatha, and Ezra the priest the scribe, and the Levites that taught the people, said unto all the people, This day *is* holy unto the LORD your God; mourn not, nor weep. For all the people wept, when they heard the words of the law.

**Ephesians 4:11 (KJV)** And he gave some, apostles; and some, prophets; and some, evangelists; and some, pastors and teachers;

3. The sole task entrusted by Jesus Christ to all His ministers is to teach the Word of God. In this divine educational framework, the lost children of God are the students, while the ministers of Christ serve as their teachers!

**Ezekiel 34:16 (KJV)** I will seek that which was lost, and bring again that which was driven away, and will bind up *that which was* broken, and will strengthen that which was sick: but I will destroy the fat and the strong; I will feed them with judgment.

**Matthew 18:11 (KJV)** For the Son of man is come to save that which was lost.

**Luke 19:10 (KJV)** For the Son of man is come to seek and to save that which was lost.

**Matthew 28:19 (KJV)** Go ye therefore, and teach all nations, baptizing them in the name of the Father, and of the Son, and of the Holy Ghost:

**Matthew 28:20 (KJV)** Teaching them to observe all things whatsoever I have commanded you: and, lo, I am with you alway, *even* unto the end of the world. Amen.

**Luke 1:2 (KJV)** Even as they delivered them unto us, which from the beginning were eyewitnesses, and ministers of the word;

**Acts 6:4 (KJV)** But we will give ourselves continually to prayer, and to the ministry of the word.

**1 Timothy 2:7 (KJV)** Whereunto I am ordained a preacher, and an apostle, (I speak the truth in Christ, *and* lie not;) a teacher of the Gentiles in faith and verity.

**2 Timothy 1:11 (KJV)** Whereunto I am appointed a preacher, and an apostle, and a teacher of the Gentiles.

4. The primary role of the Holy Spirit on Earth is centered around education. This divine entity is tasked with enlightening and guiding believers, offering wisdom, understanding, and insight into the depths of God's Word and His will. Through teaching, the Holy Spirit empowers individuals to navigate their spiritual journey, interpret biblical truths, and apply these teachings to their lives, thereby fulfilling a pivotal educational function in the lives of believers!

   **John 14:26 (KJV)** But the Comforter, *which is* the Holy Ghost, whom the Father will send in my name, he shall teach you all things, and bring all things to your remembrance, whatsoever I have said unto you.

   **Matthew 7:28 (KJV)** And it came to pass, when Jesus had ended these sayings, the people were astonished at his doctrine:

   **Matthew 7:29 (KJV)** For he taught them as *one* having authority, and not as the scribes.

   **Mark 1:21 (KJV)** And they went into Capernaum; and straightway on the sabbath day he entered into the synagogue, and taught.

   **Mark 1:22 (KJV)** And they were astonished at his doctrine: for he taught them as one that had authority, and not as the scribes.

5. The form of human progress that truly pleases God is for individuals to earnestly seek, day and night, an understanding of God through His textbook, the Holy Bible, and to

live by its teachings. This pursuit embodies the essence of Christianity. Analogous to university students who dedicate themselves to mastering mathematics, adhering to its rules, and applying its principles to practical scenarios like road design and construction to succeed in their studies, followers of Christianity are similarly engaged in a rigorous educational process. In this "University of Christianity," the objective is to internalize and implement the divine knowledge and principles outlined in the Holy Bible into one's life:

> **Hosea 4:1 (KJV)** Hear the word of the LORD, ye children of Israel: for the LORD hath a controversy with the inhabitants of the land, because *there is* no truth, nor mercy, nor knowledge of God in the land.

> **Hosea 6:6 (KJV)** For I desired mercy, and not sacrifice; and the knowledge of God more than burnt offerings.

> **1 Corinthians 15:34 (KJV)** Awake to righteousness, and sin not; for some have not the knowledge of God: I speak *this* to your shame.

> **2 Corinthians 4:6 (KJV)** For God, who commanded the light to shine out of darkness, hath shined in our hearts, to *give* the light of the knowledge of the glory of God in the face of Jesus Christ.

> **2 Corinthians 10:5 (KJV)** Casting down imaginations, and every high thing that exalteth itself against the knowledge of God, and bringing into captivity every thought to the obedience of Christ;

> **Ephesians 1:17 (KJV)** That the God of our Lord Jesus Christ, the Father of glory, may give unto you the spirit of wisdom and revelation in the knowledge of him:

> **Ephesians 4:13 (KJV)** Till we all come in the unity of the faith, and of the knowledge of the Son of God, unto a perfect man, unto the measure of the stature of the fulness of Christ:

> **Colossians 1:10 (KJV)** That ye might walk worthy of the Lord unto all pleasing, being fruitful in every good work, and increasing in the knowledge of God;

> **2 Peter 1:2 (KJV)** Grace and peace be multiplied unto you through the knowledge of God, and of Jesus our Lord,

This concludes the introductory chapter. In the chapters that follow, we will delve deeper into various themes and doctrines briefly touched upon here, including fasting, worship, salvation, Christianity, the Doctrine of Spiritual Father-Son Relationship, among others. Each of these topics will be explored in greater detail, providing a comprehensive understanding of their significance and application.

# CHAPTER 1

## IT IS RIGHTEOUSNESS THAT SANCTIFIES THE FASTING!

========================

**DZINUDZEZI**

(SYMBOL OF WOMANHOOD)

Ewe symbol of womanhood

========================

Fasting, a practice embraced by churches around the globe, often follows the guidance of a Pastor or Prophet, or emerges from a personal commitment. This leads to fasting durations that can span from 10 to even 100 days, a commitment made even amidst prevalent sin within the congregation.

Biblically, the efficacy of fasting transcends the mere abstention from food; it is deeply intertwined with the spiritual integrity of the individual. Scripture teaches that the true measure of fasting's worth is not found in the act itself but in the righteousness that fuels it. **Isaiah 58:6-7**, for instance, shifts the focus from fasting as a mere ritual to a call for justice, freeing the oppressed, and caring for those in need, illustrating that the divine approval of a fast is contingent upon the ethical conduct it inspires.

Therefore, fasting, absent of righteous intent and action, is as futile as cow dung, particularly when sin remains unaddressed. In contrast, fasting that is rooted in a sincere heart and righteous living is potent and meaningful. The New Testament further underscores this by highlighting fasting coupled with prayer and acts of piety, done not for outward show but as a profound, internal spiritual discipline (**Matthew 6:16-18**).

Exploring specific scriptural references further illuminates this principle, revealing that the transformative power of fasting is unlocked not through the physical deprivation alone but through a sanctified life that aligns with God's will.

> **Isaiah 58:1 (KJV)** Cry aloud, spare not, lift up thy voice like a trumpet, and shew my people their transgression, and the house of Jacob their sins.

**Isaiah 58:2 (KJV)** Yet they seek me daily, and delight to know my ways, as a nation that did righteousness, and forsook not the ordinance of their God: they ask of me the ordinances of justice; they take delight in approaching to God.

**Isaiah 58:3 (KJV)** Wherefore have we fasted, *say they*, and thou seest not? *wherefore* have we afflicted our soul, and thou takest no knowledge? Behold, in the day of your fast ye find pleasure, and exact all your labours.

**Isaiah 58:4 (KJV)** Behold, ye fast for strife and debate, and to smite with the fist of wickedness: ye shall not fast as *ye do this* day, to make your voice to be heard on high.

**Isaiah 58:5 (KJV)** Is it such a fast that I have chosen? a day for a man to afflict his soul? *is it* to bow down his head as a bulrush, and to spread sackcloth and ashes *under him*? wilt thou call this a fast, and an acceptable day to the LORD?

This presents another instance where individuals engaged in the act of fasting, ostensibly a spiritual discipline, concurrently commit murder against an innocent person during their fast, with the aim of depriving the victim of his inheritance.

**1 Kings 21:5 (KJV)** But Jezebel his wife came to him, and said unto him, Why is thy spirit so sad, that thou eatest no bread?

**1 Kings 21:6 (KJV)** And he said unto her, Because I spake unto Naboth the Jezreelite, and said unto him, Give me thy vineyard for money; or else, if it please thee, I will give thee *another* vineyard for it: and he answered, I will not give thee my vineyard.

**1 Kings 21:7 (KJV)** And Jezebel his wife said unto him, Dost thou now govern the kingdom of Israel? arise, *and* eat bread, and let thine heart be merry: I will give thee the vineyard of Naboth the Jezreelite.

**1 Kings 21:8 (KJV)** So she wrote letters in Ahab's name, and sealed *them* with his seal, and sent the letters unto the elders and to the nobles that *were* in his city, dwelling with Naboth.

**1 Kings 21:9 (KJV)** And she wrote in the letters, saying, Proclaim a fast, and set Naboth on high among the people:

**1 Kings 21:10 (KJV)** And set two men, sons of Belial, before him, to bear witness against him, saying, Thou didst blaspheme God and the king. And *then* carry him out, and stone him, that he may die.

**1 Kings 21:11 (KJV)** And the men of his city, *even* the elders and the nobles who were the inhabitants in his city, did as Jezebel had sent unto them, *and* as it *was* written in the letters which she had sent unto them.

**1 Kings 21:12 (KJV)** They proclaimed a fast, and set Naboth on high among the people.

**1 Kings 21:13 (KJV)** And there came in two men, children of Belial, and sat before him: and the men of Belial witnessed against him, *even* against Naboth, in the presence of the people, saying, Naboth did blaspheme God and the king. Then they carried him forth out of the city, and stoned him with stones, that he died.

**1 Kings 21:14 (KJV)** Then they sent to Jezebel, saying, Naboth is stoned, and is dead.

**1 Kings 21:15 (KJV)** And it came to pass, when Jezebel heard that Naboth was stoned, and was dead, that Jezebel said to Ahab, Arise, take possession of the vineyard of Naboth the Jezreelite, which he refused to give thee for money: for Naboth is not alive, but dead.

Conversely, we find instances in scripture where fasting is acknowledged by Heaven, not merely for the act of fasting itself, but for the righteousness that imbues the fasting with spiritual significance. This is because fasting, in isolation, holds no intrinsic spiritual value; it gains efficacy only when it is sanctified through righteous living. Isaiah 58 highlights this principle by contrasting the empty ritual of fasting with a fast that pleases God—a fast accompanied by acts of justice, kindness, and humility. Thus, it is the righteous behavior accompanying the fast, not the fast alone, that renders it effective and meaningful in the eyes of Heaven.

**Jonah 3:1 (KJV)** And the word of the LORD came unto Jonah the second time, saying,

**Jonah 3:2 (KJV)** Arise, go unto Nineveh, that great city, and preach unto it the preaching that I bid thee.

**Jonah 3:3 (KJV)** So Jonah arose, and went unto Nineveh, according to the word of the LORD. Now Nineveh was an exceeding great city of three days' journey.

**Jonah 3:4 (KJV)** And Jonah began to enter into the city a day's journey, and he cried, and said, Yet forty days, and Nineveh shall be overthrown.

**Jonah 3:5 (KJV)** So the people of Nineveh believed God, and proclaimed a fast, and put on sackcloth, from the greatest of them even to the least of them.

**Jonah 3:6 (KJV)** For word came unto the king of Nineveh, and he arose from his throne, and he laid his robe from him, and covered *him* with sackcloth, and sat in ashes.

**Jonah 3:7 (KJV)** And he caused *it* to be proclaimed and published through Nineveh by the decree of the king and his nobles, saying, Let neither man nor beast, herd nor flock, taste any thing: let them not feed, nor drink water:

**Jonah 3:8 (KJV)** But let man and beast be covered with sackcloth, and cry mightily unto God: yea, let them turn every one from his evil way, and from the violence that *is* in their hands.

**Jonah 3:9 (KJV)** Who can tell *if* God will turn and repent, and turn away from his fierce anger, that we perish not?

**Jonah 3:10 (KJV)** And God saw their works, that they turned from their evil way; and God repented of the evil, that he had said that he would do unto them; and he did *it* not.

**Jonah 3:8** provides a clear example of how righteousness imbues fasting with its true value, making it acceptable to Heaven: "Let everyone turn from his evil way and from the violence that is in their hands." This verse underscores the biblical principle that the merit of a fast is significantly enhanced by a genuine commitment to repentance and moral transformation.

During a previous Bible study session, I shared insights on the authentic biblical perspective of fasting, as revealed to me by the Holy Spirit. Contrary to common teachings in many churches that Moses was merely abstaining from food and water on Mount Horeb, I explained that Moses was, in fact, partaking in a different kind of sustenance.

Moses's experience of fasting for 40 days and nights was not an absence of nourishment but involved consuming a spiritual food and drink, far surpassing any earthly provisions. This divine sustenance that Moses encountered on Mount Horeb was of such a quality that it could be described as sweeter than honey, illustrating the profound and often misunderstood nature of biblical fasting. This exemplifies that fasting, as portrayed in the Bible, transcends physical abstention, pointing instead to a deeper spiritual engagement and nourishment.

> **Ezekiel 3:1 (KJV)** Moreover he said unto me, Son of man, eat that thou findest; eat this roll, and go speak unto the house of Israel.
>
> **Ezekiel 3:2 (KJV)** So I opened my mouth, and he caused me to eat that roll.
>
> **Ezekiel 3:3 (KJV)** And he said unto me, Son of man, cause thy belly to eat, and fill thy bowels with this roll that I give thee. Then did I eat *it*; and it was in my mouth as honey for sweetness.
>
> **Ezekiel 3:4 (KJV)** And he said unto me, Son of man, go, get thee unto the house of Israel, and speak with my words unto them.

Here's an alternative perspective to consider regarding the practice of fasting, particularly the traditional view of abstaining from food and water. It's essential to recognize that in the eyes of God Almighty, the spiritual significance of fasting is not inherently found in the act itself but in the righteousness of the individual engaging in the fast. This righteousness is what truly consecrates the fast, rather than the mere physical abstention, which on its own, lacks spiritual merit.

Take, for example, the common interpretation of Moses' and Elijah's fasting periods. While it might seem that they were merely forsaking physical sustenance, the deeper truth is both were nourished by a divine form of sustenance. Moses, during his time on Mount Horeb, and Elijah, throughout his

40-day journey, were actually partaking in spiritual food and drink provided by God. This illustrates that, biblically speaking, fasting can be a period of profound spiritual feeding and communion with God, rather than a mere physical denial. This understanding invites us to view fasting through a more nuanced lens, appreciating the deeper spiritual engagement it signifies.

> **1 Kings 19:1 (KJV)** And Ahab told Jezebel all that Elijah had done, and withal how he had slain all the prophets with the sword.

> **1 Kings 19:2 (KJV)** Then Jezebel sent a messenger unto Elijah, saying, So let the gods do *to me*, and more also, if I make not thy life as the life of one of them by to morrow about this time.

> **1 Kings 19:3 (KJV)** And when he saw *that*, he arose, and went for his life, and came to Beer-sheba, which *belongeth* to Judah, and left his servant there.

> **1 Kings 19:4 (KJV)** But he himself went a day's journey into the wilderness, and came and sat down under a juniper tree: and he requested for himself that he might die; and said, It is enough; now, O LORD, take away my life; for I *am* not better than my fathers.

> **1 Kings 19:5 (KJV)** And as he lay and slept under a juniper tree, behold, then an angel touched him, and said unto him, Arise *and* eat.

> **1 Kings 19:6 (KJV)** And he looked, and, behold, *there was* a cake baken on the coals, and a cruse of water at his head. And he did eat and drink, and laid him down again.

> **1 Kings 19:7 (KJV)** And the angel of the LORD came again the second time, and touched him, and said, Arise *and* eat; because the journey *is* too great for thee.

> **1 Kings 19:8 (KJV)** And he arose, and did eat and drink, and went in the strength of that meat forty days and forty nights unto Horeb the mount of God.

Thus, it becomes clear that righteousness is what truly uplifts a nation, rather than engaging in practices like extended 100-day fasting rituals without meaningful spiritual foundation. It's the pursuit of genuine righteousness that holds transformative power for individuals and communities alike.

> **Proverbs 14:34 (KJV)** Righteousness exalteth a nation: but sin *is* a reproach to any people.

Hence, prioritizing righteousness over mere fasting is advisable, as righteousness encompasses both the essence of spiritual fasting and its rewards. Engaging in righteousness ensures that you embody the true spirit of fasting, coupled with the benefits it brings. Conversely, if one observes physical fasting while continuing to indulge in sin, including those hidden from the eyes of others, such fasting becomes futile, comparable to filthy rags.

Fasting should be viewed as a gesture of humility before God, not as a badge of holiness, divine approval, or acceptance in Heaven.

> **Psalm 35:13 (KJV)** But as for me, when they were sick, my clothing *was* sackcloth: I humbled my soul with fasting; and my prayer returned into mine own bosom.

Here we have priests, pastors, and prophets deeply committed to the spiritual discipline of fasting, seeking God Almighty's endorsement for their decades-long practice, extending over 70 years. However, upon seeking divine affirmation, they were met with a startling revelation from God Almighty Himself. He declared that the fasts they had observed for more than 70 years were ineffectual, devoid of spiritual significance, unrecognized in Heaven, and ultimately, futile.

> **Zechariah 7:3 (KJV)** *And* to speak unto the priests which *were* in the house of the LORD of hosts, and to the prophets, saying, Should I weep in the fifth month, separating myself, as I have done these so many years?

> **Zechariah 7:4 (KJV)** Then came the word of the LORD of hosts unto me, saying,

> **Zechariah 7:5 (KJV)** Speak unto all the people of the land, and to the priests, saying, When ye fasted and mourned in the fifth and seventh *month*, even those seventy years, did ye at all fast unto me, *even* to me?

> **Zechariah 7:6 (KJV)** And when ye did eat, and when ye did drink, did not ye eat *for yourselves*, and drink *for yourselves*?

Undoubtedly, those priests, pastors, and prophets felt a profound sense of astonishment—much like the surprise you might be experiencing now upon hearing that your fasting efforts have not borne any spiritual fruit. But there's a way forward. Consider the guidance offered in **Zechariah 7:8-10,** which presents an approach fully acknowledged by Heaven and far surpasses the previous, merely physical practice of fasting you might have adhered to.

> **Zechariah 7:7 (KJV)** *Should ye* not *hear* the words which the LORD hath cried by the former prophets, when Jerusalem was inhabited and in prosperity, and the cities thereof round about her, when *men* inhabited the south and the plain?

> **Zechariah 7:8 (KJV)** And the word of the LORD came unto Zechariah, saying,

> **Zechariah 7:9 (KJV)** Thus speaketh the LORD of hosts, saying, Execute true judgment, and shew mercy and compassions every man to his brother:

> **Zechariah 7:10 (KJV)** And oppress not the widow, nor the fatherless, the stranger, nor the poor; and let none of you imagine evil against his brother in your heart.

> **Zechariah 7:11 (KJV)** But they refused to hearken, and pulled away the shoulder, and stopped their ears, that they should not hear.

**Zechariah 7:12 (KJV)** Yea, they made their hearts *as* an adamant stone, lest they should hear the law, and the words which the LORD of hosts hath sent in his spirit by the former prophets: therefore came a great wrath from the LORD of hosts.

**Zechariah 7:13 (KJV)** Therefore it is come to pass, *that* as he cried, and they would not hear; so they cried, and I would not hear, saith the LORD of hosts:

**Zechariah 7:14 (KJV)** But I scattered them with a whirlwind among all the nations whom they knew not. Thus the land was desolate after them, that no man passed through nor returned: for they laid the pleasant land desolate.

The LORD Jesus Christ be with your spirit. The LORD Jesus Christ give you understanding.

# CHAPTER 2

## HOW CAN I WORSHIP GOD IN SPIRIT AND IN TRUTH?

===========================

LAMB OF GOD

Ewe symbol for Lamb of God

===========================

1.  The encounter between Yeshua (Jesus Christ) and the Samaritan woman at Jacob's well is a significant event documented in the Christian New Testament. This story is found in the Gospel of John. The account is rich with theological insights, cultural contexts, and profound teachings, serving as a critical element in understanding Jesus' ministry and approach towards inclusivity, social norms, and spiritual conversation:

    **John 4:3 (KJV)** He left Judaea, and departed again into Galilee.

    **John 4:4 (KJV)** And he must needs go through Samaria.

    **John 4:5 (KJV)** Then cometh he to a city of Samaria, which is called Sychar, near to the parcel of ground that Jacob gave to his son Joseph.

    **John 4:6 (KJV)** Now Jacob's well was there. Jesus therefore, being wearied with *his* journey, sat thus on the well: *and* it was about the sixth hour.

    **John 4:7 (KJV)** There cometh a woman of Samaria to draw water: Jesus saith unto her, Give me to drink.

    **John 4:8 (KJV)** (For his disciples were gone away unto the city to buy meat.)

2.  The Samaritan woman represents an individual with a nominal Christian faith, characterized by her engagement in behaviors such as fornication and adultery, despite professing belief in God Almighty. Despite her limited understanding of God's Word, her ability to recognize a prophet suggests she possesses some degree of spiritual discernment. This combination of factors highlights the complexity of her faith journey

and underscores the varied paths individuals may take in their spiritual lives, grappling with personal shortcomings while still retaining a connection to divine knowledge!

**John 4:19 (KJV)** The woman saith unto him, Sir, I perceive that thou art a prophet.

3. The Samaritan woman, much like many Christians today who do not engage with the Bible directly, had inherited her understanding of Christianity and worship practices through tradition, upbringing, and the teachings of her elders, without independently verifying these beliefs against Scripture as the Bereans did. Her approach to faith, rooted in custom rather than personal investigation of the Scriptures, led her to a point where, despite her foundational ignorance, she felt confident enough to discuss worship practices and the essence of true church service with Jesus Christ, the very embodiment of divine truth. This scenario, depicted in **John 4:20 (KJV),** illustrates the gap between cultural or traditional religiosity and the informed faith that comes from direct engagement with God's Word.

**John 4:20 (KJV)** Our fathers worshipped in this mountain; and ye say, that in Jerusalem is the place where men ought to worship.

**Acts 17:11 (KJV)** These were more noble than those in Thessalonica, in that they received the word with all readiness of mind, and searched the scriptures daily, whether those things were so.

4. Jesus Christ, in His divine wisdom, takes the opportunity to impart crucial spiritual knowledge to the Samaritan woman, revealing to her two essential truths of heavenly significance:

- **ONE** The appropriate place for worshipping God Almighty, and

- **TWO** The proper way to engage in worship that pleases God Almighty.

**John 4:21 (KJV)** Jesus saith unto her, Woman, believe me, the hour cometh, when ye shall neither in this mountain, nor yet at Jerusalem, worship the Father.

**John 4:22 (KJV)** Ye worship ye know not what: we know what we worship: for salvation is of the Jews.

5. In **John 4:21-22**, Lord Yeshua the Messiah enlightens the Samaritan woman with key teachings:

**ONE** The cessation of worshiping God Almighty in any physical place, location, or building.

**TWO** The assertion that those who worship God Almighty in any physical place, location, or building engage in a form of worship without true understanding, implying they believe they are worshiping God, yet in reality, they do not fully comprehend the essence of their worship.

6. During this conversation, Lord Jesus Christ chose not to disclose to the woman the true identity of the entity being worshiped in those physical structures they mistakenly refer to as "church." However, subsequent revelations by the Holy Spirit indicated that the entity often revered in these physical church buildings might not align with divine worship as intended, leading some to believe it diverges from God's true presence.

> **Mark 11:17 (KJV)** And he taught, saying unto them, Is it not written, My house shall be called of all nations the house of prayer? but ye have made it a den of thieves.

> **2 Thessalonians 2:3 (KJV)** Let no man deceive you by any means: for *that day shall not come*, except there come a falling away first, and that man of sin be revealed, the son of perdition;

> **2 Thessalonians 2:4 (KJV)** Who opposeth and exalteth himself above all that is called God, or that is worshipped; so that he as God sitteth in the temple of God, shewing himself that he is God.

> **2 Thessalonians 2:5 (KJV)** Remember ye not, that, when I was yet with you, I told you these things?

7. Stemming from the insights shared in **2 Thessalonians 2:3-5**, it was for this reason that Lord Jesus Christ advocated for the dismantling of the physical Temple!

> **Matthew 16:18 (KJV)** And I say also unto thee, That thou art Peter, and upon this rock I will build my church; and the gates of hell shall not prevail against it.

> **Matthew 26:61 (KJV)** And said, This *fellow* said, I am able to destroy the temple of God, and to build it in three days.

> **Mark 14:58 (KJV)** We heard him say, I will destroy this temple that is made with hands, and within three days I will build another made without hands.

> **John 2:19 (KJV)** Jesus answered and said unto them, Destroy this temple, and in three days I will raise it up.

8. In defiance of the explicit teachings of Lord Jesus Christ, there is still a marked emphasis on erecting elaborate physical structures such as temples, mega-churches, sanctuaries, domes, and cathedrals, adorned with discotheque-style lighting and gold-plated pulpits and altars. Many are unaware that these edifices frequently serve as venues for financial exploitation and deceit, cloaked in the preaching of the gospel, thus transforming into contemporary havens of wrongdoing. This practice persists, undiminished by time.

9. Despite the instructions given by Lord Jesus Christ, there continues to be a trend where individuals construct physical temples, mega-churches, sanctuaries, domes, and

cathedrals. These actions persist today, raising concerns about their true purpose and alignment with divine will.

10. Another compelling reason to reconsider the practice of worshiping God Almighty in physical locations is based on a revelation that was not initially disclosed to the Samaritan woman by Jesus Christ but was later revealed by the Holy Spirit: God Almighty does not dwell in any physical worship spaces, mountains, or church buildings. This insight challenges traditional notions of worship and the significance of physical places of worship.

11. Despite Lord Jesus Christ's guidance, the focus on building physical temples, mega-churches, sanctuaries, domes, and cathedrals remains prevalent. This ongoing trend prompts reflection on the true intentions behind these projects and how they align with spiritual principles.

12. Additionally, the practice of allocating substantial time and resources, including the accrual of significant debt from secular financial institutions, to enhance physical structures for worship raises concerns, especially when such efforts contradict the essence of worship as taught by the Lord. This approach not only places churches in financial jeopardy but also deviates from the spiritual path outlined by Jesus Christ. The Holy Spirit's later revelation—that God Almighty's presence is not confined to any physical location, mountain, or church building— further emphasizes the need to reassess our priorities in worship. This insight challenges us to consider the true meaning of worship and the sanctity of the spaces we deem holy.

> **Acts 7:46 (KJV)** Who found favour before God, and desired to find a tabernacle for the God of Jacob.
>
> **Acts 7:47 (KJV)** But Solomon built him an house.
>
> **Acts 7:48 (KJV)** Howbeit the most High dwelleth not in temples made with hands; as saith the prophet,
>
> **Acts 17:24 (KJV)** God that made the world and all things therein, seeing that he is Lord of heaven and earth, dwelleth not in temples made with hands;
>
> **Acts 17:25 (KJV)** Neither is worshipped with men's hands, as though he needed any thing, seeing he giveth to all life, and breath, and all things;

13. As Lord Yeshua the Messiah engaged with the Samaritan woman, He compassionately instructed her, emphasizing the immediacy of His teachings and commands. He conveyed to her that the **revelations** and directives He was sharing were to be acted upon "**RIGHT NOW, THIS HOUR,**" underlining the urgency and present relevance of His message.

> **John 4:23 (KJV)** But the hour cometh, and now is, when the true worshippers shall worship the Father in spirit and in truth: for the Father seeketh such to worship him.

14. Lord Yeshua the Messiah's teachings to the Samaritan woman extended further, as He enlightened her on the inefficacy of seeking physical spaces for worship. He explained that considering God's nature as a spirit, the pursuit of physical locations for worship does not align with true spiritual communion, highlighting a crucial understanding: "GOD IS A SPIRIT," and thus, the spiritual realm and the physical realm do not intermix. This insight serves to emphasize the profound spiritual truth that worship transcends physical boundaries!

> **John 4:24 (KJV)** God *is* a Spirit: and they that worship him must worship *him* in spirit and in truth.

> **John 4:25 (KJV)** The woman saith unto him, I know that Messias cometh, which is called Christ: when he is come, he will tell us all things.

> **John 4:26 (KJV)** Jesus saith unto her, I that speak unto thee am *he.*

> **1 Corinthians 15:50 (KJV)** Now this I say, brethren, that flesh and blood cannot inherit the kingdom of God; neither doth corruption inherit incorruption.

> **Galatians 5:17 (KJV)** For the flesh lusteth against the Spirit, and the Spirit against the flesh: and these are contrary the one to the other: so that ye cannot do the things that ye would.

> **Romans 8:13 (KJV)** For if ye live after the flesh, ye shall die: but if ye through the Spirit do mortify the deeds of the body, ye shall live.

15. Brethren, why would you attempt to use water as fuel in your car when you know well that its engine is not designed to run on water?

16. Now, Brethren, you may ask:

   • Given that Jesus Christ taught, "the true worshippers shall worship the Father in spirit and in truth," and considering that I am of flesh and blood, how can I fulfill or adhere to this directive in my physical existence?

   • Allow me to share a revelation with you, my brothers and sisters in Christ Jesus!

17. Here is the revelation my Brothers and Sisters in Christ Jesus!

> **Romans 1:9 (KJV)** For God is my witness, whom I serve with my spirit in the gospel of his Son, that without ceasing I make mention of you always in my prayers;

18. It is essential that you worship God Almighty "with your spirit through the Gospel of His Son."

19. You may wonder, "Where is my spirit?"

20. Your spirit resides in your mind, located within your head, where you read, contemplate, and reflect upon the Word of God, the Gospel of Jesus Christ.

> **Romans 7:25 (KJV)** I thank God through Jesus Christ our Lord. So then with the mind I myself serve the law of God; but with the flesh the law of sin.

21. Engaging daily with the Gospel of Jesus Christ—reading it, pondering its teachings, living by its directives, consistently speaking the truth, and extending assistance to the poor, needy, widows, strangers, orphans, and destitute—embodies authentic church service and genuine worship of God. By embracing these actions, you become the true Temple of God!

> **Joshua 1:7 (KJV)** Only be thou strong and very courageous, that thou mayest observe to do according to all the law, which Moses my servant commanded thee: turn not from it *to* the right hand or *to* the left, that thou mayest prosper whithersoever thou goest.

> **Joshua 1:8 (KJV)** This book of the law shall not depart out of thy mouth; but thou shalt meditate therein day and night, that thou mayest observe to do according to all that is written therein: for then thou shalt make thy way prosperous, and then thou shalt have good success.

> **Zechariah 8:16 (KJV)** These *are* the things that ye shall do; Speak ye every man the truth to his neighbour; execute the judgment of truth and peace in your gates:

> **Zechariah 8:17 (KJV)** And let none of you imagine evil in your hearts against his neighbour; and love no false oath: for all these *are things* that I hate, saith the LORD.

> **Matthew 18:20 (KJV)** For where two or three are gathered together in my name, there am I in the midst of them.

> **1 Corinthians 3:16 (KJV)** Know ye not that ye are the temple of God, and that the Spirit of God dwelleth in you?

> **1 Corinthians 3:17 (KJV)** If any man defile the temple of God, him shall God destroy; for the temple of God is holy, which temple ye are.

> **1 Corinthians 6:19 (KJV)** What? know ye not that your body is the temple of the Holy Ghost which is in you, which ye have of God, and ye are not your own?

22. Here we see the Holy Spirit graciously assisting the Ethiopian Eunuch, who was engaging in authentic and proper worship by himself, as previously described.

> **Acts 8:26 (KJV)** And the angel of the Lord spake unto Philip, saying, Arise, and go toward the south unto the way that goeth down from Jerusalem unto Gaza, which is desert.

**Acts 8:27 (KJV)** And he arose and went: and, behold, a man of Ethiopia, an eunuch of great authority under Candace queen of the Ethiopians, who had the charge of all her treasure, and had come to Jerusalem for to worship,

**Acts 8:28 (KJV)** Was returning, and sitting in his chariot read Esaias the prophet.

**Acts 8:29 (KJV)** Then the Spirit said unto Philip, Go near, and join thyself to this chariot.

**Acts 8:30 (KJV)** And Philip ran thither to *him*, and heard him read the prophet Esaias, and said, Understandest thou what thou readest?

**Acts 8:31 (KJV)** And he said, How can I, except some man should guide me? And he desired Philip that he would come up and sit with him.

**Acts 8:32 (KJV)** The place of the scripture which he read was this, He was led as a sheep to the slaughter; and like a lamb dumb before his shearer, so opened he not his mouth:

**Acts 8:33 (KJV)** In his humiliation his judgment was taken away: and who shall declare his generation? for his life is taken from the earth.

**Acts 8:34 (KJV)** And the eunuch answered Philip, and said, I pray thee, of whom speaketh the prophet this? of himself, or of some other man?

**Acts 8:35 (KJV)** Then Philip opened his mouth, and began at the same scripture, and preached unto him Jesus.

23. It's important to observe in **Acts 8:26-35** that the Holy Spirit came to aid the Ethiopian Eunuch, not while he was in the church building in Jerusalem—a place he visited for worship, similar to contemporary practices—but rather after he left this man-made structure, often considered sacred, and began to engage in meaningful spiritual activities.

24. Similarly, we see Jesus Christ guiding another individual along the path followed by the Ethiopian Eunuch, leading to genuine salvation. This highlights that salvation is an educational journey, one that requires direct instruction to navigate successfully towards Heaven, as Jesus Christ elucidates in **Matthew 13:52.** Salvation is thus rooted in the engagement with and teaching of the Word of God, the Gospel of Jesus Christ, rather than merely an emotional experience.

**Matthew 13:52 (KJV)** Then said he unto them, Therefore every scribe *which is* instructed unto the kingdom of heaven is like unto a man *that is* an householder, which bringeth forth out of his treasure *things* new and old.

**Luke 10:25 (KJV)** And, behold, a certain lawyer stood up, and tempted him, saying, Master, what shall I do to inherit eternal life?

**Luke 10:26 (KJV)** He said unto him, What is written in the law? how readest thou?

**Luke 10:27 (KJV)** And he answering said, Thou shalt love the Lord thy God with all thy heart, and with all thy soul, and with all thy strength, and with all thy mind; and thy neighbour as thyself.

**Luke 10:28 (KJV)** And he said unto him, Thou hast answered right: this do, and thou shalt live.

25. Given that salvation involves a process of learning and instruction, requiring someone to guide another towards Heaven, this teaching activity, which can span hours, days, weeks, months, and even years, is recognized as labor deserving of compensation. This is because it represents a significant investment of time, a resource God Almighty has blessed us with. As God has stated, compensation is due for "the loss of his time." God grants us time and talents as free gifts, with the intention that we enhance their value and, in turn, use them to generate resources for our necessities such as shelter, clothing, and sustenance.

> **Genesis 47:15 (KJV)** And when money failed in the land of Egypt, and in the land of Canaan, all the Egyptians came unto Joseph, and said, Give us bread: for why should we die in thy presence? for the money faileth.
>
> **Genesis 47:16 (KJV)** And Joseph said, Give your cattle; and I will give you for your cattle, if money fail.
>
> **Exodus 21:19 (KJV)** If he rise again, and walk abroad upon his staff, then shall he that smote him be quit: only he shall pay for the loss of his time, and shall cause him to be thoroughly healed.
>
> **Deuteronomy 2:2 (KJV)** And the LORD spake unto me, saying,
>
> **Deuteronomy 2:6 (KJV)** Ye shall buy meat of them for money, that ye may eat; and ye shall also buy water of them for money, that ye may drink.
>
> **Deuteronomy 2:28 (KJV)** Thou shalt sell me meat for money, that I may eat; and give me water for money, that I may drink: only I will pass through on my feet;
>
> **Ecclesiastes 2:21 (KJV)** For there is a man whose labour is in wisdom, and in knowledge, and in equity; yet to a man that hath not laboured therein shall he leave it for his portion. This also is vanity and a great evil.
>
> **Luke 19:15 (KJV)** And it came to pass, that when he was returned, having received the kingdom, then he commanded these servants to be called unto him, to whom he had given the money, that he might know how much every man had gained by trading.

**Luke 22:35 (KJV)** And he said unto them, When I sent you without purse, and scrip, and shoes, lacked ye any thing? And they said, Nothing.

**Luke 22:36 (KJV)** Then said he unto them, But now, he that hath a purse, let him take *it*, and likewise *his* scrip: and he that hath no sword, let him sell his garment, and buy one.

**Matthew 25:20 (KJV)** And so he that had received five talents came and brought other five talents, saying, Lord, thou deliveredst unto me five talents: behold, I have gained beside them five talents more.

**Matthew 25:21 (KJV)** His lord said unto him, Well done, *thou* good and faithful servant: thou hast been faithful over a few things, I will make thee ruler over many things: enter thou into the joy of thy lord.

**Matthew 10:10 (KJV)** Nor scrip for *your* journey, neither two coats, neither shoes, nor yet staves: for the workman is worthy of his meat.

**Luke 10:7 (KJV)** And in the same house remain, eating and drinking such things as they give: for the labourer is worthy of his hire. Go not from house to house.

**1 Timothy 5:18 (KJV)** For the scripture saith, Thou shalt not muzzle the ox that treadeth out the corn. And, The labourer is worthy of his reward

26. This serves as another among numerous instances found within the Bible that affirm the principle of Christian giving in return for receiving guidance in the understanding of God's knowledge!

**1 Corinthians 9:3 (KJV)** Mine answer to them that do examine me is this,

**Corinthians 9:4 (KJV)** Have we not power to eat and to drink?

**1 Corinthians 9:5 (KJV)** Have we not power to lead about a sister, a wife, as well as other apostles, and *as* the brethren of the Lord, and Cephas?

**1 Corinthians 9:6 (KJV)** Or I only and Barnabas, have not we power to forbear working?

**1 Corinthians 9:7 (KJV)** Who goeth a warfare any time at his own charges? who planteth a vineyard, and eateth not of the fruit thereof? or who feedeth a flock, and eateth not of the milk of the flock?

**1 Corinthians 9:8 (KJV)** Say I these things as a man? or saith not the law the same also?

**1 Corinthians 9:9 (KJV)** For it is written in the law of Moses, Thou shalt not muzzle the mouth of the ox that treadeth out the corn. Doth God take care for oxen?

**1 Corinthians 9:10 (KJV)** Or saith he *it* altogether for our sakes? For our sakes, no doubt, *this* is written: that he that ploweth should plow in hope; and that he that thresheth in hope should be partaker of his hope.

**1 Corinthians 9:11 (KJV)** If we have sown unto you spiritual things, *is it* a great thing if we shall reap your carnal things?

**1 Corinthians 9:12 (KJV)** If others be partakers of *this* power over you, *are* not we rather? Nevertheless we have not used this power; but suffer all things, lest we should hinder the gospel of Christ

**1 Corinthians 9:13 (KJV)** Do ye not know that they which minister about holy things live *of the things* of the temple? and they which wait at the altar are partakers with the altar?

**1 Corinthians 9:14 (KJV)** Even so hath the Lord ordained that they which preach the gospel should live of the gospel.

27. This represents yet another example from the multitude of biblical confirmations regarding the practice of Christian giving as a means to acquire instruction in the divine knowledge of God

    **Romans 15:26 (KJV)** For it hath pleased them of Macedonia and Achaia to make a certain contribution for the poor saints which are at Jerusalem.

    **Romans 15:27 (KJV)** It hath pleased them verily; and their debtors they are. For if the Gentiles have been made partakers of their spiritual things, their duty is also to minister unto them in carnal things.

28. To truly worship God Almighty, one must enter the genuine and correct Temple of God, which is embodied by Yeshua the Christ. Since Jesus Christ is synonymous with the Word of God, engaging with the Gospel of Jesus Christ becomes the means through which we can authentically worship God. This approach stands in contrast to entering physical, man-made structures, which do not hold the same sacred value. This principle is further illuminated in scriptures such as **John 1:1, John 2:21, Hebrews 8:2,** and **Revelation 19:13**, each underscoring the importance of finding spiritual communion within the living Word, rather than within any earthly edifice.

    **John 1:1 (KJV)** In the beginning was the Word, and the Word was with God, and the Word was God.

    **John 2:19 (KJV)** Jesus answered and said unto them, Destroy this temple, and in three days I will raise it up

    **John 2:20 (KJV)** Then said the Jews, Forty and six years was this temple in building, and wilt thou rear it up in three days?

**John 2:21 (KJV)** But he spake of the temple of his body.

**1 Corinthians 3:10 (KJV)** According to the grace of God which is given unto me, as a wise masterbuilder, I have laid the foundation, and another buildeth thereon. But let every man take heed how he buildeth thereupon.

**1 Corinthians 3:11 (KJV)** For other foundation can no man lay than that is laid, which is Jesus Christ.

**Hebrews 8:1 (KJV)** Now of the things which we have spoken *this is* the sum: We have such an high priest, who is set on the right hand of the throne of the Majesty in the heavens;

**Hebrews 8:2 (KJV)** A minister of the sanctuary, and of the true tabernacle, which the Lord pitched, and not man.

**Revelation 19:13 (KJV)** And he was clothed with a vesture dipped in blood: and his name is called The Word of God.

29. Brethren, consider the manner in which Apostle Paul chose to worship God Almighty. Paul never sought out man-made temples for his worship; instead, he consistently turned to the Gospel of the Lord Jesus Christ as his place of worship. This example serves as a guide for anyone aspiring to live in accordance with true Christian principles—worshiping through engagement with the Gospel is essential.

    **Romans 1:9 (KJV)** For God is my witness, whom I serve with my spirit in the gospel of his Son, that without ceasing I make mention of you always in my prayers;

    **Romans 7:25 (KJV)** I thank God through Jesus Christ our Lord. So then with the mind I myself serve the law of God; but with the flesh the law of sin.

30. Brethren, the guidance that the Holy Spirit provided to Philip the Evangelist, leading him to assist the Ethiopian Eunuch, mirrors what I have endeavored to achieve for you through this letter.

31. While I have addressed this specific biblical inquiry, I wish to point you towards further enlightenment found in the Book of **Job, chapter 26**. This passage can aid you on your spiritual journey towards Heaven, as you seek a deeper comprehension of the Word from the Lord.

# REFERENCE DIRECTORY

## FOR CHAPTER TOPICS – JOB CHAPTER 26

1. The Word of God serves as the Light for the living; thus, an individual without the Word of God resides in darkness and is, essentially, spiritually deceased.

2. **In Genesis 1:1-5,** we are presented with how the LORD God distinguished between darkness (associated with death) and light (symbolizing life) at the dawn of Creation.

   **Genesis 1:1 (KJV)** In the beginning God created the heaven and the earth.

   **Genesis 1:2 (KJV)** And the earth was without form, and void; and darkness *was* upon the face of the deep. And the Spirit of God moved upon the face of the waters.

   **Genesis 1:3 (KJV)** And God said, Let there be light: and there was light.

   **Genesis 1:4 (KJV)** And God saw the light, that *it was* good: and God divided the light from the darkness.

   **Genesis 1:5 (KJV)** And God called the light Day, and the darkness he called Night. And the evening and the morning were the first day.

   **Job 33:30 (KJV)** To bring back his soul from the pit, to be enlightened with the light of the living.

   **Psalm 119:105 (KJV)** NUN. Thy word *is* a lamp unto my feet, and a light unto my path.

   **John 1:1 (KJV)** In the beginning was the Word, and the Word was with God, and the Word was God.

   **John 1:2 (KJV)** The same was in the beginning with God.

   **John 1:3 (KJV)** All things were made by him; and without him was not any thing made that was made.

   **John 1:4 (KJV)** In him was life; and the life was the light of men.

   **John 1:5 (KJV)** And the light shineth in darkness; and the darkness comprehended it not.

3. The LORD God Almighty is revealing that the spirit of man travels in his words!

   **Job 26:4 (KJV)** To whom hast thou uttered words? and whose spirit came from thee?

4. Essentially, to understand the spirit residing within a person, pay attention to their words to determine if they align with God's teachings.

   **Matthew 12:34 (KJV)** O generation of vipers, how can ye, being evil, speak good things? for out of the abundance of the heart the mouth speaketh.

> **Luke 6:45 (KJV)** A good man out of the good treasure of his heart bringeth forth that which is good; and an evil man out of the evil treasure of his heart bringeth forth that which is evil: for of the abundance of the heart his mouth speaketh.

5. This further validation from Jesus Christ highlights that words possess a spiritual nature. Given that the LORD God Almighty embodies Spirit, it follows that His Words also carry spiritual vitality!

> **John 4:24 (KJV)** God *is* a Spirit: and they that worship him must worship *him* in spirit and in truth.

> **John 6:63 (KJV)** It is the spirit that quickeneth; the flesh profiteth nothing: the words that I speak unto you, *they* are spirit, and *they* are life.

> **John 14:10 (KJV)** Believest thou not that I am in the Father, and the Father in me? the words that I speak unto you I speak not of myself: but the Father that dwelleth in me, he doeth the works.

6. That is why you worship God in His Word and NOT with any other activities we are led to practice in our churches!

> **Romans 1:9 (KJV)** For God is my witness, whom I serve with my spirit in the gospel of his Son, that without ceasing I make mention of you always in my prayers;

> **Romans 7:25 (KJV)** I thank God through Jesus Christ our Lord. So then with the mind I myself serve the law of God; but with the flesh the law of sin.

7. This illuminates the reason blessings are bestowed upon readers of His Word and underscores how salvation is achieved through connecting with the Word of God.

> **Luke 10:25 (KJV)** And, behold, a certain lawyer stood up, and tempted him, saying, Master, what shall I do to inherit eternal life?

> **Luke 10:26 (KJV)** He said unto him, What is written in the law? how readest thou?

> **Luke 10:27 (KJV)** And he answering said, Thou shalt love the Lord thy God with all thy heart, and with all thy soul, and with all thy strength, and with all thy mind; and thy neighbour as thyself.

> **Luke 10:28 (KJV)** And he said unto him, Thou hast answered right: this do, and thou shalt live.

> **Revelation 1:3 (KJV)** Blessed *is* he that readeth, and they that hear the words of this prophecy, and keep those things which are written therein: for the time *is* at hand.

8. Understand, then, that in the spiritual realm, might and strength are not gauged by physical attributes such as muscle mass or the robustness of one's limbs, nor are they

determined by physical vigor. Rather, in the spirit realm, true power and strength are quantified by the depth of one's knowledge!

>**Job 36:5 (KJV)** Behold, God *is* mighty, and despiseth not *any: he is* mighty in strength *and* wisdom.

9. Therefore, a person who possesses profound knowledge, especially the knowledge of God, is considered strong and mighty in the spiritual realm.

>**Acts 18:24 (KJV)** And a certain Jew named Apollos, born at Alexandria, an eloquent man, *and* mighty in the scriptures, came to Ephesus.

>**Zechariah 4:6 (KJV)** Then he answered and spake unto me, saying, This *is* the word of the LORD unto Zerubbabel, saying, Not by might, nor by power, but by my spirit, saith the LORD of hosts.

>**1 John 2:14 (KJV)** I have written unto you, fathers, because ye have known him *that is* from the beginning. I have written unto you, young men, because ye are strong, and the word of God abideth in you, and ye have overcome the wicked one.

10. Within the spiritual realm, a meticulous hierarchy exists, placing those who wield physical force, energy, and cause destruction at a lower tier compared to individuals endowed with knowledge, particularly the knowledge of God!

>**1 Corinthians 6:3 (KJV)** Know ye not that we shall judge angels? how much more things that pertain to this life?

>**Psalm 91:11 (KJV)** For he shall give his angels charge over thee, to keep thee in all thy ways.

>**Matthew 13:41 (KJV)** The Son of man shall send forth his angels, and they shall gather out of his kingdom all things that offend, and them which do iniquity;

11. In the spiritual hierarchy, entities that engage in destruction and exhibit physical might are subordinate to those who possess and uphold the knowledge of God. This arrangement underscores the supremacy of spiritual wisdom over mere physical force.

12. Pursuing knowledge in the heavenly realm equates to aspiring for the utmost echelon of existence. The LORD God holds in high esteem those who earnestly seek knowledge, particularly, the knowledge that pertains to understanding His divine nature and will. This pursuit is viewed as aligning with the highest virtues and aspirations in the spiritual order.

>**2 Chronicles 1:10 (KJV)** Give me now wisdom and knowledge, that I may go out and come in before this people: for who can judge this thy people, *that is so* great?

**2 Chronicles 1:11 (KJV)** And God said to Solomon, Because this was in thine heart, and thou hast not asked riches, wealth, or honour, nor the life of thine enemies, neither yet hast asked long life; but hast asked wisdom and knowledge for thyself, that thou mayest judge my people, over whom I have made thee king:

**2 Chronicles 1:12 (KJV)** Wisdom and knowledge *is* granted unto thee; and I will give thee riches, and wealth, and honour, such as none of the kings have had that *have been* before thee, neither shall there any after thee have the like.

13. To embark on the journey of acquiring knowledge is essentially to journey towards understanding the LORD God Himself, as God is intrinsically the embodiment of all knowledge. This pursuit of enlightenment and understanding is not merely an academic or intellectual endeavor, but a profound spiritual quest that leads one closer to comprehending the nature and essence of the Divine. Through seeking knowledge, one is essentially seeking to connect with and understand the LORD God, who is the ultimate source and foundation of all wisdom and understanding.

**1 Samuel 2:3 (KJV)** Talk no more so exceeding proudly; let *not* arrogancy come out of your mouth: for the LORD *is* a God of knowledge, and by him actions are weighed.

**2 Chronicles 30:22 (KJV)** And Hezekiah spake comfortably unto all the Levites that taught the good knowledge of the LORD: and they did eat throughout the feast seven days, offering peace offerings, and making confession to the LORD God of their fathers.

14. This explains why individuals who scorn the pursuit of knowledge, especially those who reject reading the Word of God as a means to gain understanding, and those who fail to incorporate the knowledge of God into their daily lives, are considered foolish. Such attitudes towards knowledge not only reflect a disregard for wisdom but also carry severe consequences. These individuals face destruction without leniency, illustrating the critical importance of valuing and integrating divine wisdom into one's existence!

**Psalm 5:5 (KJV)** The foolish shall not stand in thy sight: thou hatest all workers of iniquity.

**Proverbs 1:7 (KJV)** The fear of the LORD *is* the beginning of knowledge: *but* fools despise wisdom and instruction.

**Proverbs 13:16 (KJV)** Every prudent *man* dealeth with knowledge: but a fool layeth open *his* folly.

**Proverbs 14:7 (KJV)** Go from the presence of a foolish man, when thou perceivest not *in him* the lips of knowledge.

**Hosea 4:6 (KJV)** My people are destroyed for lack of knowledge: because thou hast rejected knowledge, I will also reject thee, that thou shalt be no priest to me: seeing thou hast forgotten the law of thy God, I will also forget thy children.

15. Wealth and prosperity are not destined for those who engage in evil and wickedness. Thus, if you encounter a pastor who is driven by greed, who dishonestly accumulates wealth by misleading his followers into giving tithes, it's clear that such riches are not a blessing from the LORD God but are instead granted by Satan. This distinction underscores the importance of recognizing the true source behind one's wealth.

16. This situation casts doubt on the ethical standing of an individual who, despite receiving generous support through donations, offerings, and tithes, enjoys a lavish lifestyle while the donors themselves face financial hardships. This stark contrast necessitates a thorough investigation into the roots of their affluence. It raises the possibility that their wealth may not derive from their role in religious service or the financial backing of their congregation; alternatively, it might even involve unethical practices such as money rituals. Such circumstances force us to critically assess whether the financial prosperity they display is a manifestation of divine blessing or the result of engaging in morally questionable activities.

**Job 36:11 (KJV)** If they obey and serve *him*, they shall spend their days in prosperity, and their years in pleasures.

**Job 36:12 (KJV)** But if they obey not, they shall perish by the sword, and they shall die without knowledge.

17. Wealth and financial gain obtained without adherence to and service of the LORD God are attributed to Satan's influence. Such prosperity, achieved through disobedience, is not a blessing from the Divine but rather a consequence of aligning with malevolent forces.

18. Drawing from **Job 36:12** there is inherent value in departing this life enriched with divine knowledge. Therefore, pursuing an understanding of God Almighty stands as a noble endeavor throughout one's lifetime. When the moment arrives to transition from this world, it is the depth of your knowledge about God and your adherence to His teachings that will play a pivotal role in determining your eternal destiny—whether you are welcomed into Heaven or turned away into Hell.

19. The exhortation from the LORD God to seek Him in one's youth, before the onset of challenging times, emphasizes the importance of dedicating one's life to the acquisition of divine knowledge. It is advised to embrace every moment, using the abundance of time afforded in youth, to diligently learn about God. This pursuit should be relentless and

thorough because, at life's end, the opportunity to learn and to grow in understanding will no longer be available!

> **Job 29:4 (KJV)** As I was in the days of my youth, when the secret of God *was* upon my tabernacle;

> **Ecclesiastes 11:9 (KJV)** Rejoice, O young man, in thy youth; and let thy heart cheer thee in the days of thy youth, and walk in the ways of thine heart, and in the sight of thine eyes: but know thou, that for all these *things* God will bring thee into judgment.

> **Ecclesiastes 12:1 (KJV)** Remember now thy Creator in the days of thy youth, while the evil days come not, nor the years draw nigh, when thou shalt say, I have no pleasure in them;

20. The essence of this message is clear: to align oneself with the LORD God, it is essential to actively pursue an understanding of God. This can be achieved by committing to read the Word of God with diligence on a daily basis!

> **John 5:39 (KJV)** Search the scriptures; for in them ye think ye have eternal life: and they are they which testify of me.

The LORD Jesus Christ be with your spirit. The LORD Jesus Christ give you understanding.

# CHAPTER 3

## THE DOCTRINE OF SPIRITUAL FATHER-SON RELATIONSHIP!

====================

Traditional ewe symbol of imperfection.

The *'zegbagbá'* (broken pot) symbol is a traditional ewe symbol of imperfection, which is taken from the proverb *'tɔmedelae gbãa ze'* literally meaning: "it is the one who fetches water that breaks the pot". This symbol teaches tolerance regarding one another's imperfections within the society. When the mishap of life happens, it should not be considered as something serious, but as one of the inevitable issues of life.

====================

1.  In the Christian faith, the notion of a "spiritual father-son relationship" is not merely a tradition but is deeply embedded in the fabric of the community, drawing its lifeblood from the Scriptures and the unwavering adherence to its teachings. This relationship is built upon a shared commitment to the principles outlined in the Bible, serving as a testament to the importance of living a life that mirrors biblical directives.

2.  The Scriptures act as the cornerstone of this sacred bond between a spiritual father and son, weaving together their relationship with threads of divine wisdom and guidance. It is through the lens of the Bible that their connection gains its depth and significance, elevating it beyond the bounds of a mere earthly relationship to something much more profound and spiritually enriching.

3.  Consequently, the moment the Bible ceases to be the pivotal axis around which the relationship revolves, or when its teachings no longer guide and influence the interactions and decisions of the individuals involved, the very soul of the "spiritual father-son relationship" dissolves. Without the Scripture as their compass, the relationship loses its spiritual context and essence.

4. This spiritual kinship is conceived and nurtured in the spiritual domain, where both the spiritual father and son pledge themselves to the teachings of the Bible and to living lives that reflect obedience to God's Word. This commitment to scripture and mutual obedience is the glue that binds them together in a relationship that transcends the physical realm. Absent this scriptural foundation and shared obedience, the relationship forfeits its right to be recognized as a genuine "spiritual father-son" bond.

5. The doctrine of the "spiritual father-son relationship" is thus comprehensively articulated through these points, providing a clear framework within the Christian doctrine. This framework is not just theoretical but is grounded in the lived experiences and practices of the faith community.

6. Historical precedence for this concept can be found in the relationship between the Israelites and God Almighty. They were acknowledged as God's children, a title and position that were contingent upon their faithful adherence to His Word and commandments. This historical example underscores the timeless principle that a true connection with the Divine, akin to that of a parent and child, is forged through obedience and living in accordance with God's will as expressed in the Scriptures.

> **Genesis 17:1 (KJV)** And when Abram was ninety years old and nine, the LORD appeared to Abram, and said unto him, I am the Almighty God; walk before me, and be thou perfect.

> **Genesis 17:2 (KJV)** And I will make my covenant between me and thee, and will multiply thee exceedingly.

> **Genesis 17:3 (KJV)** And Abram fell on his face: and God talked with him, saying,

7. Observe how the concept of fatherhood is firmly established and rooted in the Covenant or the Word of God!

> **Genesis 17:4 (KJV)** As for me, behold, my covenant *is* with thee, and thou shalt be a father of many nations.

> **Genesis 17:5 (KJV)** Neither shall thy name any more be called Abram, but thy name shall be Abraham; for a father of many nations have I made thee.

> **Genesis 17:7 (KJV)** And I will establish my covenant between me and thee and thy seed after thee in their generations for an everlasting covenant, to be a God unto thee, and to thy seed after thee.

> **Jeremiah 24:7 (KJV)** And I will give them an heart to know me, that I *am* the LORD: and they shall be my people, and I will be their God: for they shall return unto me with their whole heart.

8. Then, it's important to recognize how both fatherhood and childhood are nullified when either party ceases to pursue the LORD God.

> **Jeremiah 10:20 (KJV)** My tabernacle is spoiled, and all my cords are broken: my children are gone forth of me, and they *are* not: *there is* none to stretch forth my tent any more, and to set up my curtains.

> **Jeremiah 10:21 (KJV)** For the pastors are become brutish, and have not sought the LORD: therefore they shall not prosper, and all their flocks shall be scattered.

This passage showcases the LORD God Almighty's declaration to disown any child who fails to adhere to His Word, thereby reinforcing the principle previously mentioned. When the Word of God is no longer the central element connecting two individuals, or when it ceases to act as their guiding and stabilizing force, the "spiritual father-son relationship" effectively ceases to exist.

> **Numbers 14:11 (KJV)** And the LORD said unto Moses, How long will this people provoke me? and how long will it be ere they believe me, for all the signs which I have shewed among them?

> **Numbers 14:12 (KJV)** I will smite them with the pestilence, and disinherit them, and will make of thee a greater nation and mightier than they.

9. This presents the fifth piece of evidence that straying from the LORD or failing to follow His commands directly results in the dissolution of the "spiritual father-son relationship."

> **Hosea 1:2 (KJV)** The beginning of the word of the LORD by Hosea. And the LORD said to Hosea, Go, take unto thee a wife of whoredoms and children of whoredoms: for the land hath committed great whoredom, *departing* from the LORD.

> **Hosea 1:3 (KJV)** So he went and took Gomer the daughter of Diblaim; which conceived, and bare him a son.

> **Hosea 1:4 (KJV)** And the LORD said unto him, Call his name Jezreel; for yet a little *while*, and I will avenge the blood of Jezreel upon the house of Jehu, and will cause to cease the kingdom of the house of Israel.

> **Hosea 1:5 (KJV)** And it shall come to pass at that day, that I will break the bow of Israel in the valley of Jezreel.

> **Hosea 1:6 (KJV)** And she conceived again, and bare a daughter. And *God* said unto him, Call her name Lo-ruhamah: for I will no more have mercy upon the house of Israel; but I will utterly take them away.

**Hosea 1:7 (KJV)** But I will have mercy upon the house of Judah, and will save them by the LORD their God, and will not save them by bow, nor by sword, nor by battle, by horses, nor by horsemen.

**Hosea 1:8 (KJV)** Now when she had weaned Lo-ruhamah, she conceived, and bare a son.

**Hosea 1:9 (KJV)** Then said *God*, Call his name Lo-ammi: for ye *are* not my people, and I will not be your *God*.

10. What has been illustrated here accurately reflects the teachings of the LORD Jesus Christ regarding the "spiritual father-son relationship," as conveyed to His followers in **Matthew 23:1-13**.

**Matthew 23:1 (KJV)** Then spake Jesus to the multitude, and to his disciples,

**Matthew 23:2 (KJV)** Saying, The scribes and the Pharisees sit in Moses' seat:

**Matthew 23:3 (KJV)** All therefore whatsoever they bid you observe, *that* observe and do; but do not ye after their works: for they say, and do not.

**Matthew 23:4 (KJV)** For they bind heavy burdens and grievous to be borne, and lay *them* on men's shoulders; but they *themselves* will not move them with one of their fingers.

**Matthew 23:5 (KJV)** But all their works they do for to be seen of men: they make broad their phylacteries, and enlarge the borders of their garments,

**Matthew 23:6 (KJV)** And love the uppermost rooms at feasts, and the chief seats in the synagogues,

**Matthew 23:7 (KJV)** And greetings in the markets, and to be called of men, Rabbi, Rabbi.

**Matthew 23:8 (KJV)** But be not ye called Rabbi: for one is your Master, *even* Christ; and all ye are brethren.

**Matthew 23:9 (KJV)** And call no *man* your father upon the earth: for one is your Father, which is in heaven.

**Matthew 23:10 (KJV)** Neither be ye called masters: for one is your Master, *even* Christ.

**Matthew 23:11 (KJV)** But he that is greatest among you shall be your servant.

**Matthew 23:12 (KJV)** And whosoever shall exalt himself shall be abased; and he that shall humble himself shall be exalted.

**Matthew 23:13 (KJV)** But woe unto you, scribes and Pharisees, hypocrites! for ye shut up the kingdom of heaven against men: for ye neither go in *yourselves*, neither suffer ye them that are entering to go in.

11. To put it another way, the Scribes and Pharisees, being of malicious intent, failed to adhere to God's Word. Instead, they manipulated the Scriptures for personal gain and exploitation of the populace, disqualifying themselves from any authentic "spiritual father-son relationship." Consequently, Jesus Christ admonished: Do not bestow upon them the title of 'Father' as they do not follow the teachings of God's Word.!

> **Matthew 23:1 (KJV)** Then spake Jesus to the multitude, and to his disciples,
>
> **Matthew 23:2 (KJV)** Saying, The scribes and the Pharisees sit in Moses' seat:
>
> **Matthew 23:3 (KJV)** All therefore whatsoever they bid you observe, *that* observe and do; but do not ye after their works: for they say, and do not.
>
> **Matthew 23:4 (KJV)** For they bind heavy burdens and grievous to be borne, and lay *them* on men's shoulders; but they *themselves* will not move them with one of their fingers.
>
> **Matthew 23:5 (KJV)** But all their works they do for to be seen of men: they make broad their phylacteries, and enlarge the borders of their garments,
>
> **Matthew 23:6 (KJV)** And love the uppermost rooms at feasts, and the chief seats in the synagogues,
>
> **Matthew 23:7 (KJV)** And greetings in the markets, and to be called of men, Rabbi, Rabbi.

12. Now, let's delve into the second tier of instruction, outlined as follows:

> Based on the scenario previously discussed,
>
> If the "spiritual father-son relationship" is effectively initiated in the spiritual domain through adherence to God's Word by both parties, and if both the spiritual father and son consistently live by these divine instructions without fail, then a genuine "spiritual father-son relationship" is in existence.
>
> Under such circumstances, as delineated above, it is then, and only then, that Jesus Christ suggests one may rightfully address them as **'Father'**.

13. Through this demonstration of when it is appropriate to refer to a religious leader as "Spiritual Father" and for him to consider you "a spiritual son," we observe the Lord Jesus Christ embodying this principle. Both He and His disciples live in accordance with God's Word, thereby establishing Him as their spiritual father—the Teacher of

God's Word—and them as His spiritual children. This relationship is evidenced in **John 13:33** and **John 21:5,** where the dynamic between Jesus and His disciples illustrates this sacred bond.

> **John 8:29 (KJV)** And he that sent me is with me: the Father hath not left me alone; for I do always those things that please him.

> **John 15:10 (KJV)** If ye keep my commandments, ye shall abide in my love; even as I have kept my Father's commandments, and abide in his love.

> **John 17:6 (KJV)** I have manifested thy name unto the men which thou gavest me out of the world: thine they were, and thou gavest them me; and they have kept thy word.

> **John 17:14 (KJV)** I have given them thy word; and the world hath hated them, because they are not of the world, even as I am not of the world.

> **John 13:33 (KJV)** Little children, yet a little while I am with you. Ye shall seek me: and as I said unto the Jews, Whither I go, ye cannot come; so now I say to you.

> **John 21:5 (KJV)** Then Jesus saith unto them, Children, have ye any meat? They answered him, No.

14. Here is another instance that illustrates when it is appropriate to refer to a religious leader as a "Spiritual Father" and to be called "a spiritual son" in return. Apostle Paul is recognized as a spiritual father with spiritual sons, similar to the way Jesus Christ had!

> **Galatians 4:19 (KJV)** My little children, of whom I travail in birth again until Christ be formed in you,

15. This is the third example demonstrating the circumstances under which you can appropriately refer to a religious leader as a "Spiritual Father" and be acknowledged as "a spiritual son." Apostle John serves as a spiritual father with spiritual sons, in a manner akin to that of Jesus Christ!

> **1 John 2:1 (KJV)** My little children, these things write I unto you, that ye sin not. And if any man sin, we have an advocate with the Father, Jesus Christ the righteous:

> **1 John 2:12 (KJV)** I write unto you, little children, because your sins are forgiven you for his name's sake.

> **1 John 2:13 (KJV)** I write unto you, fathers, because ye have known him *that is* from the beginning. I write unto you, young men, because ye have overcome the wicked one. I write unto you, little children, because ye have known the Father.

> **1 John 2:18 (KJV)** Little children, it is the last time: and as ye have heard that antichrist shall come, even now are there many antichrists; whereby we know that it is the last time.

**1 John 2:28 (KJV)** And now, little children, abide in him; that, when he shall appear, we may have confidence, and not be ashamed before him at his coming.

**1 John 3:7 (KJV)** Little children, let no man deceive you: he that doeth righteousness is righteous, even as he is righteous.

**1 John 3:18 (KJV)** My little children, let us not love in word, neither in tongue; but in deed and in truth.

**1 John 4:4 (KJV)** Ye are of God, little children, and have overcome them: because greater is he that is in you, than he that is in the world.

**1 John 5:21 (KJV)** Little children, keep yourselves from idols. Amen.

16. Another important insight emerges from the concept of "spiritual father-son relationship" within the Christian community, which is closely linked to the frequently discussed belief in "once saved, always saved."

17. Specifically, there are pastors who erroneously preach that simply by acknowledging the foundational beliefs of Christianity — the Birth, Death, and Resurrection of Jesus Christ — one is eternally saved. According to them, this assurance of salvation remains unshaken, even if an individual continues to sin, suggesting that salvation is irrevocable and the risk of damnation is nonexistent.

18. However, when the LORD explicitly states in **Numbers 14:11 12** that God can disinherit a child due to their sins, it raises a critical question: Is God's warning to be disregarded?

    **Numbers 14:11 (KJV)** And the LORD said unto Moses, How long will this people provoke me? and how long will it be ere they believe me, for all the signs which I have shewed among them?

    **Numbers 14:12 (KJV)** I will smite them with the pestilence, and disinherit them, and will make of thee a greater nation and mightier than they.

19. Is it then to suggest that the Lord Jesus Christ was also being untruthful when He spoke of such matters below? **Absolutely not!**

    **Matthew 8:11 (KJV)** And I say unto you, That many shall come from the east and west, and shall sit down with Abraham, and Isaac, and Jacob, in the kingdom of heaven.

    **Matthew 8:12 (KJV)** But the children of the kingdom shall be cast out into outer darkness: there shall be weeping and gnashing of teeth.

20. Was the Holy Spirit also deceiving us when He conveyed this message? Certainly not!

**Revelation 21:7 (KJV)** He that overcometh shall inherit all things; and I will be his God, and he shall be my son.

**Revelation 21:8 (KJV)** But the fearful, and unbelieving, and the abominable, and murderers, and whoremongers, and sorcerers, and idolaters, and all liars, shall have their part in the lake which burneth with fire and brimstone: which is the second death

**Revelation 21:27 (KJV)** And there shall in no wise enter into it any thing that defileth, neither *whatsoever* worketh abomination, or *maketh* a lie: but they which are written in the Lamb's book of life.

**Revelation 22:15 (KJV)** For without *are* dogs, and sorcerers, and whoremongers, and murderers, and idolaters, and whosoever loveth and maketh a lie.

21. Was Jesus Christ being untruthful when He proclaimed that entrance into Heaven is conditional upon obeying God's Commandments? Absolutely not!

**Matthew 5:20 (KJV)** For I say unto you, That except your righteousness shall exceed *the righteousness* of the scribes and Pharisees, ye shall in no case enter into the kingdom of heaven.

**Matthew 7:21 (KJV)** Not every one that saith unto me, Lord, Lord, shall enter into the kingdom of heaven; but he that doeth the will of my Father which is in heaven.

**Revelation 22:14 (KJV)** Blessed *are* they that do his commandments, that they may have right to the tree of life, and may enter in through the gates into the city.

**Revelation 22:15 (KJV)** For without *are* dogs, and sorcerers, and whoremongers, and murderers, and idolaters, and whosoever loveth and maketh a lie.

**Revelation 22:16 (KJV)** I Jesus have sent mine angel to testify unto you these things in the churches. I am the root and the offspring of David, *and* the bright and morning star.

22. Is the Word of God misleading, allowing some preachers and pastors to propagate the erroneous doctrine that accepting the Birth, Death, and Resurrection of the Lord Jesus Christ grants automatic entry into Heaven, regardless of continuing to live in sin? Certainly not!

**1 Timothy 1:8 (KJV)** But we know that the law *is* good, if a man use it lawfully;

**1 Timothy 1:9 (KJV)** Knowing this, that the law is not made for a righteous man, but for the lawless and disobedient, for the ungodly and for sinners, for unholy and profane, for murderers of fathers and murderers of mothers, for manslayers,

**1 Timothy 1:10 (KJV)** For whoremongers, for them that defile themselves with mankind, for menstealers, for liars, for perjured persons, and if there be any other thing that is contrary to sound doctrine;

23. Brothers and Sisters, let me share with you the reality:

The concept of a "spiritual father-son relationship" ceases to exist without ongoing adherence to God's Word.

24. To conclude, what I am revealing to you about the concept of "spiritual father-son relationship" within the Christian community is that, just as physical children are conceived through biological means, similarly, spiritual offspring can be generated in the spiritual realm. However, the means of this spiritual procreation is through the Word of God. Here's the proof!

**Philippians 2:19 (KJV)** But I trust in the Lord Jesus to send Timotheus shortly unto you, that I also may be of good comfort, when I know your state.

**Philippians 2:20 (KJV)** For I have no man likeminded, who will naturally care for your state.

**Philippians 2:21 (KJV)** For all seek their own, not the things which are Jesus Christ's.

**Philippians 2:22 (KJV)** But ye know the proof of him, that, as a son with the father, he hath served with me in the gospel.

**Philippians 2:23 (KJV)** Him therefore I hope to send presently, so soon as I shall see how it will go with me.

**1 Corinthians 4:14 (KJV)** I write not these things to shame you, but as my beloved sons I warn *you*.

**1 Corinthians 4:15 (KJV)** For though ye have ten thousand instructors in Christ, yet *have ye* not many fathers: for in Christ Jesus I have begotten you through the gospel.

**Timothy 1:10 (KJV)** But is now made manifest by the appearing of our Saviour Jesus Christ, who hath abolished death, and hath brought life and immortality to light through the gospel:

May the Lord Jesus Christ be with your spirit. May the Lord Jesus Christ grant you understanding.

# CHAPTER 4

## SPIRITUAL INTERPRETATION OF THE LORD'S PRAYER!

========================

The Ewe symbol of light is referred to as '**gomekaɖi**' (lantern). It is taken from the adage '*Kekeli*' meaning 'there is light'. The symbol expresses the essence of light in that, wherever light is, it overpowers darkness. In other words, wherever there is positivity, knowledge, wisdom, progress and growth; negativity, ignorance, foolishness, retrogression, and stagnation are overpowered.

========================

In the Sermon on the Mount, recorded in Matthew chapters 5 through 7, Jesus Christ initiates His teachings during His three-year ministry with profound insights. Starting in Matthew 5, Jesus undertakes a significant reinterpretation of several Old Testament laws and doctrines, offering deeper and more accurate understandings, meanings, and practices.

As He progresses into Matthew 6, Jesus addresses the issue of performative acts of charity prevalent in His time, a practice sadly mirrored in some contemporary churches. Here, pastors or prophets might publicly announce their charitable acts, sometimes even broadcasting the plight of the poor on television, a direct contradiction to Jesus' teachings against such public displays of piety for self-aggrandizement.

Furthermore, Jesus critiques the ostentatious manner of public prayer observed in churches and religious gatherings, where the emphasis often lies on eloquence and outward display of spirituality rather than genuine communication with God. This includes the use of elaborate language and the performance of speaking in tongues for the sake of impressing others. Jesus asserts that such prayers, aimed at garnering human admiration rather than divine connection, are not only ineffectual but are also misguided, essentially receiving no acknowledgment from God.

To underscore these teachings, let us reflect on the specific verses that highlight the essence of genuine worship and devotion, free from hypocrisy and focused on sincere, heartfelt connection with the Divine.

**Matthew 6:5 (KJV)** And when thou prayest, thou shalt not be as the hypocrites *are*: for they love to pray standing in the synagogues and in the corners of the streets, that they may be seen of men. Verily I say unto you, They have their reward.

Following His critique of insincere and performative practices in prayer, Jesus Christ then guides us towards the authentic and appropriate approach to prayer, one that ensures our communication reaches God Almighty. This instruction emphasizes the importance of sincerity, humility, and privacy in our prayer life, directing us away from seeking human approval and towards cultivating a genuine relationship with God.

1. The initial key theme highlighted in Matthew 6:9 (KJV) emphasizes the importance of privacy in prayer. This advises that prayers should be conducted discreetly, where others may observe the act of prayer, akin to Hannah's prayer in the temple, but the content of the prayer remains a personal conversation between the individual and God Almighty. The focus is on ensuring a private and sincere dialogue with God, irrespective of one's surroundings, including within a church setting!

   **1 Samuel 1:12 (KJV)** And it came to pass, as she continued praying before the LORD, that Eli marked her mouth.

   **1 Samuel 1:13 (KJV)** Now Hannah, she spake in her heart; only her lips moved, but her voice was not heard: therefore Eli thought she had been drunken.

   **1 Samuel 1:14 (KJV)** And Eli said unto her, How long wilt thou be drunken? put away thy wine from thee.

   **1 Samuel 1:15 (KJV)** And Hannah answered and said, No, my lord, I *am* a woman of a sorrowful spirit: I have drunk neither wine nor strong drink, but have poured out my soul before the LORD.

   **1 Samuel 1:16 (KJV)** Count not thine handmaid for a daughter of Belial: for out of the abundance of my complaint and grief have I spoken hitherto.

   **1 Samuel 1:17 (KJV)** Then Eli answered and said, Go in peace: and the God of Israel grant *thee* thy petition that thou hast asked of him.

   **Matthew 6:6 (KJV)** But thou, when thou prayest, enter into thy closet, and when thou hast shut thy door, pray to thy Father which is in secret; and thy Father which seeth in secret shall reward thee openly.

2. Jesus Christ warns against the use of redundant phrases and mindless repetition in prayer, equating such practices with those of non-believers or idolaters. According to Matthew 6:7 (KJV), engaging in repetitive prayers does not enhance their effectiveness, as God does not measure prayers by their length or verbosity.

3. Jesus further enlightens us that God Almighty is already aware of our needs even before we voice them. Thus, He suggests that the essence of a true Christian's prayer should focus on seeking divine guidance through the Word of God (Judgment) and striving for a life of integrity and blamelessness before both God and fellow humans (Righteousness). This perspective shifts the focus of prayer from mere requests to a deeper yearning for spiritual growth and alignment with God's will!

> **Matthew 6:8 (KJV)** Be not ye therefore like unto them: for your Father knoweth what things ye have need of, before ye ask him.

4. A testament to the power of concise prayer can be found in the example Jesus gives us, often referred to as the Lord's Prayer. This model prayer is succinct yet encompasses all essential elements that should be part of our communication with God. It highlights the importance of acknowledging God's holiness, submitting to His will, requesting daily needs, seeking forgiveness, and asking for guidance away from temptation and evil. This prayer serves as a powerful example that effectiveness in prayer is not about length but about the sincerity and content of our petitions to God!

> **Philippians 4:6 (KJV)** Be careful for nothing; but in every thing by prayer and supplication with thanksgiving let your requests be made known unto God.
>
> **1 Thessalonians 5:18 (KJV)** In every thing give thanks: for this is the will of God in Christ Jesus concerning you.

5. Upholding truthfulness is also a vital form of prayer. Unfortunately, it's not uncommon for Christians and pastors to deviate from truthfulness in their daily lives. When they are confronted with the truths of Scripture, their reaction is often one of anger rather than acceptance. Embracing honesty and integrity in all interactions is not only a mark of genuine faith but also an act of living prayer that aligns with God's will!

> **Proverbs 12:17 (KJV)** *He that* speaketh truth sheweth forth righteousness: but a false witness deceit.
>
> **Zechariah 8:16 (KJV)** These *are* the things that ye shall do; Speak ye every man the truth to his neighbour; execute the judgment of truth and peace in your gates:
>
> **Zechariah 8:17 (KJV)** And let none of you imagine evil in your hearts against his neighbour; and love no false oath: for all these *are things* that I hate, saith the LORD.
>
> **2 Corinthians 4:1 (KJV)** Therefore seeing we have this ministry, as we have received mercy, we faint not;
>
> **2 Corinthians 4:2 (KJV)** But have renounced the hidden things of dishonesty, not walking in craftiness, nor handling the word of God deceitfully; but by manifestation of the truth commending ourselves to every man's conscience in the sight of God.

Jesus Christ instructs us that our prayers to God Almighty should either directly utilize His teachings or should be deeply reflective of the themes and principles found within His words. This guidance ensures that our prayers remain aligned with the spirit of His teachings, emphasizing the importance of a prayer life that is rooted in the teachings of Christ!

> **Matthew 6:9 (KJV)** After this manner therefore pray ye: Our Father which art in heaven, Hallowed be thy name.

6. The second significant theme identified in Matthew 6:9 (KJV) pertains to the exaltation and praise of God Almighty. It is essential for a genuine Christian or a true Man of God to commence their prayers by glorifying and praising God. This sets the right tone for prayer, focusing the mind on God's sovereignty and majesty.

One way to honor God at the beginning of your prayer is by addressing Him as Father, signifying a relationship of intimacy and respect. This approach not only prepares your heart for sincere worship but also serves as a spiritual guard against trivial or insincere prayer.

- Praising and glorifying God Almighty, as taught in Matthew 6:9 (KJV), involves recognizing His supreme authority and expressing reverence for His divine nature. This can be achieved through words that uplift His name and acknowledge His greatness.

- An integral part of your prayer should be the acknowledgment of God's heavenly domain. This recognition places God above all earthly realms and situations, highlighting His omnipresence and omnipotence.

- Additionally, acknowledging God's holiness is crucial. This reflects your understanding of God's absolute purity and the distinction between His divine nature and human imperfection. Recognizing God's holiness sets a foundation of respect and awe in your prayer.

> **Revelation 4:8 (KJV)** And the four beasts had each of them six wings about *him*; and *they were* full of eyes within: and they rest not day and night, saying, Holy, holy, holy, Lord God Almighty, which was, and is, and is to come.

> **Revelation 4:11 (KJV)** Thou art worthy, O Lord, to receive glory and honour and power: for thou hast created all things, and for thy pleasure they are and were created.

7. Subsequently, your prayer should express faith and anticipation for the realization of God's Kingdom and the fulfillment of His will on Earth, just as it already prevails in Heaven. This demonstrates your desire for divine principles and righteousness to govern earthly life, aligning with God's eternal purpose!

**Matthew 6:10 (KJV)** Thy kingdom come. Thy will be done in earth, as *it is* in heaven.

8. Following the initial praise and glorification of God Almighty in your prayer, as outlined in **Matthew 6:9,** the next step involves presenting your requests to God. However, these requests should transcend mere earthly or material desires, focusing instead on seeking a sufficient measure of God's Word in your life. This emphasizes the importance of spiritual nourishment and wisdom over temporal needs!

   **Matthew 6:11 (KJV)** Give us this day our daily bread.

9. The Word of God is identified as the true sustenance for our spiritual lives, which highlights the notion that relying solely on physical symbols like man-made bread and wine without understanding their spiritual significance can lead one away from the true essence of Holy Communion as intended in the Bible. This underscores the necessity of seeking spiritual truth and life in God's Word rather than in ritualistic practices alone.

10. Jesus Christ, in **Matthew 6:11,** is emphasizing the spiritual nourishment that the soul requires, which is fulfilled through the Word of God. This concept is supported by passages such as **Jeremiah 15:16,** where the prophet finds joy and delight in God's words as if he had eaten them; **Ezekiel 3:1-4,** which describes Ezekiel's call to eat a scroll of lamentations and warnings yet find it as sweet as honey; and **Revelation 10:8-11,** where John is instructed to eat a small scroll that tastes sweet but turns bitter in his stomach. These passages collectively illustrate that the true sustenance and fulfillment for the believer come from digesting and living according to God's Word.

   **Jeremiah 15:16 (KJV)** Thy words were found, and I did eat them; and thy word was unto me the joy and rejoicing of mine heart: for I am called by thy name, O LORD God of hosts.

   **Ezekiel 3:1 (KJV)** Moreover he said unto me, Son of man, eat that thou findest; eat this roll, and go speak unto the house of Israel.

   **Ezekiel 3:2 (KJV)** So I opened my mouth, and he caused me to eat that roll.

   **Ezekiel 3:3 (KJV)** And he said unto me, Son of man, cause thy belly to eat, and fill thy bowels with this roll that I give thee. Then did I eat *it*; and it was in my mouth as honey for sweetness.

   **Ezekiel 3:4 (KJV)** And he said unto me, Son of man, go, get thee unto the house of Israel, and speak with my words unto them.

   **Revelation 10:8 (KJV)** And the voice which I heard from heaven spake unto me again, and said, Go *and* take the little book which is open in the hand of the angel which standeth upon the sea and upon the earth.

**Revelation 10:9 (KJV)** And I went unto the angel, and said unto him, Give me the little book. And he said unto me, Take *it*, and eat it up; and it shall make thy belly bitter, but it shall be in thy mouth sweet as honey.

**Revelation 10:10 (KJV)** And I took the little book out of the angel's hand, and ate it up; and it was in my mouth sweet as honey: and as soon as I had eaten it, my belly was bitter.

**Revelation 10:11 (KJV)** And he said unto me, Thou must prophesy again before many peoples, and nations, and tongues, and kings.

11. In **Matthew 6:11**, Jesus Christ teaches that during prayer, it's essential to request from God Almighty the provision of His Word that will adequately nourish, shield, and liberate you for the day at hand. This instruction emphasizes the importance of seeking daily spiritual sustenance and guidance through God's Word!

> **Exodus 16:15 (KJV)** And when the children of Israel saw *it*, they said one to another, It *is* manna: for they wist not what it *was*. And Moses said unto them, This *is* the bread which the LORD hath given you to eat.

> **Exodus 16:16 (KJV)** This *is* the thing which the LORD hath commanded, Gather of it every man according to his eating, an omer for every man, *according to* the number of your persons; take ye every man for *them* which *are* in his tents.

> **Exodus 16:17 (KJV)** And the children of Israel did so, and gathered, some more, some less.

> **Exodus 16:18 (KJV)** And when they did mete it with an omer, he that gathered much had nothing over, and he that gathered little had no lack; they gathered every man according to his eating.

> **Exodus 16:19 (KJV)** And Moses said, Let no man leave of it till the morning.

> **Matthew 6:34 (KJV)** Take therefore no thought for the morrow: for the morrow shall take thought for the things of itself. Sufficient unto the day is the evil thereof.

12. The fourth significant aspect of prayer highlighted in Matthew 6:9 involves seeking forgiveness for our transgressions, whether they occur in thought, word, or deed. Equally important is the act of forgiving those who have wronged us, entrusting any retribution to God Almighty's just judgment. This emphasizes the need for a heart that both acknowledges personal faults and extends grace to others, in alignment with divine mercy!

> **Matthew 6:12 (KJV)** And forgive us our debts, as we forgive our debtors.

> **Romans 12:19 (KJV)** Dearly beloved, avenge not yourselves, but rather give place unto wrath: for it is written, Vengeance is mine; I will repay, saith the Lord.

**2 Thessalonians 1:6 (KJV)** Seeing it is a righteous thing with God to recompense tribulation to them that trouble you;

**James 5:16 (KJV)** Confess your faults one to another, and pray one for another, that ye may be healed. The effectual fervent prayer of a righteous man availeth much.

**1 John 1:7 (KJV)** But if we walk in the light, as he is in the light, we have fellowship one with another, and the blood of Jesus Christ his Son cleanseth us from all sin.

**1 John 1:8 (KJV)** If we say that we have no sin, we deceive ourselves, and the truth is not in us.

**1 John 1:9 (KJV)** If we confess our sins, he is faithful and just to forgive us *our* sins, and to cleanse us from all unrighteousness.

**1 John 1:10 (KJV)** If we say that we have not sinned, we make him a liar, and his word is not in us.

13. The focus on seeking forgiveness and extending it to others, as highlighted in **Matthew 6:9**, is pivotal as it reinforces the truth that the Word of God cannot dwell fully in a heart that is tainted by sin or malice and still expect to be effective in divine service. Clinging to bitterness or sin while endeavoring to perform God's work can only lead to spiritual defeat. Ironically, the Word, which is meant to impart life, can cause harm if one's heart is not rightly aligned with God's principles.

14. Brethren, recall the instance in **2 Chronicles 1** where God appeared to Solomon after his significant offering and asked what Solomon wished for. Instead of desiring riches or the downfall of his enemies, Solomon chose to ask for wisdom and knowledge to lead God's people effectively. God was so pleased with Solomon's request that He granted him not only the wisdom he sought but also wealth and honor beyond any of his contemporaries. This story prompts us to reflect: What would we ask for in Solomon's place? Would we seek the demise of our adversaries and worldly gains, or would we pursue divine wisdom and understanding?

This narrative serves as a powerful reminder of the necessity to purify our hearts from sin and embrace forgiveness. Such a heart is a fertile ground for the Word of God, enabling us to harness its transformative power effectively!

**2 Chronicles 1:1(KJV)** "And God said to Solomon, "Because this was in thine heart, and thou hast not asked riches, wealth, or honour, nor the life of thine enemies, neither yet hast asked long life; but hast asked wisdom and knowledge for thyself, that thou mayest judge my people, over whom I have made thee king:

**2 Chronicles 1:1(KJV)** Wisdom and knowledge is granted unto thee; and I will give thee riches, and wealth, and honour, such as none of the kings have had that have been before thee, neither shall there any after thee have the like."

**Psalm 50:16 (KJV)** But unto the wicked God saith, What hast thou to do to declare my statutes, or *that* thou shouldest take my covenant in thy mouth?

**2 Corinthians 4:1 (KJV)** Therefore seeing we have this ministry, as we have received mercy, we faint not;

**2 Corinthians 4:2 (KJV)** But have renounced the hidden things of dishonesty, not walking in craftiness, nor handling the word of God deceitfully; but by manifestation of the truth commending ourselves to every man's conscience in the sight of God.

**1 Timothy 3:9 (KJV)** Holding the mystery of the faith in a pure conscience.

15. The fifth critical theme in prayer, as presented in **Matthew 6:9,** involves asking God Almighty to guide your actions according to His Word, ensuring you do not stumble in your walk with Him. Additionally, it's a plea to God to sustain your faith so that it does not waver, protecting you from becoming susceptible to Satan's attacks. This aspect of prayer emphasizes the believer's reliance on divine guidance and strength to navigate life's challenges and spiritual battles!

   **Psalm 119:133 (KJV)** Order my steps in thy word: and let not any iniquity have dominion over me.

   **Matthew 6:13 (KJV)** And lead us not into temptation, but deliver us from evil: For thine is the kingdom, and the power, and the glory, for ever. Amen.

   **Luke 22:31 (KJV)** And the Lord said, Simon, Simon, behold, Satan hath desired *to have* you, that he may sift *you* as wheat:

   **Luke 22:32 (KJV)** But I have prayed for thee, that thy faith fail not: and when thou art converted, strengthen thy brethren.

   **John 14:30 (KJV)** Hereafter I will not talk much with you: for the prince of this world cometh, and hath nothing in me.

   **1 Corinthians 10:12 (KJV)** Wherefore let him that thinketh he standeth take heed lest he fall.

   **1 Timothy 3:1 (KJV)** This *is* a true saying, If a man desire the office of a bishop, he desireth a good work.

   **1 Timothy 3:2 (KJV)** A bishop then must be blameless, the husband of one wife, vigilant, sober, of good behaviour, given to hospitality, apt to teach;

   **1 Timothy 3:6 (KJV)** Not a novice, lest being lifted up with pride he fall into the condemnation of the devil.

**In summary, the Lord's Prayer encompasses five essential components:**

16. Engage in prayer privately, ensuring your communication with God is personal and sincere.

17. Begin with Praise and Adoration for God Almighty:

xviii. Recognize God's sovereign presence in Heaven.

xix. Acknowledge the holiness of God.

xx. Declare your faith in and anticipation for the Kingdom of God to manifest on Earth as it is in Heaven.

21. Present Your Requests: Focus your petitions on spiritual needs, particularly the desire for God's Word to nourish and guide you, rather than on material or earthly desires

22. Seek Forgiveness: Request forgiveness for your own transgressions, whether in thought, word, or deed, and extend forgiveness to those who have wronged you, fostering a spirit of grace and reconciliation.

23. Ask for Divine Guidance and Protection: Request that God direct your actions according to His Word to prevent spiritual falter and ask for faith that remains strong in the face of trials and temptations.

May the Lord Jesus Christ accompany your spirit and grant you deep understanding.

# CHAPTER 5

## ARE CHRISTIANS PRACTISING THE BIBLE?

=====================

ANANSE NTENTAN

"Spider's web"

Asante philosophical symbol of Wisdom,
Creativity, Craftiness, Shrewdness

==========================

Is love for one another and humility considered the highest teachings in the Bible? Are believers truly living according to biblical principles? What causes the world to become increasingly perilous? And why do some churches and their leaders contribute to the world's wrongdoings?

1. The first and greatest commandment in the Bible is highlighted in the Gospel of Matthew, where Jesus himself articulates it in response to a question about the most important commandment. Let's look at the specific scripture to confirm this doctrine:

In **Matthew 22:37-38** Jesus said to him, "'Love the Lord your God with all your heart and with all your soul and with all your mind.' This is the first and greatest commandment."

This commandment emphasizes the total devotion to God with every aspect of one's being. It serves as a fundamental principle that underpins the entire doctrine of Christianity, focusing on the importance of loving God as the paramount duty of every believer. This core teaching is not only pivotal for understanding Christian ethics but also sets the stage for the second commandment, which deals with loving one's neighbor as oneself, further elaborating on the theme of love as central to Christian faith and practice.

**Deuteronomy 6:4 (KJV)** Hear, O Israel: The LORD our God *is* one LORD:

**Mark 12:28 (KJV)** And one of the scribes came, and having heard them reasoning together, and perceiving that he had answered them well, asked him, Which is the first commandment of all?

**Mark 12:29 (KJV)** And Jesus answered him, The first of all the commandments *is*, Hear, O Israel; The Lord our God is one Lord:

**Mark 12:30 (KJV)** And thou shalt love the Lord thy God with all thy heart, and with all thy soul, and with all thy mind, and with all thy strength: this *is* the first commandment.

The second greatest commandment, as articulated by Jesus, is pivotal in understanding the depth and breadth of Christian ethics and love. Found in the Gospel of Matthew, this commandment directs us to "Love your neighbor as yourself," underscoring the vital importance of empathy, compassion, and mutual respect in all our interactions. This principle not only calls for treating others with the kindness and consideration we seek for ourselves but also affirms the inherent worth of every person.

When combined, the greatest commandment to love God wholly and this second commandment to love others as ourselves, lay the cornerstone of Christian ethical teachings. They remind us that our love for God is reflected in our love for others, establishing a direct link between our spiritual devotion and our practical, everyday actions towards those around us. These commandments together encapsulate the essence of what it means to live a life guided by Christian principles.

**Mark 12:31 (KJV)** And the second *is* like, *namely* this, Thou shalt love thy neighbour as thyself. There is none other commandment greater than these.

The profound spiritual insight derived from these commandments is that by adhering to them, one essentially upholds the entirety of the Old Testament. Jesus' teaching reveals that the essence of the law and the prophets is encapsulated in these two principles: love for God and love for others.

This synthesis of commandments simplifies the myriad laws into core actions that reflect true devotion and righteousness.

2. The ability to genuinely love others is predicated on having a foundational love for God Almighty. This teaching underscores that all attempts to exercise love, devoid of a relationship with God, are likely to lead to disappointment and hardship. The reason behind this is the belief that love, in its truest form, originates from God; hence, loving outside of this divine context is seen as inherently flawed. It's posited that love directed towards God creates the capacity for love towards others, drawing a metaphorical line between **vertical** (towards God) and **horizontal** (towards people) love. Without the foundational love for God, extending love to one's neighbor or spouse becomes a challenge, reinforcing the scriptural declaration that **"God is love."** This concept stresses the interconnectedness of divine love with human love, emphasizing the necessity of loving God as a prerequisite for loving others effectively.

**1 John 4:7 (KJV)** Beloved, let us love one another: for love is of God; and every one that loveth is born of God, and knoweth God.

**1 John 4:8 (KJV)** He that loveth not knoweth not God; for God is love.

**1 John 4:10 (KJV)** Herein is love, not that we loved God, but that he loved us, and sent his Son *to be* the propitiation for our sins.

**1 John 4:11 (KJV)** Beloved, if God so loved us, we ought also to love one another.

**1 John 4:20 (KJV)** If a man say, I love God, and hateth his brother, he is a liar: for he that loveth not his brother whom he hath seen, how can he love God whom he hath not seen?

**1 John 4:21 (KJV)** And this commandment have we from him, That he who loveth God love his brother also.

3. Love towards God is primarily manifested through one's consistent obedience to the Word of God, which serves as the clearest measure of a person's devotion to the divine. This form of love is not merely lip service or confined to moments of convenience; rather, it is demonstrated through a steadfast commitment to follow God's teachings, even when such obedience entails personal sacrifice or suffering. This concept underscores the principle that true love for God goes beyond emotions or declarations—it is deeply rooted in actions that align with God's commandments, reflecting a willingness to prioritize divine will above personal comfort or worldly gains. Thus, the genuine measure of love towards God is seen in how individuals live out their faith in their everyday lives, particularly in their readiness to uphold God's Word amidst challenges:

**Exodus 20:6 (KJV)** And shewing mercy unto thousands of them that love me, and keep my commandments.

**Deuteronomy 5:10 (KJV)** And shewing mercy unto thousands of them that love me and keep my commandments.

**Mark 10:29 (KJV)** And Jesus answered and said, Verily I say unto you, There is no man that hath left house, or brethren, or sisters, or father, or mother, or wife, or children, or lands, for my sake, and the gospel's,

**Mark 10:30 (KJV)** But he shall receive an hundredfold now in this time, houses, and brethren, and sisters, and mothers, and children, and lands, with persecutions; and in the world to come eternal life.

**John 14:15 (KJV)** If ye love me, keep my commandments.

**John 14:23 (KJV)** Jesus answered and said unto him, If a man love me, he will keep my words: and my Father will love him, and we will come unto him, and make our abode with him.

**2 Timothy 3:12 (KJV)** Yea, and all that will live godly in Christ Jesus shall suffer persecution.

4. Humility, while not explicitly commanded, emerges naturally as a byproduct of the Holy Spirit's presence within an individual. When the Holy Spirit resides in a person, humility manifests effortlessly, becoming visible to others without any need for proclamation or solicitation. This virtue is intrinsically linked to obedience to the Word of God; a humble person exemplifies this through daily adherence to divine teachings in every decision made. Thus, humility is not just an attribute but a testament to one's obedience and the indwelling of the Holy Spirit, recognized and acknowledged by those around without being outwardly declared:

**1 Peter 5:5 (KJV)** Likewise, ye younger, submit yourselves unto the elder. Yea, all *of you* be subject one to another, and be clothed with humility: for God resisteth the proud, and giveth grace to the humble.

5. Evidence that humility encompasses turning away from evil can be found in its definition as a disposition towards selflessness and a rejection of wrongful actions. Humility involves recognizing one's limitations and dependence on God, leading to a life that avoids evil in favor of righteousness. This concept of humility is not merely about modest behavior or low self-regard but fundamentally about choosing a path that aligns with moral and ethical principles. By turning away from evil, a person demonstrates a humble submission to God's will and a commitment to living according to divine standards, embodying humility through actions that reflect a deep respect for God's commandments and a dedication to goodness.

**2 Chronicles 7:14 (KJV)** If my people, which are called by my name, shall humble themselves, and pray, and seek my face, and turn from their wicked ways; then will I hear from heaven, and will forgive their sin, and will heal their land.

6. A humble person follows God's guidance unconditionally, akin to the unquestioning trust and obedience of a young child.

**Matthew 18:4 (KJV)** Whosoever therefore shall humble himself as this little child, the same is greatest in the kingdom of heaven.

7. To summarize, an individual lacking in humility is essentially one who does not adhere to God's commands!

**Numbers 12:3 (KJV)** (Now the man Moses *was* very meek, above all the men which *were* upon the face of the earth.)

**Hebrews 3:2 (KJV)** Who was faithful to him that appointed him, as also Moses *was faithful* in all his house.

**Hebrews 3:5 (KJV)** And Moses verily *was* faithful in all his house, as a servant, for a testimony of those things which were to be spoken after;

8. **Are Christians practicing the Bible?** The extent to which Christians practice the teachings of the Bible varies widely among individuals and communities. While many strive to live in accordance with biblical principles, applying them to daily life, challenges, and interpretations can differ. The faith's diverse expressions and denominations contribute to a broad spectrum of adherence and practice. Ultimately, the degree of biblical practice among Christians is influenced by personal conviction, understanding, and the context within which one's faith is nurtured and expressed.

9. The true essence of being a Christian is not defined by outward appearances but by one's inner faith and convictions, which inevitably manifest in external actions. Not everyone who identifies as a Christian may embody the principles and teachings of Christianity at their core. Authentic Christianity is characterized by a transformation from the inside out, where a genuine relationship with God influences one's behavior and choices. A hallmark of true Christian faith is a profound aversion to committing acts that are evil, deceitful, or dishonest. Instead, a true Christian is committed to upholding the truth, even in the face of personal harm or the risk of death. This integrity and adherence to truth, regardless of the consequences, signify the depth of one's faith and the presence of a transformed heart!

> **Romans 2:28 (KJV)** For he is not a Jew, which is one outwardly; neither *is that* circumcision, which is outward in the flesh:
>
> **Romans 2:29 (KJV)** But he *is* a Jew, which is one inwardly; and circumcision *is that* of the heart, in the spirit, *and* not in the letter; whose praise *is* not of men, but of God.
>
> **Revelation 2:10 (KJV)** Fear none of those things which thou shalt suffer: behold, the devil shall cast *some* of you into prison, that ye may be tried; and ye shall have tribulation ten days: be thou faithful unto death, and I will give thee a crown of life.

10. Consistently, the true Christian is someone who may face animosity for their unwavering commitment to speaking the truth:

> **Mark 13:13 (KJV)** And ye shall be hated of all *men* for my name's sake: but he that shall endure unto the end, the same shall be saved.
>
> **John 14:17 (KJV)** *Even* the Spirit of truth; whom the world cannot receive, because it seeth him not, neither knoweth him: but ye know him; for he dwelleth with you, and shall be in you.

**John 15:26 (KJV)** But when the Comforter is come, whom I will send unto you from the Father, *even* the Spirit of truth, which proceedeth from the Father, he shall testify of me:

**John 16:13 (KJV)** Howbeit when he, the Spirit of truth, is come, he will guide you into all truth: for he shall not speak of himself; but whatsoever he shall hear, *that* shall he speak: and he will shew you things to come.

**Ephesians 5:9 (KJV)** (For the fruit of the Spirit *is* in all goodness and righteousness and truth;)

11. Christianity loses its essence when an individual professing to be a Christian persists in living in sin. A true Christian emulates Christ, and since Jesus Christ was never disobedient to God, the definitive sign of genuine Christianity is obedience to the Word of God:

    **Romans 2:25 (KJV)** For circumcision verily profiteth, if thou keep the law: but if thou be a breaker of the law, thy circumcision is made uncircumcision.

    **Romans 2:26 (KJV)** Therefore if the uncircumcision keep the righteousness of the law, shall not his uncircumcision be counted for circumcision?

    **Romans 2:27 (KJV)** And shall not uncircumcision which is by nature, if it fulfil the law, judge thee, who by the letter and circumcision dost transgress the law?

12. A true Christian is defined as someone who has a genuine faith in Jesus Christ as their Savior and Lord, embracing His teachings and striving to live in accordance with His example. This involves a personal relationship with God through Jesus, characterized by repentance, faith, and obedience. A true Christian seeks to embody the love, grace, and truth of Christ, reflecting His character in their actions, decisions, and interactions with others. Their faith is not merely intellectual agreement with Christian doctrines but a transformed life that evidences the work of the Holy Spirit within them. Through prayer, study of the Scriptures, and participation in the life of the Church, they grow in their understanding of God and His will for their lives, endeavoring to serve Him and extend His kingdom on Earth.

    **2 John 9 (KJV)** Whosoever transgresseth, and abideth not in the doctrine of Christ, hath not God. He that abideth in the doctrine of Christ, he hath both the Father and the Son.

13. Being a Christian goes beyond mere outward practices or the visible study of the Bible. A lack of engagement with the Word of God, such as refusing, neglecting, or showing disdain for reading and meditating on Scripture, significantly indicates a person's distance

from the Christian faith. True Christianity involves a deep, personal connection with God's Word, reflecting a commitment to understand and live by its teachings!

**Leviticus 26:15 (KJV)** And if ye shall despise my statutes, or if your soul abhor my judgments, so that ye will not do all my commandments, *but* that ye break my covenant:

**Nehemiah 9:26 (KJV)** Nevertheless they were disobedient, and rebelled against thee, and cast thy law behind their backs, and slew thy prophets which testified against them to turn them to thee, and they wrought great provocations.

**Proverbs 1:7 (KJV)** The fear of the LORD *is* the beginning of knowledge: *but* fools despise wisdom and instruction.

**Proverbs 28:9 (KJV)** He that turneth away his ear from hearing the law, even his prayer *shall be* abomination.

14. Within the Christian community, a distinction exists between carnal Christians and true Christians. Carnal Christians, who might still be influenced heavily by worldly desires and attitudes, tend to be more prevalent. In contrast, true Christians, characterized by a deep, genuine commitment to living according to God's will and embodying the teachings of Christ, constitute only a small fraction and a remnant of the broader Christian population. This disparity highlights the challenge of spiritual growth and the importance of striving for a faith that transcends mere surface-level adherence.

**Romans 9:27 (KJV)** Esaias also crieth concerning Israel, Though the number of the children of Israel be as the sand of the sea, a remnant shall be saved:

**Romans 11:5 (KJV)** Even so then at this present time also there is a remnant according to the election of grace.

**1 Corinthians 3:3 (KJV)** For ye are yet carnal: for whereas *there is* among you envying, and strife, and divisions, are ye not carnal, and walk as men?

**1 Corinthians 3:4 (KJV)** For while one saith, I am of Paul; and another, I *am* of Apollos; are ye not carnal?

**1 Peter 4:17 (KJV)** For the time *is come* that judgment must begin at the house of God: and if *it* first *begin* at us, what shall the end *be* of them that obey not the gospel of God?

**1 Peter 4:18 (KJV)** And if the righteous scarcely be saved, where shall the ungodly and the sinner appear?

15. Carnal Christians are sometimes metaphorically referred to as "Tares" or described in terms of being distant from the core teachings of Christianity. While they may

present themselves in a manner similar to devout Christians in outward appearances and behaviors, their private actions and beliefs may not align with scriptural values. This contrast highlights the discrepancy between external conformity to Christian practices and the internal embodiment of Christian principles and teachings.

**Matthew 13:25 (KJV)** But while men slept, his enemy came and sowed tares among the wheat, and went his way.

**Matthew 13:27 (KJV)** So the servants of the householder came and said unto him, Sir, didst not thou sow good seed in thy field? from whence then hath it tares?

**Matthew 13:28 (KJV)** He said unto them, An enemy hath done this. The servants said unto them, Wilt thou then that we go and gather them up?

**Matthew 13:29 (KJV)** But he said, Nay; lest while ye gather up the tares, ye root up also the wheat with them.

**Matthew 13:30 (KJV)** Let both grow together until the harvest: and in the time of harvest I will say to the reapers, Gather ye together first the tares, and bind them in bundles to burn them: but gather the wheat into my barn.

**Matthew 13:38 (KJV)** The field is the world; the good seed are the children of the kingdom; but the tares are the children of the wicked *one*;

**1 John 3:10 (KJV)** In this the children of God are manifest, and the children of the devil: whosoever doeth not righteousness is not of God, neither he that loveth not his brother.

**John 8:42 (KJV)** Jesus said unto them, If God were your Father, ye would love me: for I proceeded forth and came from God; neither came I of myself, but he sent me.

**John 8:43 (KJV)** Why do ye not understand my speech? *even* because ye cannot hear my word.

**John 8:44 (KJV)** Ye are of *your* father the devil, and the lusts of your father ye will do. He was a murderer from the beginning, and abode not in the truth, because there is no truth in him. When he speaketh a lie, he speaketh of his own: for he is a liar, and the father of it.

**John 8:45 (KJV)** And because I tell *you* the truth, ye believe me not.

**Revelation 21:8 (KJV)** But the fearful, and unbelieving, and the abominable, and murderers, and whoremongers, and sorcerers, and idolaters, and all liars, shall have their part in the lake which burneth with fire and brimstone: which is the second death.

16. The distinction previously mentioned sheds light on why, although many are labeled as Christians, discerning the genuine from those whose faith may not be as deeply rooted

can be challenging. This raises the question: Do Christians live by the teachings of the Bible? Indeed, true Christians actively embody and practice the principles found within Scripture. However, those who might be considered insincere in their faith do not adhere to these biblical teachings, highlighting the contrast between authentic and superficial expressions of Christianity:

> **Ecclesiastes 7:20 (KJV)** For *there is* not a just man upon earth, that doeth good, and sinneth not.

> **1 John 3:6 (KJV)** Whosoever abideth in him sinneth not: whosoever sinneth hath not seen him, neither known him.

> **1 John 5:18 (KJV)** We know that whosoever is born of God sinneth not; but he that is begotten of God keepeth himself, and that wicked one toucheth him not.

> **1 John 1:7 (KJV)** But if we walk in the light, as he is in the light, we have fellowship one with another, and the blood of Jesus Christ his Son cleanseth us from all sin.

17. The increasing danger and prevalence of evil in the world can be attributed to a variety of complex factors. One fundamental reason is the gradual departure from ethical and moral standards, often rooted in spiritual and traditional values. As societies become more secular and materialistic, the emphasis on compassion, integrity, and community welfare may diminish, leading to a rise in selfishness, greed, and indifference. Additionally, technological advancements, while beneficial in many ways, have also facilitated new avenues for crime, exploitation, and the spread of harmful ideologies. The combination of these elements, alongside a lack of accountability and the erosion of family and social structures, contributes to a world that can seem increasingly perilous and morally compromised.

> **2 Timothy 3:13 (KJV)** But evil men and seducers shall wax worse and worse, deceiving, and being deceived.

> **Luke 17:26 (KJV)** And as it was in the days of Noe, so shall it be also in the days of the Son of man.

> **Luke 17:27 (KJV)** They did eat, they drank, they married wives, they were given in marriage, until the day that Noe entered into the ark, and the flood came, and destroyed them all.

> **Luke 17:28 (KJV)** Likewise also as it was in the days of Lot; they did eat, they drank, they bought, they sold, they planted, they builded;

> **Luke 17:29 (KJV)** But the same day that Lot went out of Sodom it rained fire and brimstone from heaven, and destroyed *them* all.

> **Luke 17:30 (KJV)** Even thus shall it be in the day when the Son of man is revealed.

18. The growing danger and prevalence of evil in the world can also be seen as an indicator of significant times ahead, according to some interpretations of Christian eschatology. This perspective suggests that the increase in global turmoil and moral decay may be aligned with the belief that such conditions precede the return of Jesus Christ. From this viewpoint, the challenges and adversities faced in the world today could be understood as part of a larger divine plan, leading towards a pivotal moment in Christian faith— the second coming of Christ. This interpretation encourages a look beyond current hardships, towards a future promise of renewal and salvation!

> **2 Thessalonians 2:3 (KJV)** Let no man deceive you by any means: for *that day shall not come*, except there come a falling away first, and that man of sin be revealed, the son of perdition;

> **2 Thessalonians 2:4 (KJV)** Who opposeth and exalteth himself above all that is called God, or that is worshipped; so that he as God sitteth in the temple of God, shewing himself that he is God.

> **2 Timothy 3:1 (KJV)** This know also, that in the last days perilous times shall come.

19. Furthermore, the increasing dangers and evils in the world can be viewed through a spiritual lens as part of God's method for discerning true faith among individuals. This perspective considers the challenges and moral complexities of our times as a means by which God tests faith and character, effectively separating those who are genuine in their commitment to His teachings (the sheep) from those who are not (the goats). This process of spiritual evaluation and distinction serves as a mechanism to reveal the depth and authenticity of one's faith, highlighting resilience, devotion, and adherence to spiritual principles amidst adversity!

> **Matthew 25:34 (KJV)** Then shall the King say unto them on his right hand, Come, ye blessed of my Father, inherit the kingdom prepared for you from the foundation of the world:

> **Matthew 25:40 (KJV)** And the King shall answer and say unto them, Verily I say unto you, Inasmuch as ye have done *it* unto one of the least of these my brethren, ye have done *it* unto me.

> **Matthew 25:41 (KJV)** Then shall he say also unto them on the left hand, Depart from me, ye cursed, into everlasting fire, prepared for the devil and his angels:

> **Matthew 25:45 (KJV)** Then shall he answer them, saying, Verily I say unto you, Inasmuch as ye did *it* not to one of the least of these, ye did *it* not to me.

> **1 John 3:17 (KJV)** But whoso hath this world's good, and seeth his brother have need, and shutteth up his bowels *of compassion* from him, how dwelleth the love of God in him?

20. If one professes to be a true child of God yet has never faced trials that test their faith, it prompts a reflection on the authenticity of their belief and self-perception. This concept is rooted in the teachings of Jesus Christ, who emphasized that his followers would encounter persecution, trials, and even the prospect of death. However, He also called for unwavering faithfulness through these challenges. It is through enduring these difficulties and remaining steadfast in faith that one's true commitment to God is revealed. Jesus assured that those who persevere to the end, maintaining their faith despite adversity, will be rewarded with the crown of life, signifying eternal salvation and victory over spiritual trials!

> **2 Timothy 1:8 (KJV)** Be not thou therefore ashamed of the testimony of our Lord, nor of me his prisoner: but be thou partaker of the afflictions of the gospel according to the power of God;

> **Revelation 2:10 (KJV)** Fear none of those things which thou shalt suffer: behold, the devil shall cast *some* of you into prison, that ye may be tried; and ye shall have tribulation ten days: be thou faithful unto death, and I will give thee a crown of life.

21. A clear indicator that "the spirit of glory and of God rests upon you" can be seen in how others respond to your refusal to engage in sinful actions and your commitment to speaking the truth in all situations. If you find that people are antagonistic towards you because of your stand against sin and your unwavering dedication to truthfulness, it may signal that you are indeed carrying the presence of God's spirit. This opposition, rather than being a negative sign, can be a testament to the strength of your spiritual convictions and the impact of living a life aligned with divine principles!

> **1 Peter 4:14 (KJV)** If ye be reproached for the name of Christ, happy *are ye*; for the spirit of glory and of God resteth upon you: on their part he is evil spoken of, but on your part he is glorified.

22. Therefore, the presence of evil in your surroundings can paradoxically be beneficial if you are a true child of God, with the definitive proof of your authenticity being your refusal to partake in evil deeds. When others observe your steadfast refusal to engage in wrongdoing, it may lead to animosity towards you. However, such hostility should be seen as a cause for joy and celebration, for it serves as tangible evidence that you have triumphed in your spiritual test. It signifies that the Spirit of God resides within you and that you are graced by God's favor. This adversarial reaction from the world, rather than disheartening you, should affirm your strong standing in faith and your alignment with divine principles!

> **2 Corinthians 11:30 (KJV)** If I must needs glory, I will glory of the things which concern mine infirmities.

**2 Corinthians 12:5 (KJV)** Of such an one will I glory: yet of myself I will not glory, but in mine infirmities.

**2 Corinthians 12:9 (KJV)** And he said unto me, My grace is sufficient for thee: for my strength is made perfect in weakness. Most gladly therefore will I rather glory in my infirmities, that the power of Christ may rest upon me.

**2 Corinthians 12:10 (KJV)** Therefore I take pleasure in infirmities, in reproaches, in necessities, in persecutions, in distresses for Christ's sake: for when I am weak, then am I strong.

**1 Peter 3:14 (KJV)** But and if ye suffer for righteousness' sake, happy *are ye*: and be not afraid of their terror, neither be troubled;

23. The involvement of some churches and their leaders in the world's evils can be explained by considering that not all individuals who hold positions of leadership in religious communities genuinely embody the principles they preach. Some individuals, referred to as leaders within churches, may in fact be acting contrary to the teachings of Christ, aligning more closely with wrongful actions and behaviors. This contradiction arises because true leadership in a Christian context demands a life free from participation in evil deeds, as alignment with Christ's teachings is fundamental. Therefore, those leaders who engage in such actions do not truly serve as ministers of Christ but rather diverge from the path of genuine spiritual guidance and stewardship.

    **2 Corinthians 11:13 (KJV)** For such *are* false apostles, deceitful workers, transforming themselves into the apostles of Christ.

    **2 Corinthians 11:14 (KJV)** And no marvel; for Satan himself is transformed into an angel of light.

    **2 Corinthians 11:15 (KJV)** Therefore *it is* no great thing if his ministers also be transformed as the ministers of righteousness; whose end shall be according to their works.

24. For those leaders within the church who engage in wrongdoing and fail to adhere to the Gospel of our Lord and Savior Jesus Christ, the consequences they face from God are in accordance with divine justice. These individuals, who hold positions of influence yet choose to act contrary to the teachings they are supposed to uphold, will encounter accountability before God. Their actions, which diverge from the path set by Christ, invite a response that aligns with the principles of righteousness and retribution as outlined in the Christian faith. This serves as a reminder that leadership within the church carries the responsibility of living in a manner that is reflective of the Gospel's core values!

**2 Peter 2:12 (KJV)** But these, as natural brute beasts, made to be taken and destroyed, speak evil of the things that they understand not; and shall utterly perish in their own corruption;

**2 Peter 2:13 (KJV)** And shall receive the reward of unrighteousness, *as* they that count it pleasure to riot in the day time. Spots *they are* and blemishes, sporting themselves with their own deceivings while they feast with you;

**2 Peter 2:14 (KJV)** Having eyes full of adultery, and that cannot cease from sin; beguiling unstable souls: an heart they have exercised with covetous practices; cursed children:

**2 Peter 2:15 (KJV)** Which have forsaken the right way, and are gone astray, following the way of Balaam *the son* of Bosor, who loved the wages of unrighteousness;

**2 Peter 2:16 (KJV)** But was rebuked for his iniquity: the dumb ass speaking with man's voice forbad the madness of the prophet.

**2 Peter 2:17 (KJV)** These are wells without water, clouds that are carried with a tempest; to whom the mist of darkness is reserved for ever.

**2 Peter 2:18 (KJV)** For when they speak great swelling *words* of vanity, they allure through the lusts of the flesh, *through much* wantonness, those that were clean escaped from them who live in error.

**2 Peter 2:19 (KJV)** While they promise them liberty, they themselves are the servants of corruption: for of whom a man is overcome, of the same is he brought in bondage

25. Indeed, the LORD God has made it clear that those who commit evil deeds, especially those in positions of spiritual leadership who fail to live by His teachings, will face consequences. The recompense for their actions will be meted out with a severity that reflects the gravity of their misconduct, receiving back double for their wrongdoings. This principle underscores the seriousness with which God views the responsibility of leading His followers and the importance of adhering to His commandments and teachings!

**Jude 11 (KJV)** Woe unto them! for they have gone in the way of Cain, and ran greedily after the error of Balaam for reward, and perished in the gainsaying of Core.

**Jude 12 (KJV)** These are spots in your feasts of charity, when they feast with you, feeding themselves without fear: clouds *they are* without water, carried about of winds; trees whose fruit withereth, without fruit, twice dead, plucked up by the roots;

**Jude 13 (KJV)** Raging waves of the sea, foaming out their own shame; wandering stars, to whom is reserved the blackness of darkness for ever.

**Jude 14 (KJV)** And Enoch also, the seventh from Adam, prophesied of these, saying, Behold, the Lord cometh with ten thousands of his saints,

**Jude 15 (KJV)** To execute judgment upon all, and to convince all that are ungodly among them of all their ungodly deeds which they have ungodly committed, and of all their hard *speeches* which ungodly sinners have spoken against him.

**Jude 16 (KJV)** These are murmurers, complainers, walking after their own lusts; and their mouth speaketh great swelling *words*, having men's persons in admiration because of advantage.

**Jude 11 (KJV)** Woe unto them! for they have gone in the way of Cain, and ran greedily after the error of Balaam for reward, and perished in the gainsaying of Core.

**Jude 12 (KJV)** These are spots in your feasts of charity, when they feast with you, feeding themselves without fear: clouds *they are* without water, carried about of winds; trees whose fruit withereth, without fruit, twice dead, plucked up by the roots;

**Jude 13 (KJV)** Raging waves of the sea, foaming out their own shame; wandering stars, to whom is reserved the blackness of darkness for ever.

**Jude 14 (KJV)** And Enoch also, the seventh from Adam, prophesied of these, saying, Behold, the Lord cometh with ten thousands of his saints,

**Jude 15 (KJV)** To execute judgment upon all, and to convince all that are ungodly among them of all their ungodly deeds which they have ungodly committed, and of all their hard *speeches* which ungodly sinners have spoken against him.

**Jude 16 (KJV)** These are murmurers, complainers, walking after their own lusts; and their mouth speaketh great swelling *words*, having men's persons in admiration because of advantage.

26. To avoid the severe judgment from God associated with disobedience and wrongdoing, there are specific steps you can take. It involves earnestly turning towards a life aligned with God's teachings and commandments. This includes sincere repentance for past sins, seeking forgiveness, and committing to a lifestyle that reflects the values and principles of the Gospel. Engaging in regular prayer, studying Scripture to deepen your understanding of God's will, and actively participating in a faith community can also support your spiritual growth and resilience. Living a life marked by love, compassion, and righteousness not only aligns you with God's desires but also serves as a protective measure against the consequences of straying from His path.

**Joshua 1:8 (KJV)** This book of the law shall not depart out of thy mouth; but thou shalt meditate therein day and night, that thou mayest observe to do according to all that is written therein: for then thou shalt make thy way prosperous, and then thou shalt have good success.

27. Farewell! May your journey be guided by wisdom and grace, and may you find strength and peace in your endeavors.

# CHAPTER 6

## MARLON, ROBERT, WILLIAM, AND DANIEL

===================

### ASASE YE DURU

"The Earth is heavy"

Asante philosophical symbol of Divinity of Mother Earth

==========================

I n the preface, I shared a deeply personal transformation that began with the profound loss of my siblings in quick succession. My journey back to faith in Christ was catalyzed by the passing of my older brother Marlon in August 2010, followed by William in September 2010, and Daniel in November 2010. This series of losses also brought to mind Robert, who had passed into eternity years earlier.

In my quest for comfort and comprehension within the scriptures, struggling with the abrupt loss of my brothers, I experienced an epiphany regarding how to honor their memory. Our beliefs, as followers of God the Father, guide us to commemorate one another not by erecting tangible monuments, but through the enduring impact of our efforts to spread the teachings of Jesus Christ. This act of recording and honoring acts of virtue, founded on a deep respect for God, becomes our genuine memorial. This concept is anchored in the Spiritual Law of Memorial and Remembrance, as described in **Exodus 17:14**, guiding us to preserve the memory of a person through the impactful works they have left behind.

> **Exodus 17:14 (KJV)** And the LORD said unto Moses, Write this *for* a memorial in a book, and rehearse *it* in the ears of Joshua: for I will utterly put out the remembrance of Amalek from under heaven.

The Lord God Almighty bestowed the Spiritual Law of Memorial and Remembrance upon Phinehas, the son of Eleazar, through an everlasting covenant. This honor was in recognition of Phinehas' valiant efforts to uphold and defend the sacred Word of the Lord and His Name. This same principle is relevant to all Christians who hold the Word of God as their paramount concern. It highlights the importance of actions taken in defense of the divine teachings and the preservation of God's Name, ensuring that such deeds are eternally remembered and rewarded by God. This law emphasizes the value of prioritizing spiritual commitments and living in a manner that reflects the teachings of the Lord.

> **Numbers 25:10 (KJV)** And the LORD spake unto Moses, saying,
>
> **Numbers 25:11 (KJV)** Phinehas, the son of Eleazar, the son of Aaron the priest, hath turned my wrath away from the children of Israel, while he was zealous for my sake among them, that I consumed not the children of Israel in my jealousy.
>
> **Numbers 25:12 (KJV)** Wherefore say, Behold, I give unto him my covenant of peace:
>
> **Numbers 25:13 (KJV)** And he shall have it, and his seed after him, *even* the covenant of an everlasting priesthood; because he was zealous for his God, and made an atonement for the children of Israel.

In the New Testament, we observe the application of the Spiritual Law of Memorial and Remembrance by the Lord Jesus Christ, who extended this principle through an everlasting covenant to Mary Magdalene. This was in recognition of her commendable actions in supporting and defending the Gospel of the Lord Jesus Christ. This law is not exclusive to her but is applicable to any Christian who prioritizes the Word of God above all else. It underscores the importance of living a life that actively contributes to the spread and defense of the Gospel, ensuring that such deeds are remembered and honored in accordance with divine principles. This tradition of memorializing through acts of faithfulness and righteousness highlights the enduring value placed on spiritual contributions over physical memorials, echoing throughout Christian teachings:

> **Matthew 26:13 (KJV)** Verily I say unto you, Wheresoever this gospel shall be preached in the whole world, *there* shall also this, that this woman hath done, be told for a memorial of her.
>
> **Mark 14:9 (KJV)** Verily I say unto you, Wheresoever this gospel shall be preached throughout the whole world, *this* also that she hath done shall be spoken of for a memorial of her.

Bible Teacher and Scribe, Nehemiah, is aware of the Spiritual Law of Memorial and Remembrance and how it can be acquired through doing good works for the Name of the LORD, therefore, Nehemiah is seen here praying to the LORD God Almighty for that mercy:

> **Nehemiah 13:14 (KJV)** Remember me, O my God, concerning this, and wipe not out my good deeds that I have done for the house of my God, and for the offices thereof.

**Nehemiah 13:22 (KJV)** And I commanded the Levites that they should cleanse themselves, and *that* they should come *and* keep the gates, to sanctify the sabbath day. Remember me, O my God, *concerning* this also, and spare me according to the greatness of thy mercy.

**Nehemiah 13:31 (KJV)** And for the wood offering, at times appointed, and for the firstfruits. Remember me, O my God, for good.

Much like the Bible teacher Nehemiah did. By recalling their contributions and the positive impacts they made in alignment with their faith, we keep their memory alive in a manner that reflects the biblical tradition of acknowledging deeds done in service to God and the community. Just as Nehemiah sought God's remembrance for his actions aimed at benefiting his people and honoring the Sabbath, we too commemorate Marlon, Robert, William, and Daniel for their righteous acts and the ways in which they lived out their faith, trusting that their legacy continues to resonate within the principles of God's kingdom.

Thus, for Marlon, William, and Daniel, we recall their good works in the LORD and before the LORD even as Bible Teacher Nehemiah did.

In remembrance of Marlon, Robert, William, and Daniel, we honor their good works in and before the Lord.

I dedicate this tribute to my sister, Favour Kpodzo, whose life and untimely passing on January 14, 2024, occurred as I was preparing to publish this book. This tribute is not only a reflection of my personal loss but also serves as a crucial discourse on the impact of religious teachings and the importance of discerning true faith from potentially misleading doctrines.

Much like the Bible teacher Nehemiah, who sought God's remembrance for his actions aimed at benefiting his people and honoring the Sabbath, we recall the contributions of Marlon, Favour, Robert, William, and Daniel, celebrating the positive impacts they made in alignment with their faith. By acknowledging their deeds done in service to God and the community, we keep their memory alive, reflecting the biblical tradition of honoring righteous acts.

Thus, in memory of Marlon, Robert, William, Daniel, and now sadly, my dear sister Favour, we honor their good works in the Lord and before the Lord, trusting that their legacy continues to resonate within the principles of God's kingdom.

# CHAPTER 7

## DID GOD PRESCRIBE WHAT ATTITUDE TO HAVE TOWARD DEATH?

===================

AYA

"Fern"

Asante philosophical symbol of Endurance, Independence, Defiance against difficulties, Hardiness, Perseverance, and Resourcefulness

===================

Death, indeed, is an inevitable aspect of human existence, and the question of whether one should prepare for it, or even welcome it, can elicit profound reflections, especially from a faith-based perspective. A true child of God, rooted in spiritual beliefs, can indeed approach death with a sense of readiness and peace, distinguishing their outlook from a more secular perspective on mortality. This attitude is underpinned by several Scriptural teachings that highlight the transient nature of earthly possessions and the eternal value of spiritual wealth. Let's explore key scriptures that reinforce this doctrine:

All the wealth and money that we gather on the Earth will serve for nothing when we die:

> **Ecclesiastes 5:15 (KJV)** As he came forth of his mother's womb, naked shall he return to go as he came, and shall take nothing of his labour, which he may carry away in his hand.

1. The perspective that death can be considered more favorable for a true child of God than for a sinner finds its roots in several scriptural passages that contrast the eternal destinies and the peace of the righteous with the fate of the wicked. These scriptures emphasize the hope and assurance that believers in Christ have regarding their eternal future, as opposed to the uncertainty and dread that may accompany those who live apart from God's ways. Let's consider some scriptures that support this view:

**Ecclesiastes 7:1 (KJV)** A good name *is* better than precious ointment; and the day of death than the day of one's birth.

2.  Hence, a true child of God will be happy to die in order to free their spirit to go and be with Jesus Christ in Heaven:

    **Philippians 1:21 (KJV)** For to me to live *is* Christ, and to die *is* gain.

    **2 Corinthians 5:8 (KJV):** "We are confident, I say, and willing rather to be absent from the body, and to be present with the Lord."

    **Philippians 1:23 (KJV):** "For I am in a strait betwixt two, having a desire to depart, and to be with Christ; which is far better:"

This perspective is deeply rooted in the Christian belief in the afterlife and the assurance of salvation and eternal life with Jesus Christ for those who have faith in Him. The sentiment that a true child of God would find joy in the prospect of death is based on the understanding that death is not the end but the beginning of a more glorious and perfect existence in the presence of the Lord. Key scriptures support and provide comfort to believers with this hope:

**2 Corinthians** expresses the confidence and preference of believers to be "absent from the body" – meaning to die – because it means being "present with the Lord," which is the ultimate goal and desire of every follower of Christ.

Similarly, in **Philippians**, Paul articulates a deep longing to depart from this life and to be with Christ, considering such a transition as "far better" than continuing in the earthly life. This reflects the profound hope and joy that comes from the belief in eternal life with Christ, transcending the fear of death.

The ultimate futility of accumulating material wealth, as one cannot take such possessions beyond this life. This teaching encourages believers to focus on what is spiritually significant and eternal, fostering an attitude that values spiritual preparedness for death over material accumulation. This perspective helps believers to welcome death not as an end but as a transition to an eternal existence with God, where the true treasures of one's life—those stored up in heaven through righteous living and faith—are everlasting.

Death is a certainty we all face, yet the question of whether to prepare for it or if anyone can genuinely embrace it with happiness may seem perplexing. Surprisingly, the response for those deeply rooted in faith is affirmative. A true child of God can indeed approach the concept of death with a positive outlook, embracing it as a transition to eternal life. This perspective is not born out of a disregard for life but from a profound understanding of what lies beyond it. To affirm this approach, we turn to Scripture, which provides the foundation for such a belief system, guiding believers on how to view death not as an end but as the beginning of a more glorious existence with God:

3. All the wealth and money that we gather on the Earth will serve for nothing when we die. This principle underscores the transient nature of material wealth in contrast to the eternal significance of spiritual treasures. Scripture teaches that the possessions we accumulate here on earth have no value in the afterlife, encouraging a focus on what truly matters in the eyes of God.

4. A true child of God may exhibit a sense of peace or even happiness at a funeral, in stark contrast to the despair often felt by those who do not share the same faith. This unique sense of contentment stems from a deep-seated hope and assurance in their spiritual journey and the promises of their faith. Thus, when encountering someone who maintains a sense of joy or peace amidst the grief of losing a brother or sister, it's insightful to inquire about the source of their hope. This conversation can reveal whether their foundation of happiness is rooted in the eternal promises found in Christ or if it derives from other, possibly less spiritual, origins. This distinction can shed light on the profound impact that faith in Christ has on one's perspective of death and the afterlife.

> **Ecclesiastes 7:2 (KJV)** *It is* better to go to the house of mourning, than to go to the house of feasting: for that *is* the end of all men; and the living will lay *it* to his heart.

5. Our connection with God is deeply rooted in the heart, underscoring the importance of nurturing a heart that is in harmony with God to serve Him more effectively. The catalyst for enhancing the condition of the heart, surprisingly, is found in the experience of "sorrow." This emotional state, when approached with a reflective and sincere spirit, has the remarkable capacity to transform and refine our hearts, making them more receptive to God's guidance and will. Sorrow, when embraced as a part of our spiritual journey, can act as a powerful agent of change, prompting introspection, growth, and a deeper commitment to aligning our hearts with God's purposes.

> **Ecclesiastes 7:3 (KJV)** Sorrow *is* better than laughter: for by the sadness of the countenance the heart is made better.

> **Ecclesiastes 7:4 (KJV)** The heart of the wise *is* in the house of mourning; but the heart of fools *is* in the house of mirth.

Conclusion – Embracing these five spiritual perspectives is deeply transformative and is particularly resonant for those committed to walking in faith as true children of God. It's important to recognize that these practices may not be understood or appreciated by everyone, especially not by those who do not share the same spiritual convictions. In fact, adopting such attitudes towards death and life's profound questions might draw criticism or disdain from those with opposing views or beliefs. Therefore, while these spiritual insights offer profound guidance for believers, they are best approached with discernment and an understanding of the potential for misunderstanding or conflict they may bring from those outside the faith.

# CHAPTER 8

## DEAR MARLON, FAVOUR, ROBERT, WILLIAM, AND DANIEL

====================

BESE SAKA

"Sack of cola nuts"

Asante philosophical symbol of Affluence, Abundance, Unity

=========================

**For the Departed...for the Bereaved...and for the Living:**

Death transcends the notion of an end; it marks the beginning of a spiritual journey, guiding us from our earthly existence to an eternal realm. Here, the essence of our lives undergoes scrutiny, our deeds determining the path ahead. This echoes the spiritual law that our actions on earth shape our fate beyond, underscoring the importance of living a life that aligns with the principles of goodness and accountability.

In moments of reflection, we face the reality of our imperfections—our sins and errors. Yet, amidst this introspection, we find solace in the promise of salvation, offered through the grace and mercy of Jesus Christ, our judge who dispenses justice with righteousness.

In remembering those who have left this world, we draw hope from the assurance that belief in Jesus offers not just solace but the promise of eternal life, a beacon of light for all, especially for our beloved Marlon, sister Favour, Robert, William, and Daniel.

As we navigate through our loss, we find refuge in prayer, seeking comfort in the profound truths found within the teachings of faith. We call upon the divine, asking for our departed to be welcomed into the everlasting embrace of God's kingdom.

In solitude, we discover resilience and comfort in the enduring words of faith that remind us of the transformative power of our belief: in Christ, death is redefined not as a final farewell but as the threshold to an unending existence in the presence of the divine.

You might already understand that death is more than a physical occurrence; it's a spiritual event. It's also recognized that what we refer to as death is essentially the gateway to the afterlife. This gateway, while marking an end to our earthly existence, signifies a definitive conclusion—a conclusion that is irrevocable and leads us directly into the realm of spiritual assessment.

Just as our actions in life can lead to judgments and consequences within our societal systems, so too are our spiritual selves evaluated based on our earthly deeds. This evaluation determines our standing in the hereafter, much like a courtroom decides the fate of an individual based on their actions. It's a transition that mirrors the principle of accountability, extending beyond our physical life into the spiritual domain.

**Psalm 142:7 (KJV)** Bring my soul out of prison, that I may praise thy name: the righteous shall compass me about; for thou shalt deal bountifully with me.

**Isaiah 42:7 (KJV)** To open the blind eyes, to bring out the prisoners from the prison, *and* them that sit in darkness out of the prison house.

In the vast expanse of human existence, questions of sin, iniquity, transgression, and unrighteousness often arise, pointing to the complexities and imperfections of our lives. Yet, amidst this, there stands a singular Judge over the spirits and souls of all—the Lord Jesus Christ. It is to Him that we belong, in life as in death, anchoring our existence in His sovereignty and mercy.

Throughout history, from the days of Noah to the earthly life of Jesus Christ, the Lord has extended His remembrance to those who have passed. This divine act of remembrance brings comfort to the notion of farewell, urging us to express those unspoken words and sentiments we've held back.

The spiritual journey towards healing and solace involves a heartfelt engagement with prayer and meditation, directing our thoughts and words towards Jesus Christ. It is a call to entrust our loved ones—our fathers, mothers, and dear ones like Robert, Marlon, William, and Daniel—to the merciful remembrance of God the Father, in the name of Jesus.

Finding peace in the midst of loss and solitude hinges on seeking solace not only for ourselves but also for those who have departed. This solace is found in the profound embrace of faith, in the assurance that our words, lifted in prayer, reach the heart of the divine, ensuring that those we miss are remembered and cherished in the presence of the Lord.

**Ecclesiastes 12:1 (KJV)** Remember now thy Creator in the days of thy youth, while the evil days come not, nor the years draw nigh, when thou shalt say, I have no pleasure in them;

**Ecclesiastes 12:2 (KJV)** While the sun, or the light, or the moon, or the stars, be not darkened, nor the clouds return after the rain:

**Ecclesiastes 12:3 (KJV)** In the day when the keepers of the house shall tremble, and the strong men shall bow themselves, and the grinders cease because they are few, and those that look out of the windows be darkened,

**Ecclesiastes 12:4 (KJV)** And the doors shall be shut in the streets, when the sound of the grinding is low, and he shall rise up at the voice of the bird, and all the daughters of musick shall be brought low;

**Ecclesiastes 12:5 (KJV)** Also *when* they shall be afraid of *that which is* high, and fears *shall be* in the way, and the almond tree shall flourish, and the grasshopper shall be a burden, and desire shall fail: because man goeth to his long home, and the mourners go about the streets:

**Ecclesiastes 12:6 (KJV)** Or ever the silver cord be loosed, or the golden bowl be broken, or the pitcher be broken at the fountain, or the wheel broken at the cistern.

**Ecclesiastes 12:7 (KJV)** Then shall the dust return to the earth as it was: and the spirit shall return unto God who gave it.

**Ecclesiastes 12:14 (KJV)** For God shall bring every work into judgment, with every secret thing, whether *it be* good, or whether *it be* evil

The LORD comfort thee Marlon, Robert, Favour William, and Daniel.

# CHAPTER 9

## THE FEAR OF DEATH GRIPPED ME
## AND I SUDDENLY REMEMBERED!

===================

BI NKA BI

"No one should bite the other"

Asante philosophical symbol of

Peace, Harmony, no backbiting, no false witnessing

==========================

In the introductory section of my preface, I delve into a reflection that resonates deeply with my experiences, as outlined in a prior passage:

*The incidents of deaths that I encountered were profoundly impactful, instilling a pervasive sense of fear not only within myself but across my entire family and community at large. During this period of uncertainty, my father of blessed memory reached out to offer solace and advice, emphasizing the importance of remaining steadfast in prayer. This conversation catalyzed a period of introspection, wherein I confronted the existential query of my own mortality. Fear gripped me and I suddenly remembered one thing that I learned during my days in one of those Sword Bible Drills competitions, specifically the verse **Matthew 10:2** And fear not them which kill the body, but are not able to kill the soul: but rather fear him which is able to destroy both soul and body in hell.. This scripture underscores the principle that our fears should not be directed towards forces that can only harm the physical body but rather towards that which holds sway over both our corporeal and spiritual essence.*

*In confronting the myriad challenges that arose, I steadfastly refused to succumb to despondency or self-pity. My resolve was fortified by an unyielding optimism and a profound faith in the Divine. This spiritual resilience was further nurtured by the recollection of scriptural wisdom, guiding me towards a path of regular church attendance. However, it is imperative to clarify that the act of attending services was not the panacea. Rather, it was my unwavering faith in the Almighty and the comforting promises contained within the Holy Scriptures that imbued me with the strength to persevere and invoke divine protection against further familial losses.*

*This profound journey of faith and introspection has significantly inspired me to author this book, aiming to illuminate the transformative power of spiritual belief and the sustenance of hope amidst life's adversities. It is a testament to the dynamic and enduring nature of faith, underscoring its role not as a static refuge but as a source of continuous strength and renewal. My narrative endeavors to contribute to the ongoing dialogue within theological and spiritual studies, recognizing that our understanding and interpretations are perpetually evolving. This work is an invitation to explore the depths of faith, resilience, and the human spirit's capacity to navigate the complexities of existence with grace and conviction.*

Dear brothers and sisters, in this section, I aim to address the topic of spiritual liberation, a concept familiar to many of you. It is common today for a significant portion of Christians to seek spiritual freedom through the services of a renowned Prophet or Spiritualist. Many of you have seen televised prophetic sessions where a group of strong individuals restrain a man or woman who seems to be in a state of delirium, exhibiting uncontrollable behavior, uttering unintelligible phrases, and demonstrating aggressive physical actions. This is often presented as a form of deliverance.

However, we must pause and reflect: Is this the method of deliverance practiced by Jesus Christ? Did He or any of the Apostles ever engage in a form of deliverance that involved physically overpowering individuals, employing force and exertion to rid them of demonic influences?

> **Luke 8:26 (KJV)** And they arrived at the country of the Gadarenes, which is over against Galilee.

> **Luke 8:27 (KJV)** And when he went forth to land, there met him out of the city a certain man, which had devils long time, and ware no clothes, neither abode in *any* house, but in the tombs

> **Luke 8:28 (KJV)** When he saw Jesus, he cried out, and fell down before him, and with a loud voice said, What have I to do with thee, Jesus, *thou* Son of God most high? I beseech thee, torment me not.

> **Luke 8:29 (KJV)** (For he had commanded the unclean spirit to come out of the man. For oftentimes it had caught him: and he was kept bound with chains and in fetters; and he brake the bands, and was driven of the devil into the wilderness.)

> **Luke 8:30 (KJV)** And Jesus asked him, saying, What is thy name? And he said, Legion: because many devils were entered into him.

**Luke 8:31 (KJV)** And they besought him that he would not command them to go out into the deep.

**Luke 8:32 (KJV)** And there was there an herd of many swine feeding on the mountain: and they besought him that he would suffer them to enter into them. And he suffered them.

**Luke 8:33 (KJV)** Then went the devils out of the man, and entered into the swine: and the herd ran violently down a steep place into the lake, and were choked.

**Luke 8:34 (KJV)** When they that fed *them* saw what was done, they fled, and went and told *it* in the city and in the country.

**Luke 8:35 (KJV)** Then they went out to see what was done; and came to Jesus, and found the man, out of whom the devils were departed, sitting at the feet of Jesus, clothed, and in his right mind: and they were afraid.

Brothers and sisters, as illustrated in the passage from **Luke 8:26-35**, the form of spiritual liberation taught by our Lord Jesus Christ emphasizes a contactless approach, aligning with the Divine Principle of Deliverance as commanded by the Lord God. This principle underscores a method of deliverance that does not rely on physical restraint or force, showcasing the power of faith and divine command over physical interventions:

**1 Samuel 2:9 (KJV)** He will keep the feet of his saints, and the wicked shall be silent in darkness; for by strength shall no man prevail.

**Psalm 107:20 (KJV)** He sent his word, and healed them, and delivered *them* from their destructions.

**Zechariah 4:6 (KJV)** Then he answered and spake unto me, saying, This *is* the word of the LORD unto Zerubbabel, saying, Not by might, nor by power, but by my spirit, saith the LORD of hosts.

Reflecting back to the Preface of my narrative, I recount my personal experience of deliverance. This moment of spiritual liberation stands as a testament to the profound impact of faith and divine intervention in my life, offering a deeply personal insight into the transformative power of surrendering to a higher will and the gentle guidance of the Holy Spirit. My journey underscores the essence of true deliverance, as taught and exemplified by the Lord Jesus Christ, marking a pivotal chapter in my spiritual walk and understanding:

*Fear gripped me and I suddenly remembered one thing that I learned during my days in one of those Sword Bible Drills competitions,* **Matthew 10:28** And fear not them which kill the body, but are not able to kill the soul: but rather fear him which is able to destroy both soul and body in hell.

Therefore, when the fear of death gripped me, then, suddenly, the Word of God, specifically, the Word of God that is in **Matthew 10:28**, came to my help and delivered me from that death!

Brethren, did not the LORD Jesus Christ rightly say in **John 8:31-32** that your deliverance comes directly from knowing the Truth of God and that it is the words of Jesus Christ that deliver a person?

> **John 8:31 (KJV)** Then said Jesus to those Jews which believed on him, If ye continue in my word, *then* are ye my disciples indeed;

> **John 8:32 (KJV)** And ye shall know the truth, and the truth shall make you free.

# CHAPTER 10

## HOW SHOULD A MINISTER DO DELIVERANCE?

======================

DAME-DAME

"Name of a board game"

Asante philosophical symbol of
Intelligence, Ingenuity, Foresightedness, Preemption

=========================

Throughout history, numerous prophets have employed a wide array of methods for deliverance, ranging from the use of salt, water, pepper, sand, ash, oil, fire, candles, anointing water, beads, and spiritual baths, to practices such as fasting, prayer, retreats to mountains, interpretation of dreams, monetary offerings, and symbolic objects like eagles. Despite this diversity, the Almighty God has disclosed a steadfast and unambiguous path for deliverance, raising the question of why prophets often resort to alternative means instead of adhering to God's direct guidance.

God's prescription for deliverance is remarkably simple and profound, emphasizing the power of "righteousness." Surprisingly, the need for elaborate rituals or materials is eliminated, as God indicates that deliverance can be effectively achieved through the singular principle of righteousness. This approach aligns with the foundational biblical teachings that prioritize the purity of one's heart and actions as the key to spiritual liberation.

To solidify this understanding, let's explore specific verses that underscore the doctrine of righteousness as the cornerstone of true deliverance, highlighting the simplicity and purity of God's way in contrast to the complex practices often observed. This reiterates the scriptural emphasis on living a life aligned with divine will and moral integrity as the most powerful means of overcoming spiritual bondage!

> **Daniel 4:27 (KJV)** Wherefore, O king, let my counsel be acceptable unto thee, and break off thy sins by righteousness, and thine iniquities by shewing mercy to the poor; if it may be a lengthening of thy tranquility.

True deliverance is evidenced not by the complexity of rituals or the use of various substances, but by the transformation of lives through the application of scriptural truths. Genuine deliverance results in a notable change in the individual's spiritual, emotional, and sometimes physical state, reflecting a newfound freedom from the bonds that previously held them. This change is marked by peace, joy, and a deeper connection with God, demonstrating the individual's liberation from oppressive forces.

The key to this deliverance lies in the power of faith, prayer, and the living out of righteousness—living in a way that aligns with God's commandments and teachings. True deliverance is thus a manifestation of God's power working through faith in His Word, showcasing the supremacy of divine intervention over any physical means or human efforts. It's a testament to the grace and mercy of God, who liberates the oppressed and sets captives free, purely through the transformative power of His love and righteousness.

> **Ezekiel 18:28 (KJV)** Because he considereth, and turneth away from all his transgressions that he hath committed, he shall surely live, he shall not die.

> **Ezekiel 33:12 (KJV)** Therefore, thou son of man, say unto the children of thy people, The righteousness of the righteous shall not deliver him in the day of his transgression: as for the wickedness of the wicked, he shall not fall thereby in the day that he turneth from his wickedness; neither shall the righteous be able to live for his *righteousness* in the day that he sinneth.

As a faithful servant of Jesus Christ, your approach to deliverance involves engaging in meaningful conversation with those seeking your guidance. The primary goal of this dialogue is to uncover any sins the individual may be grappling with. Upon identifying these transgressions, it's your responsibility to gently reveal these to the person, grounding your insights in Scripture, and advising them to renounce their sinful behaviors. This act of repentance is the genuine remedy for the troubles they face, embodying the heart of true spiritual healing and liberation!

> **Lamentations 2:14 (KJV)** Thy prophets have seen vain and foolish things for thee: and they have not discovered thine iniquity, to turn away thy captivity; but have seen for thee false burdens and causes of banishment.

In the New Testament, we witness numerous instances where Jesus Christ performs deliverance, exemplifying his divine authority and compassion. One notable example is when He encounters a man tormented by demons in the region of the Gerasenes. With a word, Jesus commands the unclean spirits to leave the man, showcasing the power of divine command over any force of darkness. This moment, like many others in the Gospels, illustrates Jesus's unparalleled ability to free individuals from spiritual bondage, healing them not just physically but also restoring their spirit and dignity through spoken Words. Through these acts of deliverance, Jesus demonstrates the kingdom of God's nearness, emphasizing love, mercy, and the transformative power of His word.

**John 8:10 (KJV)** When Jesus had lifted up himself, and saw none but the woman, he said unto her, Woman, where are those thine accusers? hath no man condemned thee?

**John 8:11 (KJV)** She said, No man, Lord. And Jesus said unto her, Neither do I condemn thee: go, and sin no more.

**John 4:16 (KJV)** Jesus saith unto her, Go, call thy husband, and come hither.

**John 4:17 (KJV)** The woman answered and said, I have no husband. Jesus said unto her, Thou hast well said, I have no husband:

**John 4:18 (KJV)** For thou hast had five husbands; and he whom thou now hast is not thy husband: in that saidst thou truly.

**John 5:14 (KJV)** Afterward Jesus findeth him in the temple, and said unto him, Behold, thou art made whole: sin no more, lest a worse thing come unto thee.

**Acts 8:22 (KJV)** Repent therefore of this thy wickedness, and pray God, if perhaps the thought of thine heart may be forgiven thee.

**Acts 8:23 (KJV)** For I perceive that thou art in the gall of bitterness, and *in* the bond of iniquity.

May the Lord Jesus Christ be with your spirit, enveloping you in His grace and peace. May He grant you understanding, illuminating your path with wisdom and guiding your heart in His ways. Through His presence, may you find clarity, strength, and a deeper connection to His divine love and truth.

# CHAPTER 11

## DOES THE PROPHET WHO RECEIVES DIVINE REVELATIONS HOLD A HIGHER STANDING THAN ONE WHO IS DEDICATED TO STUDYING THE SCRIPTURES?

====================

DUAFE

"Wooden comb"

Asante philosophical symbol of Beauty, Hygiene, Feminine Qualities

==========================

In truth, an individual well-versed in the teachings of the Bible holds a greater authority than a prophet who claims to hear voices, regardless of their origin. The scriptures emphasize that God's favor rests with those who diligently study His Word, suggesting that salvation itself is an experience cultivated through learning about God. The pathway to heaven is illuminated by gaining knowledge of the Divine.

Moreover, irrespective of how sacred a voice might seem, if its message doesn't align with the biblical text, then it cannot be considered as originating from God. God communicates within the boundaries set by His Word, underscoring the importance of scripture as the ultimate standard for discerning divine truth. Let's explore specific verses that reinforce this principle, ensuring our understanding and practices are firmly rooted in scriptural teachings.

> **Psalm 119:7 (KJV)** I will praise thee with uprightness of heart, when I shall have learned thy righteous judgments.

> **Isaiah 29:11 (KJV)** And the vision of all is become unto you as the words of a book that is sealed, which *men* deliver to one that is learned, saying, Read this, I pray thee: and he saith, I cannot; for it *is* sealed:

**Isaiah 29:12 (KJV)** And the book is delivered to him that is not learned, saying, Read this, I pray thee: and he saith, I am not learned.

**Isaiah 50:4 (KJV)** The Lord GOD hath given me the tongue of the learned, that I should know how to speak a word in season to *him that is* weary: he wakeneth morning by morning, he wakeneth mine ear to hear as the learned.

**Isaiah 50:5 (KJV)** The Lord GOD hath opened mine ear, and I was not rebellious, neither turned away back.

**John 6:45 (KJV)** It is written in the prophets, And they shall be all taught of God. Every man therefore that hath heard, and hath learned of the Father, cometh unto me.

**Acts 7:22 (KJV)** And Moses was learned in all the wisdom of the Egyptians, and was mighty in words and in deeds.

**Romans 16:17 (KJV)** Now I beseech you, brethren, mark them which cause divisions and offences contrary to the doctrine which ye have learned; and avoid them.

**Philippians 4:9 (KJV)** Those things, which ye have both learned, and received, and heard, and seen in me, do: and the God of peace shall be with you.

The LORD Jesus Christ be with your spirit. The LORD Jesus Christ give you understanding.

# CHAPTER 12

## WHERE IS THE RIGHT PLACE TO PRAY?

====================

EPA

"Handcuffs"

Asante philosophical symbol of Law, Justice, Slavery, Captivity, and the Crime of white people's Colonization of Black People, including both Physical Colonization on the Continent of Africa and Spiritual and Mental Colonization of all Black People in the Diaspora through the economic shackles of Racism and false historical narratives about the Black People

==========================

Prayer undeniably forms a cornerstone of a true Christian's life, raising the question of the appropriate settings for prayer. Should it be a private affair, or is public prayer acceptable? The life and teachings of Jesus Christ offer insights into this, alongside examples from the Bible, such as King Solomon's public prayers witnessed by the assembly.

The New Testament provides several instances of Jesus praying in both private and public settings, highlighting the significance of the intention and heart behind the prayer rather than the location. For instance, Jesus taught the Lord's Prayer to His disciples as a model of how to pray, emphasizing simplicity, sincerity, and a focus on God's will. This model serves as a guideline for Christians on the essence of prayer, which can transcend the confines of privacy or public exposure.

Moreover, instances like King Solomon's public prayer during the dedication of the temple showcase that there are moments in communal life where public prayer plays a pivotal role in expressing collective faith and dedication to God. These verses and examples suggest that the right place to pray is less about the physical location and more about the state of the heart, encouraging believers to maintain a constant and sincere dialogue with God, whether in solitude or in the company of others. Let's delve into specific verses and narratives that shed light on this nuanced understanding of prayer in a Christian's life:

**1 Chronicles 6:12 (KJV)** And he stood before the altar of the LORD in the presence of all the congregation of Israel, and spread forth his hands:

**2 Chronicles 6:13 (KJV)** For Solomon had made a brasen scaffold, of five cubits long, and five cubits broad, and three cubits high, and had set it in the midst of the court: and upon it he stood, and kneeled down upon his knees before all the congregation of Israel, and spread forth his hands toward heaven,

**2 Chronicles 6:14 (KJV)** And said, O LORD God of Israel, *there is* no God like thee in the heaven, nor in the earth; which keepest covenant, and *shewest* mercy unto thy servants, that walk before thee with all their hearts:

**2 Chronicles 6:15 (KJV)** Thou which hast kept with thy servant David my father that which thou hast promised him; and spakest with thy mouth, and hast fulfilled *it* with thine hand, as *it is* this day.

**2 Chronicles 6:16 (KJV)** Now therefore, O LORD God of Israel, keep with thy servant David my father that which thou hast promised him, saying, There shall not fail thee a man in my sight to sit upon the throne of Israel; yet so that thy children take heed to their way to walk in my law, as thou hast walked before me.

**2 Chronicles 6:17 (KJV)** Now then, O LORD God of Israel, let thy word be verified, which thou hast spoken unto thy servant David.

**2 Chronicles 6:18 (KJV)** But will God in very deed dwell with men on the earth? behold, heaven and the heaven of heavens cannot contain thee; how much less this house which I have built!

Jesus Christ's teachings often emphasize the purity of intention behind acts of worship and charity, cautioning against the performative display of piety for the sake of human admiration. Specifically, He addresses the issue of almsgiving in His teachings, urging His followers to conduct such acts in secrecy rather than for public accolade. In the Sermon on the Mount, Jesus instructs:

"When you give to the needy, do not announce it with trumpets, as the hypocrites do in the synagogues and on the streets, to be honored by others. Truly I tell you, they have received their reward in full. But when you give to the needy, do not let your left hand know what your right hand is doing, so that your giving may be in secret. Then your Father, who sees what is done in secret, will reward you." (**Matthew 6:2-4**)

This directive seeks to cultivate a spirit of humility and genuine compassion, emphasizing that acts of charity are a matter of the heart and should be directed towards God's recognition rather than human approval. Jesus' teachings advocate for a discreet approach to helping others, suggesting that the true essence of giving and worship lies in the unseen devotion and sincerity towards God, rather than in the outward display of religiosity!

**Matthew 6:2 (KJV)** "Therefore when thou doest thine alms, do not sound a trumpet before thee, as the hypocrites do in the synagogues and in the streets, that they may have glory of men. Verily I say unto you, They have their reward."

**Matthew 6:3 (KJV)** But when thou doest alms, let not thy left hand know what thy right hand doeth:

**Matthew 6:4 (KJV)** That thine alms may be in secret: and thy Father which seeth in secret himself shall reward thee openly.

Indeed, Jesus Christ addresses the matter of public prayer with caution, highlighting concerns over the intentions behind such practices. In Matthew 6:5-6 (KJV), He says, "And when thou prayest, thou shalt not be as the hypocrites are: for they love to pray standing in the synagogues and in the corners of the streets, that they may be seen of men. Verily I say unto you, They have their reward. But thou, when thou prayest, enter into thy closet, and when thou hast shut thy door, pray to thy Father which is in secret; and thy Father which seeth in secret shall reward thee openly."

This teaching urges followers to seek a private communion with God rather than performing prayers for the acknowledgment of others. Jesus emphasizes the value of sincere and heartfelt prayer conducted away from the public eye, where the focus is on the personal relationship between the individual and God. This approach ensures that prayer remains an authentic expression of faith and dependence on God, free from the influences of vanity and the desire for human approval!

**Matthew 6:5 (KJV)** And when thou prayest, thou shalt not be as the hypocrites *are*: for they love to pray standing in the synagogues and in the corners of the streets, that they may be seen of men. Verily I say unto you, They have their reward.

Jesus Christ's teachings indeed encourage a personal and private approach to prayer, underscoring the importance of a sincere and intimate connection with God. In **Matthew 6:6** (KJV), He instructs, "But thou, when thou prayest, enter into thy closet, and when thou hast shut thy door, pray to thy Father which is in secret; and thy Father which seeth in secret shall reward thee openly." This guidance suggests that the most profound and genuine moments of prayer occur in solitude, away from the potential distractions or influences of public observation.

The emphasis is on the quality of the relationship between the believer and God, highlighting that prayer is a deeply personal act of communication and should not be performed for the sake of public display or recognition. This teaching fosters an environment where individuals can engage with God in their most vulnerable and honest state, free from the need to curate their prayers for an audience. It reflects the heart of Christian practice: a focus on the inward journey of faith and the personal cultivation of a relationship with the Divine, rather than external expressions meant to be seen by others!

**Matthew 6:6 (KJV)** But thou, when thou prayest, enter into thy closet, and when thou hast shut thy door, pray to thy Father which is in secret; and thy Father which seeth in secret shall reward thee openly.

Jesus Christ's teachings in the Sermon on the Mount caution against the repetition of prayers and long-windedness, as practiced by those who do not understand the essence of prayer. In **Matthew 6:7-8,** His instruction highlights the importance of sincerity and trust in God over the quantity or repetition of words.

The emphasis here is on the quality of prayer, suggesting that true communication with God doesn't require endless repetitions or elaborate phrasing to be effective. Instead, Jesus teaches that prayer should come from a place of faith and genuine dialogue with God, who is already aware of our needs and desires. This approach seeks to shift the focus from performative practices to a more heartfelt and authentic engagement with the Divine!

**Matthew 6:7 (KJV)** But when ye pray, use not vain repetitions, as the heathen *do*: for they think that they shall be heard for their much speaking.

**Matthew 6:8 (KJV)** Be not ye therefore like unto them: for your Father knoweth what things ye have need of, before ye ask him.

**Matthew 6:9 (KJV)** After this manner therefore pray ye: Our Father which art in heaven, Hallowed be thy name.

Following the spiritual guidance on prayer offered by Jesus Christ, when you engage in private prayer, you are encouraged to use the template He provided, known as the Lord's Prayer. This prayer is found in **Matthew 6:9-13** and serves as a model for how to pray with sincerity, reverence, and faith:

This prayer encompasses acknowledgment of God's sovereignty, a request for daily needs, a plea for forgiveness and the strength to forgive others, guidance away from temptation, and deliverance from evil. It reflects a comprehensive approach to communicating with God, embodying humility, dependence, and a deep desire for alignment with God's will. Through this prayer, Jesus teaches us to prioritize our spiritual relationship with the Father, ensuring our prayers are both meaningful and reflective of our faith.

Then, after you have learned the above spiritual lesson, when you pray in secret, use these words that Jesus Christ gave you!

**Matthew 6:10 (KJV)** Thy kingdom come. Thy will be done in earth, as *it is* in heaven.

**Matthew 6:11 (KJV)** Give us this day our daily bread.

**Matthew 6:12 (KJV)** And forgive us our debts, as we forgive our debtors.

**Matthew 6:13 (KJV)** And lead us not into temptation, but deliver us from evil: For thine is the kingdom, and the power, and the glory, for ever. Amen.

Jesus Christ's approach to prayer often involved seeking solitude away from the crowds and His disciples, emphasizing personal communion with the Father. While there are instances in the Gospels where Jesus prays in the presence of others, such as before performing miracles or at significant moments like the Last Supper, His most profound moments of prayer were conducted in private. An example of this is His prayer in the Garden of Gethsemane, where, despite being accompanied by Peter, James, and John, He went a little farther away from them to pray deeply and earnestly to God **(Matthew 26:36-44).**

This practice underlines the principle that the essence of prayer lies in the sincerity and depth of one's relationship with God, rather than the public display of piety. Jesus taught by example that while communal prayer and worship have their place within the faith community, the core of one's prayer life should be rooted in a personal, intimate dialogue with God. This approach reinforces the importance of setting aside dedicated time for private prayer, allowing for a deep, personal engagement with the Divine!

**Matthew 14:23 (KJV)** And when he had sent the multitudes away, he went up into a mountain apart to pray: and when the evening was come, he was there alone.

**Mark 6:46 (KJV)** And when he had sent them away, he departed into a mountain to pray.

**Luke 6:12 (KJV)** And it came to pass in those days, that he went out into a mountain to pray, and continued all night in prayer to God.

In the Gospels, particularly in Matthew 19:13-15, we find the account of people bringing children to Jesus Christ, hoping He would lay His hands on them and pray. The scripture notes that Jesus "laid his hands on them," but does not specifically mention Him praying aloud for them in the presence of the crowd. This moment underscores Jesus' approach to blessing and interacting with individuals, emphasizing personal touch and connection.

Jesus' actions reflect His emphasis on the significance of personal engagement and the impartation of blessings in a manner that doesn't necessarily require public verbal prayers. It highlights His ability to convey spiritual blessings through actions, demonstrating the depth and variety of ways in which divine grace can be imparted. This episode illustrates that the essence of prayer and blessing lies not in the outward display but in the heartfelt intention and the powerful, yet often quiet, exchange between Jesus and those He ministered to!

**Matthew 19:13 (KJV)** Then were there brought unto him little children, that he should put *his* hands on them, and pray: and the disciples rebuked them.

**Matthew 19:14 (KJV)** But Jesus said, Suffer little children, and forbid them not, to come unto me: for of such is the kingdom of heaven.

**Matthew 19:15 (KJV)** And he laid *his* hands on them, and departed thence.

As a devoted follower of Christ, a genuine Christian, and a faithful servant of God, it is important to model your actions on the example set by Jesus Christ, including His approach to prayer. Jesus often chose to pray in private, away from public view and even outside the earshot of His disciples.

This pattern of seeking solitude for prayer, rather than engaging in public prayers upon request, emphasizes the value of a personal, intimate relationship with God. It suggests that the most profound communications with the Divine are those conducted in the quiet of one's heart, rather than those performed for an audience. This principle serves as a guide for maintaining the sincerity and depth of your prayer life, highlighting the importance of personal devotion over public display.

**Matthew 26:36 (KJV)** Then cometh Jesus with them unto a place called Gethsemane, and saith unto the disciples, Sit ye here, while I go and pray yonder.

**Mark 14:32 (KJV)** And they came to a place which was named Gethsemane: and he saith to his disciples, Sit ye here, while I shall pray.

In the account of the Transfiguration, found in the Gospels, Jesus Christ brings Peter, James, and John to a high mountain, separate from the others. This event, detailed **in Matthew 17:1-9, Mark 9:2-8, and Luke 9:28-36**, underscores Jesus' practice of seeking solitude for prayer, even when accompanied by His closest disciples. Upon reaching the mountaintop, Jesus separates Himself from Peter, James, and John to pray alone, further illustrating His commitment to personal communion with the Father.

This moment of profound spiritual significance, where Jesus is transfigured and speaks with Moses and Elijah, occurs while He is in prayer, highlighting the transformative power and deep connection with God that private prayer fosters. It teaches the importance of setting aside dedicated time and space for solitary prayer, demonstrating that even in moments of great spiritual importance, the practice of withdrawing from even the closest of companions to seek a personal encounter with God is vital. This principle serves as a model for believers, emphasizing the value of solitary prayer in nurturing one's relationship with God!

**Luke 9:28 (KJV)** And it came to pass about an eight days after these sayings, he took Peter and John and James, and went up into a mountain to pray.

**Luke 9:29 (KJV)** And as he prayed, the fashion of his countenance was altered, and his raiment *was* white *and* glistering.

**Luke 9:30 (KJV)** And, behold, there talked with him two men, which were Moses and Elias:

**Luke 9:31 (KJV)** Who appeared in glory, and spake of his decease which he should accomplish at Jerusalem.

**Luke 9:32 (KJV)** But Peter and they that were with him were heavy with sleep: and when they were awake, they saw his glory, and the two men that stood with him.

**Luke 9:33 (KJV)** And it came to pass, as they departed from him, Peter said unto Jesus, Master, it is good for us to be here: and let us make three tabernacles; one for thee, and one for Moses, and one for Elias: not knowing what he said.

**Luke 9:34 (KJV)** While he thus spake, there came a cloud, and overshadowed them: and they feared as they entered into the cloud.

**Luke 9:35 (KJV)** And there came a voice out of the cloud, saying, This is my beloved Son: hear him.

**Luke 9:36 (KJV)** And when the voice was past, Jesus was found alone. And they kept *it* close, and told no man in those days any of those things which they had seen.

Indeed, Jesus Christ provided His disciples with guidance on how to pray, exemplified by the Lord's Prayer, as detailed in the Gospels (Matthew 6:9-13, Luke 11:2-4). This instruction served as a template for approaching God in prayer, emphasizing simplicity, reverence, and a focus on God's will. However, the Gospels do not record instances where Jesus prays alongside His disciples in a public setting as part of this instructional process!

**Luke 11:1 (KJV)** And it came to pass, that, as he was praying in a certain place, when he ceased, one of his disciples said unto him, Lord, teach us to pray, as John also taught his disciples.

**Luke 11:2 (KJV)** And he said unto them, When ye pray, say, Our Father which art in heaven, Hallowed be thy name. Thy kingdom come. Thy will be done, as in heaven, so in earth.

Revisiting the inquiry regarding the appropriate setting and manner for prayer, we are reminded of the parable of the Pharisee and the tax collector in **Luke 18:9-14 (KJV),** which serves as a direct response from Jesus Christ to these considerations. Through this teaching, Jesus emphasizes the significance of humility and sincerity in prayer, contrasting the boastful, public prayers of the Pharisee with the humble, private plea of the tax collector!

**Luke 18:9 (KJV)** And he spake this parable unto certain which trusted in themselves that they were righteous, and despised others:

**Luke 18:10 (KJV)** Two men went up into the temple to pray; the one a Pharisee, and the other a publican.

**Luke 18:11 (KJV)** The Pharisee stood and prayed thus with himself, God, I thank thee, that I am not as other men *are*, extortioners, unjust, adulterers, or even as this publican.

**Luke 18:12 (KJV)** I fast twice in the week, I give tithes of all that I possess.

**Luke 18:13 (KJV)** And the publican, standing afar off, would not lift up so much as *his* eyes unto heaven, but smote upon his breast, saying, God be merciful to me a sinner.

**Luke 18:14 (KJV)** I tell you, this man went down to his house justified *rather* than the other: for every one that exalteth himself shall be abased; and he that humbleth himself shall be exalted.

**In Luke 18:9-14,** Jesus Christ critiques the ostentatious manner in which some people pray publicly, underscoring the importance of humility and sincerity in one's prayer life. Reflecting on Jesus' overall teachings on prayer, it is understood that the prayer Jesus offers in **John 17:1** was not performed in a public spectacle. Instead, it is believed that the Holy Spirit provided insight into the words of Jesus' prayer, allowing it to be recorded in the Scriptures for posterity. This perspective reinforces the notion that the essence and content of prayer, rather than the setting in which it is offered, are of paramount importance, aligning with the spiritual intimacy and depth that Jesus consistently advocated for.

**John 17:1 (KJV)** These words spake Jesus, and lifted up his eyes to heaven, and said, Father, the hour is come; glorify thy Son, that thy Son also may glorify thee:

The Apostle Peter, in emulating the example set by Jesus Christ, also sought solitude for his moments of prayer, illustrating the practice of withdrawing from others to engage in private communion with God. This behavior is consistent with the pattern Jesus demonstrated throughout His ministry, where He frequently retreated to quiet places to pray. Peter's actions reflect an understanding of the significance of solitary prayer as a means of fostering a deeper, more personal relationship with God. By choosing to pray in secret, Peter and other early followers of Christ underscored the value they placed on privacy and introspection in their spiritual practices, following the model of prayer that Jesus Himself lived by!

**Acts 9:40 (KJV)** But Peter put them all forth, and kneeled down, and prayed; and turning *him* to the body said, Tabitha, arise. And she opened her eyes: and when she saw Peter, she sat up.

**Acts 10:9 (KJV)** On the morrow, as they went on their journey, and drew nigh unto the city, Peter went up upon the housetop to pray about the sixth hour:

Indeed, **Romans 8:26** touches on the profound reality that we often do not know how to pray as we ought, highlighting our reliance on the Spirit to intercede for us with groanings too deep for words. This acknowledgment of our limitations in understanding the perfect will of God in prayer calls for humility rather than public displays of piety that may not capture the essence of heartfelt communion with God. The scripture serves as a reminder of the genuine struggle and complexity in prayer, encouraging believers to seek a more intimate, private dialogue with God where the Spirit can truly guide and intercede.

Given this insight, the wisdom in following the examples of Jesus Christ, Apostle Peter, and Paul becomes even more apparent. Their practices of seeking solitude for prayer and focusing on the sincerity and depth of their communication with God, rather than on external appearances, serve as models for genuine spiritual practice. This approach not only aligns with the humble acknowledgment of our limitations in prayer but also fosters a personal relationship with God that is authentic and unaffected by the desire for human approval.

> **Romans 8:26 (KJV)** Likewise the Spirit also helpeth our infirmities: for we know not what we should pray for as we ought: but the Spirit itself maketh intercession for us with groanings which cannot be uttered.

The directive to pray everywhere, as taught in the Scriptures, emphasizes the omnipresence of God and the believer's ability to communicate with Him at any time and place, reflecting a personal and continuous relationship with the Divine. However, this command is harmonized with the principle exemplified by Jesus Christ and the Apostle Peter, who both sought moments of solitude for their prayers, away from public view and the hearing of the crowd. This approach underscores the distinction between maintaining an unceasing attitude of prayer, as encouraged in **1 Thessalonians 5:17** ("pray without ceasing"), and the manner in which these prayers are offered—privately, in a way that fosters a sincere and intimate dialogue with God, rather than for the sake of being seen or heard by others. It suggests that while believers are encouraged to live in a state of constant prayerfulness, the expression of deeper, personal petitions to God is best conducted in privacy, aligning with the examples set by Jesus and His early followers.

> **1 Timothy 2:8 (KJV)** I will therefore that men pray every where, lifting up holy hands, without wrath and doubting.

May the Lord Jesus Christ be with your spirit, guiding and enriching you with His wisdom and understanding. Through His presence, may you find clarity, strength, and a deeper connection to His divine love and truth.

# CHAPTER 13

## THE DOCTRINE OF SALVATION BY ACCEPTING JESUS CHRIST!

========================

### ESE NE TEKREMA

"The teeth and the tongue"

Asante philosophical symbol of Friendship, Interdependence,
Co-Existence, Tolerance

==============================

Anyone identifying as a Christian is likely familiar with the salvation doctrine taught by pastors and evangelists, which asserts that upon accepting Jesus Christ as your Lord and Savior, you instantly become a child of God. This immediate reception of salvation is based on the belief that Jesus Christ has long been waiting, metaphorically knocking at the heart's door, ready to enter as soon as one opens it. To substantiate this teaching, let's examine the relevant biblical verses:

> **Revelation 3:20 (KJV)** Behold, I stand at the door, and knock: if any man hear my voice, and open the door, I will come in to him, and will sup with him, and he with me.

If I were to suggest that pastors, evangelists, churches, and Bible colleges have misrepresented the doctrine of Salvation, teaching a version that is incorrect and potentially leading you towards condemnation, it could evoke a range of emotions. Such a statement might cause surprise, confusion, disbelief, or even anger, as it challenges fundamental beliefs and trust in religious teachings and institutions. It would likely prompt a serious reevaluation of those teachings and a deeper personal exploration of religious doctrines and their interpretations.

> **John 10:1 (KJV)** Verily, verily, I say unto you, He that entereth not by the door into the sheepfold, but climbeth up some other way, the same is a thief and a robber.

**John 10:2 (KJV)** But he that entereth in by the door is the shepherd of the sheep.

**John 10:3 (KJV)** To him the porter openeth; and the sheep hear his voice: and he calleth his own sheep by name, and leadeth them out.

**John 10:4 (KJV)** And when he putteth forth his own sheep, he goeth before them, and the sheep follow him: for they know his voice.

**John 10:5 (KJV)** And a stranger will they not follow, but will flee from him: for they know not the voice of strangers.

**John 10:6 (KJV)** This parable spake Jesus unto them: but they understood not what things they were which he spake unto them.

**John 10:7 (KJV)** Then said Jesus unto them again, Verily, verily, I say unto you, I am the door of the sheep.

**John 10:8 (KJV)** All that ever came before me are thieves and robbers: but the sheep did not hear them.

**John 10:9 (KJV)** I am the door: by me if any man enter in, he shall be saved, and shall go in and out, and find pasture.

**John 10:10 (KJV)** The thief cometh not, but for to steal, and to kill, and to destroy: I am come that they might have life, and that they might have *it* more abundantly.

Learning that one has not been diligent as a Christian and has neglected to critically engage with the Word of God might lead to feelings of guilt, regret, or self-reproach. Realizing a failure to verify the teachings of pastors and evangelists against the Holy Scriptures could prompt a sense of responsibility for one's spiritual journey and a desire to seek a deeper understanding of biblical truths. This revelation might serve as a wake-up call to take personal ownership of one's faith, encouraging a more active and discerning approach to religious study and practice.

**Acts 17:10 (KJV)** And the brethren immediately sent away Paul and Silas by night unto Berea: who coming *thither* went into the synagogue of the Jews.

**Acts 17:11 (KJV)** These were more noble than those in Thessalonica, in that they received the word with all readiness of mind, and searched the scriptures daily, whether those things were so.

**1 Thessalonians 5:21 (KJV)** Prove all things; hold fast that which is good.

**1 John 4:1 (KJV)** Beloved, believe not every spirit, but try the spirits whether they are of God: because many false prophets are gone out into the world.

Imagine finding out that the concept of achieving salvation by "accepting Jesus Christ as your Lord and Savior" is not explicitly stated in the Holy Scriptures. Despite the term "accept" appearing 25 times in the Bible, none of these instances involve an individual accepting God or Jesus Christ for salvation. Similarly, "accepting" is mentioned only once and does not refer to accepting God or Jesus Christ for salvation. Moreover, the word "accepted" appears 28 times, yet it never describes someone accepting God or Jesus Christ for the purpose of salvation.

The Scriptures underscore a stark warning: preaching or teaching anything not founded in the Word of God brings a curse, indicating such teachings and their followers may not be aligned with true salvation.

> **Isaiah 8:20 (KJV)** To the law and to the testimony: if they speak not according to this word, *it is* because *there is* no light in them.

> **John 7:49 (KJV)** But this people who knoweth not the law are cursed.

> **Galatians 1:8 (KJV)** But though we, or an angel from heaven, preach any other gospel unto you than that which we have preached unto you, let him be accursed.

> **Galatians 1:9 (KJV)** As we said before, so say I now again, If any *man* preach any other gospel unto you than that ye have received, let him be accursed.

This statement challenges the integrity and authenticity of those who teach salvation inaccurately. It confronts individuals who, despite their prominent religious roles and leadership over large congregations, may have propagated false doctrines. The concern raised is about the responsibility of guiding others spiritually without a solid grounding in the Word of God. On the Day of Judgment, such leaders might be asked to account for their stewardship of their followers, implying that misleading them equates to failing in their pastoral duties. The imagery of leading the flock to slaughter underscores the severity of the accusation, suggesting that their actions have had dire consequences for their congregations' spiritual well-being

> **Jeremiah 23:15 (KJV)** Therefore thus saith the LORD of hosts concerning the prophets; Behold, I will feed them with wormwood, and make them drink the water of gall: for from the prophets of Jerusalem is profaneness gone forth into all the land.

> **Lamentations 2:14 (KJV)** Thy prophets have seen vain and foolish things for thee: and they have not discovered thine iniquity, to turn away thy captivity; but have seen for thee false burdens and causes of banishment.

To all the pastors, evangelists, churches, and Bible colleges implicated in leading countless individuals astray: if salvation is central to the teachings of Jesus Christ and your doctrine of salvation is flawed—lacking any scriptural backing for the concept of "accept Jesus Christ and become saved"—then who are you truly serving? The absence of biblical evidence for this doctrine raises a critical question about the spiritual destiny of those under your guidance. It seems that such teachings would please Satan rather than align with the teachings of Jesus Christ, as revealed in the scriptures.

> **John 10:8 (KJV)** All that ever came before me are thieves and robbers: but the sheep did not hear them.

**John 10:9 (KJV)** I am the door: by me if any man enter in, he shall be saved, and shall go in and out, and find pasture.

**John 10:10 (KJV)** The thief cometh not, but for to steal, and to kill, and to destroy: I am come that they might have life, and that they might have *it* more abundantly.

In the Kingdom of God, as a servant called by Jesus Christ, you lack the liberty to arbitrarily choose words or create doctrines for your ministry. If indeed it was Jesus Christ who summoned you to serve, you must adhere strictly to the teachings and words that align with His directives, without fabricating or altering the doctrinal truths.

**Isaiah 58:13 (KJV)** If thou turn away thy foot from the sabbath, *from* doing thy pleasure on my holy day; and call the sabbath a delight, the holy of the LORD, honourable; and shalt honour him, not doing thine own ways, nor finding thine own pleasure, nor speaking *thine own* words:

**Ezekiel 3:4 (KJV)** And he said unto me, Son of man, go, get thee unto the house of Israel, and speak with my words unto them.

**John 3:34 (KJV)** For he whom God hath sent speaketh the words of God: for God giveth not the Spirit by measure *unto him.*

**John 7:16 (KJV)** Jesus answered them, and said, My doctrine is not mine, but his that sent me.

To achieve the outcomes and meet the expectations set by God Almighty, you must employ the words given from Heaven. Words resonate in two distinct realms: the Spirit Realm of Heaven and the spirit realm of Satan. For words to effectively carry out God's purpose and resonate in Heaven, they must be divinely bestowed upon you as a true servant of God before you can use them. This underscores the importance of speaking with divine authority and guidance to ensure alignment with God's will.

**Isaiah 55:11 (KJV)** So shall my word be that goeth forth out of my mouth: it shall not return unto me void, but it shall accomplish that which I please, and it shall prosper *in the thing* whereto I sent it.

**Lamentations 3:37 (KJV)** Who *is* he *that* saith, and it cometh to pass, *when* the Lord commandeth *it* not?

**Amos 3:8 (KJV)** The lion hath roared, who will not fear? the Lord GOD hath spoken, who can but prophesy?

**John 12:49 (KJV)** For I have not spoken of myself; but the Father which sent me, he gave me a commandment, what I should say, and what I should speak.

**John 12:50 (KJV)** And I know that his commandment is life everlasting: whatsoever I speak therefore, even as the Father said unto me, so I speak.

Given that the phrase "accept Jesus Christ and become saved" used in your purported salvation teachings finds no recognition in Heaven, one must question the true beneficiary of these so-called salvations. Whose realm are these souls being prepared for—Satan's or God's?

For a genuine understanding of salvation, consider the scriptural language that truly defines the path to being saved. Reflect on **Psalm 119:58** which illustrates the proper plea for salvation: "be merciful unto me according to thy Word." This underscores that salvation is sought through God's Word, not the interpretations or teachings of a pastor.

> **Psalm 56:1 (KJV)** To the chief Musician upon Jonath-elem-rechokim, Michtam of David, when the Philistines took him in Gath. Be merciful unto me, O God: for man would swallow me up; he fighting daily oppresseth me.
>
> **Psalm 57:1 (KJV)** To the chief Musician, Al-taschith, Michtam of David, when he fled from Saul in the cave. Be merciful unto me, O God, be merciful unto me: for my soul trusteth in thee: yea, in the shadow of thy wings will I make my refuge, until *these* calamities be overpast.
>
> **Psalm 119:58 (KJV)** I intreated thy favour with *my* whole heart: be merciful unto me according to thy word.
>
> **Luke 18:13 (KJV)** And the publican, standing afar off, would not lift up so much as *his* eyes unto heaven, but smote upon his breast, saying, God be merciful to me a sinner.
>
> **Luke 18:14 (KJV)** I tell you, this man went down to his house justified *rather* than the other: for every one that exalteth himself shall be abased; and he that humbleth himself shall be exalted.

This second example further clarifies the authentic language of salvation, which again shows no evidence of the notion that merely "accepting Jesus Christ leads to salvation." It underscores that the genuine concept of salvation, as presented in scripture, does not align with the simplified formula of acceptance often preached.

> **Luke 19:1 (KJV)** And *Jesus* entered and passed through Jericho.
>
> **Luke 19:2 (KJV)** And, behold, *there was* a man named Zacchaeus, which was the chief among the publicans, and he was rich.
>
> **Luke 19:3 (KJV)** And he sought to see Jesus who he was; and could not for the press, because he was little of stature.
>
> **Luke 19:4 (KJV)** And he ran before, and climbed up into a sycomore tree to see him: for he was to pass that *way*.

**Luke 19:5 (KJV)** And when Jesus came to the place, he looked up, and saw him, and said unto him, Zacchaeus, make haste, and come down; for to day I must abide at thy house.

**Luke 19:6 (KJV)** And he made haste, and came down, and received him joyfully.

**Luke 19:7 (KJV)** And when they saw *it*, they all murmured, saying, That he was gone to be guest with a man that is a sinner.

**Luke 19:8 (KJV)** And Zacchaeus stood, and said unto the Lord; Behold, Lord, the half of my goods I give to the poor; and if I have taken any thing from any man by false accusation, I restore *him* fourfold.

**Luke 19:9 (KJV)** And Jesus said unto him, This day is salvation come to this house, forsomuch as he also is a son of Abraham.

**Luke 19:10 (KJV)** For the Son of man is come to seek and to save that which was lost.

The misuse of the phrase "accepting Jesus Christ to become saved" has led many Christians astray, resulting in a lifestyle focused on acquiring material wealth, properties, and fame, which starkly contradicts the teachings found in **Luke 19:8**. This verse exemplifies the behavior of a truly saved individual, like Zacchaeus, who pledged to give away half of his possessions and rectify any wrongdoing. In contrast, those who are not genuinely saved tend to accumulate and hoard wealth, revealing a disconnect between their professed beliefs and their actions.

**Luke 19:8 (KJV)** And Zacchaeus stood, and said unto the Lord; Behold, Lord, the half of my goods I give to the poor; and if I have taken any thing from any man by false accusation, I restore *him* fourfold.

**Luke 19:9 (KJV)** And Jesus said unto him, This day is salvation come to this house, forsomuch as he also is a son of Abraham.

To properly understand salvation, we should revisit **Luke 19:8**, which illustrates that true salvation is not merely about uttering words of "repentance and accepting Jesus Christ to become saved." It involves a genuine turning away from sin, as demonstrated by the actions of Zacchaeus, who committed to giving back and rectifying his wrongs. This concept of transformation and repentance, rather than just verbal acknowledgment, is the essence of salvation taught throughout the Holy Bible.

**Psalm 37:8 (KJV)** Cease from anger, and forsake wrath: fret not thyself in any wise to do evil.

**Isaiah 1:16 (KJV)** Wash you, make you clean; put away the evil of your doings from before mine eyes; cease to do evil;

**Zechariah 8:16 (KJV)** These *are* the things that ye shall do; Speak ye every man the truth to his neighbour; execute the judgment of truth and peace in your gates:

**Zechariah 8:17 (KJV)** And let none of you imagine evil in your hearts against his neighbour; and love no false oath: for all these *are things* that I hate, saith the LORD.

**Acts 3:26 (KJV)** Unto you first God, having raised up his Son Jesus, sent him to bless you, in turning away every one of you from his iniquities.

**2 Peter 2:14 (KJV)** Having eyes full of adultery, and that cannot cease from sin; beguiling unstable souls: an heart they have exercised with covetous practices; cursed children:

Following salvation or baptism, the subsequent step is to demonstrate the evidence of your salvation through a continuous and steadfast adherence to the teachings of Jesus Christ. This means living in accordance with His Word, reflecting a genuine transformation and commitment to the Christian faith.

**John 8:31 (KJV)** Then said Jesus to those Jews which believed on him, If ye continue in my word, *then* are ye my disciples indeed;

**Colossians 1:23 (KJV)** If ye continue in the faith grounded and settled, and *be* not moved away from the hope of the gospel, which ye have heard, *and* which was preached to every creature which is under heaven; whereof I Paul am made a minister;

**1 John 2:24 (KJV)** Let that therefore abide in you, which ye have heard from the beginning. If that which ye have heard from the beginning shall remain in you, ye also shall continue in the Son, and in the Father.

The authenticity of one's salvation can be seen in the consistent manifestation of a life aligned with the teachings of Jesus Christ. True salvation should result in a sustained walk in the light of the Gospel. In contrast, individuals who experience a superficial form of salvation, often promoted by the "accept Jesus Christ and be saved" rhetoric, might revert to previous behaviors such as dishonesty, anger, and other sins.

A genuine transformation through salvation is marked by a continuous practice of righteousness and adherence to the Word of God. If this transformation is absent, it raises questions about the authenticity of one's conversion and faith.

Maintaining a life of spiritual integrity and obedience to God's Word is challenging. Many who claim to have accepted Jesus Christ struggle to live out their faith consistently. This struggle is often reflected in how infrequently they engage with the Bible or discuss spiritual matters, quickly shifting focus back to worldly concerns and old habits. True change, as evidenced in a believer's life, involves more than a momentary declaration of faith; it requires ongoing commitment and transformation in accordance with God's Word.

**John 8:31 (KJV)** Then said Jesus to those Jews which believed on him, If ye continue in my word, *then* are ye my disciples indeed;

**1 John 1:6 (KJV)** If we say that we have fellowship with him, and walk in darkness, we lie, and do not the truth:

**1 John 1:7 (KJV)** But if we walk in the light, as he is in the light, we have fellowship one with another, and the blood of Jesus Christ his Son cleanseth us from all sin.

**1 John 2:18 (KJV)** Little children, it is the last time: and as ye have heard that antichrist shall come, even now are there many antichrists; whereby we know that it is the last time.

**1 John 2:19 (KJV)** They went out from us, but they were not of us; for if they had been of us, they would *no doubt* have continued with us: but *they went out*, that they might be made manifest that they were not all of us.

The LORD Jesus Christ be with your spirit. The LORD Jesus Christ give you understanding.

# CHAPTER 14

## WHO QUALIFIES AS A GENUINE FOLLOWER OF JESUS CHRIST?

====================

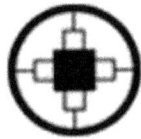

HWEMUDUA

"Measuring stick"

Asante philosophical symbol of Examination, Quality Control, Standardization, Research

=========================

1. True believer, in the context of Christian faith, is someone who genuinely believes in the Lord Jesus Christ. A true believer in Jesus Christ embodies more than mere intellectual acceptance of His existence and doctrines. Instead, this belief is deeply rooted in a personal trust and dedication to live according to His teachings. This comprehensive faith is evident through several key characteristics:

Firstly, a true believer consistently adheres to the Commandments of Jesus, demonstrating faith through actions and a lifestyle that echoes His principles of love, compassion, honesty, humility, and forgiveness. This obedience is not forced but flows naturally from genuine faith.

Such a believer maintains a personal and dynamic connection with Jesus, cultivated through regular prayer, worship, and Bible study, aiming to discern and align with His will.

The transformative power of belief in Jesus manifests in changed behaviors and attitudes, signifying a life reshaped by faith and aligned with Jesus' teachings.

Furthermore, the presence of the "fruit of the Spirit," as outlined **in Galatians 5:22-23,** including attributes like love, joy, peace, patience, kindness, goodness, faithfulness, gentleness, and self-control, is a hallmark of a true believer.

Lastly, true believers actively contribute to their religious communities, engaging in service and charity, inspired by Jesus' own example of service to others.

In essence, a true believer in Jesus Christ is one who integrates faith intellectually and practically, leading a transformed life, fostering a close relationship with Him, embodying the fruit of the Spirit, and committing to acts of service and charity.

> **John 14:21 (KJV)** He that hath my commandments, and keepeth them, he it is that loveth me: and he that loveth me shall be loved of my Father, and I will love him, and will manifest myself to him.

> **John 14:24 (KJV)** He that loveth me not keepeth not my sayings: and the word which ye hear is not mine, but the Father's which sent me.

2. A true believer is often described as a friend of Jesus Christ, indicating a close, personal relationship with Him. This friendship goes beyond mere belief in Jesus' existence or teachings; it involves a deep, personal connection that influences the believer's entire life. Such a believer not only acknowledges Jesus intellectually but also embraces His teachings, strives to live by them, and maintains a relationship characterized by love, trust, and obedience.

This concept emphasizes that the true believer of Jesus is not just a follower in name but in action and spirit. The friendship with Jesus is reflected in how they live their life, prioritize His values, and commit to His commandments. The relationship is active and dynamic, involving regular communication through prayer, reflection on His words, and a heartfelt desire to align one's actions with His teachings.

In summary, being a true believer in Jesus Christ means establishing a friendship with Him that is evident in one's faith, actions, and lifestyle, showcasing a commitment to living in accordance with His principles and teachings

The friend of Jesus Christ is the true believer of Jesus!

> **John 15:13 (KJV)** Greater love hath no man than this, that a man lay down his life for his friends.

> **John 15:14 (KJV)** Ye are my friends, if ye do whatsoever I command you.

> **John 15:15 (KJV)** Henceforth I call you not servants; for the servant knoweth not what his lord doeth: but I have called you friends; for all things that I have heard of my Father I have made known unto you.

3. The statement "The true believer of Jesus Christ is the one who did NOT accept Jesus or choose Jesus Christ as his personal LORD and Saviour" appears to contradict the traditional Christian understanding of faith and belief. However, if we consider this statement in light of **John 15:16**, where Jesus says, "You did not choose me, but I chose you and appointed you so that you might go and bear fruit—fruit that will last,"

In this context, the emphasis shifts from the believer's initial act of choosing or accepting Jesus to the idea that it is Jesus who chooses the believer. This perspective highlights the notion of divine election and the calling to live a life that bears lasting fruit in accordance with Jesus' teachings and purposes.

Therefore, a true believer in Jesus Christ, in this sense, is not defined merely by a moment of personal decision or verbal profession of faith but by the ongoing evidence of Jesus' choosing and appointing. This is manifested in a life that consistently bears fruit in alignment with His will and teachings, indicating a deeper, transformative relationship initiated by Jesus Himself.

> **John 15:16 (KJV)** Ye have not chosen me, but I have chosen you, and ordained you, that ye should go and bring forth fruit, and *that* your fruit should remain: that whatsoever ye shall ask of the Father in my name, he may give it you.

4. A true believer in Jesus Christ is characterized by their unwavering commitment to fulfilling the will of God the Father. This individual's faith is not merely a nominal or superficial declaration but is deeply rooted in a life that actively seeks and adheres to God's directives and desires. Their actions, decisions, and entire way of living are guided by an earnest desire to align with God's will, reflecting a genuine and profound dedication to the path set forth by divine instruction!

> **Matthew 12:50 (KJV)** For whosoever shall do the will of my Father which is in heaven, the same is my brother, and sister, and mother.

5. A true believer in Jesus Christ embodies a transformative faith journey that is not rooted in self-initiated acts or decisions. This individual:

Did not come to faith by merely accepting Jesus Christ through a formal or superficial act!

Did not initiate their own salvation, indicating that the process of becoming saved was not a result of their own effort or decision.

Did not choose to become saved or a believer simply by deciding to adopt the Christian identity at a specific moment.

Never consciously decided to dedicate their life to Jesus Christ as a result of a personal decision-making process.

Was not swayed into belief by external pressures, such as a directive from a pastor in a church setting to perform a ritualistic prayer without genuine understanding or conviction.

Is often unaware of the exact moment they became a child of God or entered the Kingdom of God, suggesting that their faith and regeneration were divinely orchestrated beyond their conscious control!

This perspective emphasizes the concept that true belief in Jesus Christ and entry into God's Kingdom are the results of divine action and grace, rather than human decision or effort.

> **John 1:12 (KJV)** But as many as received him, to them gave he power to become the sons of God, *even* to them that believe on his name:

> **John 1:13 (KJV)** Which were born, not of blood, nor of the will of the flesh, nor of the will of man, but of God.

> **John 3:3 (KJV)** Jesus answered and said unto him, Verily, verily, I say unto thee, Except a man be born again, he cannot see the kingdom of God.

> **John 3:4 (KJV)** Nicodemus saith unto him, How can a man be born when he is old? can he enter the second time into his mother's womb, and be born?

> **John 3:5 (KJV)** Jesus answered, Verily, verily, I say unto thee, Except a man be born of water and *of* the Spirit, he cannot enter into the kingdom of God.

> **John 3:6 (KJV)** That which is born of the flesh is flesh; and that which is born of the Spirit is spirit.

> **John 3:7 (KJV)** Marvel not that I said unto thee, Ye must be born again.

> **John 3:8 (KJV)** The wind bloweth where it listeth, and thou hearest the sound thereof, but canst not tell whence it cometh, and whither it goeth: so is every one that is born of the Spirit.

> **Matthew 28:18 (KJV)** And Jesus came and spake unto them, saying, All power is given unto me in heaven and in earth.

> **Matthew 28:19 (KJV)** Go ye therefore, and teach all nations, baptizing them in the name of the Father, and of the Son, and of the Holy Ghost:

> **Matthew 28:20 (KJV)** Teaching them to observe all things whatsoever I have commanded you: and, lo, I am with you alway, *even* unto the end of the world. Amen.

6. A good believer in Jesus Christ, as described in this context, is one who does not engage in the practice of collecting or paying tithes to a pastor or church. This perspective suggests that true devotion and faith are not measured by financial transactions or contributions to religious institutions but are instead based on personal conviction and the individual's relationship with God. The emphasis here is on the belief that one's spiritual integrity and commitment to Jesus Christ are not dependent on monetary practices but are manifested through other expressions of faith and service!

> **Matthew 17:24 (KJV)** And when they were come to Capernaum, they that received tribute *money* came to Peter, and said, Doth not your master pay tribute?

**Matthew 17:25 (KJV)** He saith, Yes. And when he was come into the house, Jesus prevented him, saying, What thinkest thou, Simon? of whom do the kings of the earth take custom or tribute? of their own children, or of strangers?

**Matthew 17:26 (KJV)** Peter saith unto him, Of strangers. Jesus saith unto him, Then are the children free.

7. A good believer in Jesus Christ is characterized by an intense desire and pursuit of God's righteousness, always striving to understand and live according to divine standards. This individual constantly seeks to align their thoughts, actions, and life with God's will, embodying a deep commitment to uphold and practice the principles of righteousness as taught in the teachings of Jesus and the broader Christian faith. Their spiritual journey is marked by a continuous effort to embody and enact the righteousness that reflects God's character and commandments!

**Matthew 5:6 (KJV)** Blessed *are* they which do hunger and thirst after righteousness: for they shall be filled.

8. A good believer in Jesus Christ is identified by their sincere and pure heart, dedicated to serving the Living God. This individual's service is driven by genuine love and devotion, free from ulterior motives or superficiality. Their commitment is rooted in a deep desire to honor and glorify God through their actions, choices, and entire way of living, reflecting a heart that is truly aligned with God's purposes and desires!

**Matthew 5:8 (KJV)** Blessed *are* the pure in heart: for they shall see God.

9. A good believer in Jesus Christ is characterized by their compassion and action towards helping the poor, needy, widows, strangers, orphans, and destitute individuals. This person actively seeks out opportunities to provide support and relief to those in vulnerable situations, reflecting Jesus' teachings on love, mercy, and service to others. Their faith is demonstrated through tangible acts of kindness and generosity, showing a commitment to living out the Christian call to care for and uplift the marginalized and disadvantaged in society!

**Matthew 5:42 (KJV)** Give to him that asketh thee, and from him that would borrow of thee turn not thou away.

10. A good believer in Jesus Christ is one who refrains from praying for the demise of their enemies. Instead of yielding to messages of hatred or vengeance, this individual follows the teachings of Jesus, who advocated for loving one's enemies and praying for those who persecute you. In many churches, it's unfortunately not uncommon to encounter practices where prayers are directed against perceived enemies, with some leaders encouraging congregations to pray for their downfall or even death. However, a

true believer recognizes the value of compassion, forgiveness, and the pursuit of peace, in alignment with Jesus' message of love and reconciliation, rather than engaging in prayers of destruction or harm against others!

> **Matthew 5:43 (KJV)** Ye have heard that it hath been said, Thou shalt love thy neighbour, and hate thine enemy.

> **Matthew 5:44 (KJV)** But I say unto you, Love your enemies, bless them that curse you, do good to them that hate you, and pray for them which despitefully use you, and persecute you;

> **Matthew 5:45 (KJV)** That ye may be the children of your Father which is in heaven: for he maketh his sun to rise on the evil and on the good, and sendeth rain on the just and on the unjust.

11. A faithful follower of Jesus Christ is one who assists the less fortunate without broadcasting their deeds, adhering to the principle of discreet charity, as highlighted in Matthew 6:3-4. This teaching encourages giving in secret, without seeking acknowledgment or praise, so that the act of kindness remains a genuine expression of compassion, visible only to God!

> **Matthew 6:1 (KJV)** Take heed that ye do not your alms before men, to be seen of them: otherwise ye have no reward of your Father which is in heaven.

> **Matthew 6:2 (KJV)** Therefore when thou doest *thine* alms, do not sound a trumpet before thee, as the hypocrites do in the synagogues and in the streets, that they may have glory of men. Verily I say unto you, They have their reward.

> **Matthew 6:3 (KJV)** But when thou doest alms, let not thy left hand know what thy right hand doeth:

> **Matthew 6:4 (KJV)** That thine alms may be in secret: and thy Father which seeth in secret himself shall reward thee openly.

12. A good believer of Jesus Christ is the one that presents a faithful Christian's approach to prayer and spiritual communication, focusing on authenticity, clarity, and intent. In **Matthew 6:7-8**, Jesus advises against repetitive and insincere prayers, indicating that God values genuine, heartfelt communication over mere words. This instruction motivates believers to pray with sincere intentions, avoiding mindless repetition. **1 Corinthians 14:15-16** sees Apostle Paul addressing the practice of speaking in tongues within the church, urging for prayer and worship that everyone can understand and benefit from. He stresses the significance of engaging both spirit and intellect in worship, advocating for expressions of faith that are not only emotionally or spiritually profound but also meaningful and comprehensible to others.

These teachings underscore that a true believer in Christ is called to participate in prayer and worship thoughtfully and meaningfully. This commitment involves shunning shallow or mechanical expressions of faith and striving for a deeper, more reflective relationship with God, along with fostering clear and beneficial communication with fellow believers about one's faith.

**Matthew 6:7 (KJV)** But when ye pray, use not vain repetitions, as the heathen *do*: for they think that they shall be heard for their much speaking.

**Matthew 6:8 (KJV)** Be not ye therefore like unto them: for your Father knoweth what things ye have need of, before ye ask him.

**1 Corinthians 14:15 (KJV)** What is it then? I will pray with the spirit, and I will pray with the understanding also: I will sing with the spirit, and I will sing with the understanding also.

**1 Corinthians 14:16 (KJV)** Else when thou shalt bless with the spirit, how shall he that occupieth the room of the unlearned say Amen at thy giving of thanks, seeing he understandeth not what thou sayest?

**1 Corinthians 14:21 (KJV)** In the law it is written, With *men of* other tongues and other lips will I speak unto this people; and yet for all that will they not hear me, saith the Lord.

**1 Corinthians 14:22 (KJV)** Wherefore tongues are for a sign, not to them that believe, but to them that believe not: but prophesying *serveth* not for them that believe not, but for them which believe.

**1 Corinthians 14:23 (KJV)** If therefore the whole church be come together into one place, and all speak with tongues, and there come in *those that are* unlearned, or unbelievers, will they not say that ye are mad?

13. A sincere believer in Jesus Christ practices fasting privately, without making it known to others, in contrast to the practices of some churches where fasting is publicly announced and mandated!

**Matthew 6:16 (KJV)** Moreover when ye fast, be not, as the hypocrites, of a sad countenance: for they disfigure their faces, that they may appear unto men to fast. Verily I say unto you, They have their reward.

**Matthew 6:17 (KJV)** But thou, when thou fastest, anoint thine head, and wash thy face;

**Matthew 6:18 (KJV)** That thou appear not unto men to fast, but unto thy Father which is in secret: and thy Father, which seeth in secret, shall reward thee openly.

14. A true follower of Jesus Christ recognizes that material wealth, such as money and possessions, is not necessarily an indicator of God's blessing, acknowledging that even negative forces can grant material success to those with ill intentions.

15. A genuine believer in Jesus Christ rejects the so-called prosperity gospel preached by some in modern churches, which wrongly equates God's favor with financial wealth and material prosperity.

16. Reflecting on personal experience, the notion that wealth signifies God's blessing is misleading. This misconception leads many to hop from one church to another seeking prophecies of wealth and miracles, ignoring the reality that being a Christian does not guarantee material wealth or prevent poverty.

>**Deuteronomy 15:11 (KJV)** For the poor shall never cease out of the land: therefore I command thee, saying, Thou shalt open thine hand wide unto thy brother, to thy poor, and to thy needy, in thy land.

>**Matthew 6:19 (KJV)** Lay not up for yourselves treasures upon earth, where moth and rust doth corrupt, and where thieves break through and steal:

>**Matthew 6:20 (KJV)** But lay up for yourselves treasures in heaven, where neither moth nor rust doth corrupt, and where thieves do not break through nor steal:

>**Matthew 13:22 (KJV)** He also that received seed among the thorns is he that heareth the word; and the care of this world, and the deceitfulness of riches, choke the word, and he becometh unfruitful.

>**Mark 4:19 (KJV)** And the cares of this world, and the deceitfulness of riches, and the lusts of other things entering in, choke the word, and it becometh unfruitful.

>**Ephesians 1:3 (KJV)** Blessed *be* the God and Father of our Lord Jesus Christ, who hath blessed us with all spiritual blessings in heavenly *places* in Christ:

17. A devoted believer in Jesus Christ prioritizes acquiring knowledge of God's Word above all else. Embedding the Word of God in one's heart, living righteously, and refraining from sin allows Christ to dwell within. Christ embodies the Word, which is the Truth and the Light. As **John 1:1** states, "In the beginning was the Word, and the Word was with God, and the Word was God." Therefore, to truly know God, a committed believer in Jesus Christ must diligently study and embrace His Word

>**Matthew 6:33 (KJV)** But seek ye first the kingdom of God, and his righteousness; and all these things shall be added unto you.

>**Habakkuk 2:14 (KJV)** For the earth shall be filled with the knowledge of the glory of the LORD, as the waters cover the sea.

**Colossians 1:9 (KJV)** For this cause we also, since the day we heard *it*, do not cease to pray for you, and to desire that ye might be filled with the knowledge of his will in all wisdom and spiritual understanding;

18. A faithful believer in Jesus Christ uses Scripture as the foundation for discernment, guiding others with humility and love. They rely on biblical teachings to distinguish right from wrong, correct those who have sinned, and oppose wickedness and unrighteousness, ensuring their actions are rooted in God's Word rather than personal righteousness!

    **Leviticus 19:17 (KJV)** Thou shalt not hate thy brother in thine heart: thou shalt in any wise rebuke thy neighbour, and not suffer sin upon him.

    **John 7:24 (KJV)** Judge not according to the appearance, but judge righteous judgment.

    **1 Corinthians 14:29 (KJV)** Let the prophets speak two or three, and let the other judge.

    **Titus 1:13 (KJV)** This witness is true. Wherefore rebuke them sharply, that they may be sound in the faith;

    **1 Timothy 5:20 (KJV)** Them that sin rebuke before all, that others also may fear

19. A good believer in Jesus Christ avoids engaging in fruitless debates and bitter arguments with unbelievers and those who reject wisdom, understanding that such interactions often lead nowhere and that, according to biblical teachings, folly is ultimately accountable to God!

    **Psalm 5:5 (KJV)** The foolish shall not stand in thy sight: thou hatest all workers of iniquity.

    **Proverbs 14:7 (KJV)** Go from the presence of a foolish man, when thou perceivest not *in him* the lips of knowledge.

    **Matthew 25:8 (KJV)** And the foolish said unto the wise, Give us of your oil; for our lamps are gone out

    **Matthew 25:9 (KJV)** But the wise answered, saying, *Not so*; lest there be not enough for us and you: but go ye rather to them that sell, and buy for yourselves.

    **Matthew 25:10 (KJV)** And while they went to buy, the bridegroom came; and they that were ready went in with him to the marriage: and the door was shut.

    **Matthew 25:11 (KJV)** Afterward came also the other virgins, saying, Lord, Lord, open to us.

**Matthew 25:12 (KJV)** But he answered and said, Verily I say unto you, I know you not.

**Titus 3:9 (KJV)** But avoid foolish questions, and genealogies, and contentions, and strivings about the law; for they are unprofitable and vain.

**Titus 3:10 (KJV)** A man that is an heretick after the first and second admonition reject;

20. A good believer in Jesus Christ possesses spiritual discernment to identify those who are dismissive or contemptuous of sacred truths, and wisely chooses not to share the precious Word of God with such individuals, as advised in scriptural teachings about casting pearls before swine!

   **Matthew 7:6 (KJV)** Give not that which is holy unto the dogs, neither cast ye your pearls before swine, lest they trample them under their feet, and turn again and rend you.

   **Matthew 15:25 (KJV)** Then came she and worshipped him, saying, Lord, help me.

   **Matthew 15:26 (KJV)** But he answered and said, It is not meet to take the children's bread, and to cast *it* to dogs.

   **Matthew 7:6 (KJV)** Give not that which is holy unto the dogs, neither cast ye your pearls before swine, lest they trample them under their feet, and turn again and rend you.

   **Luke 10:5 (KJV)** And into whatsoever house ye enter, first say, Peace *be* to this house.

   **Luke 10:6 (KJV)** And if the son of peace be there, your peace shall rest upon it: if not, it shall turn to you again.

21. A devoted believer in Jesus Christ is endowed with the ability to impart God's peace to those who wholeheartedly accept the Word of God and also has the discernment to withhold that peace from those who reject the Word, reflecting the deep spiritual responsibility and discernment called for in their faith.

   **Matthew 10:12 (KJV)** And when ye come into an house, salute it.

   **Matthew 10:13 (KJV)** And if the house be worthy, let your peace come upon it: but if it be not worthy, let your peace return to you.

   **Matthew 10:14 (KJV)** And whosoever shall not receive you, nor hear your words, when ye depart out of that house or city, shake off the dust of your feet.

   **Matthew 10:15 (KJV)** Verily I say unto you, It shall be more tolerable for the land of Sodom and Gomorrha in the day of judgment, than for that city.

**Luke 10:16 (KJV)** He that heareth you heareth me; and he that despiseth you despiseth me; and he that despiseth me despiseth him that sent me.

22. A true believer in Jesus Christ recognizes that many follow the broad path leading to destruction and thus remains committed to the narrow path that leads to life with Christ. Understanding that not all that glitters is gold, they are cautious of the allure of worldly possessions, aware that such desires can obstruct one's salvation. The believer knows the danger of money's power to overshadow the spiritual truth they hold. This caution is rooted in the teachings of Jesus, who warned of the pitfalls of wealth in Luke 6:24, highlighting the spiritual risk associated with prioritizing material gain!

**Matthew 7:13 (KJV)** Enter ye in at the strait gate: for wide *is* the gate, and broad *is* the way, that leadeth to destruction, and many there be which go in thereat:

**Matthew 7:14 (KJV)** Because strait *is* the gate, and narrow *is* the way, which leadeth unto life, and few there be that find it.

**Matthew 13:22 (KJV)** He also that received seed among the thorns is he that heareth the word; and the care of this world, and the deceitfulness of riches, choke the word, and he becometh unfruitful.

**Mark 4:19 (KJV)** And the cares of this world, and the deceitfulness of riches, and the lusts of other things entering in, choke the word, and it becometh unfruitful.

**Luke 6:24 (KJV)** But woe unto you that are rich! for ye have received your consolation.

A good believer in Jesus Christ possesses the spiritual discernment to recognize a false prophet through the fruits of their speech, namely, by evaluating the content and integrity of their teachings and preaching!

**Matthew 7:15 (KJV)** Beware of false prophets, which come to you in sheep's clothing, but inwardly they are ravening wolves.

**Matthew 7:16 (KJV)** Ye shall know them by their fruits. Do men gather grapes of thorns, or figs of thistles?

**Matthew 7:17 (KJV)** Even so every good tree bringeth forth good fruit; but a corrupt tree bringeth forth evil fruit.

**Matthew 7:18 (KJV)** A good tree cannot bring forth evil fruit, neither *can* a corrupt tree bring forth good fruit.

**Matthew 7:19 (KJV)** Every tree that bringeth not forth good fruit is hewn down, and cast into the fire.

**Matthew 7:20 (KJV)** Wherefore by their fruits ye shall know them.

23. A true believer in Jesus Christ comprehends that miracles, signs, and wonders do not guarantee entry into Heaven, emphasizing that faith and obedience to God's will are what truly matter in the pursuit of eternal life!

**Matthew 7:21 (KJV)** Not every one that saith unto me, Lord, Lord, shall enter into the kingdom of heaven; but he that doeth the will of my Father which is in heaven.

**Matthew 7:22 (KJV)** Many will say to me in that day, Lord, Lord, have we not prophesied in thy name? and in thy name have cast out devils? and in thy name done many wonderful works?

**Matthew 7:23 (KJV)** And then will I profess unto them, I never knew you: depart from me, ye that work iniquity.

**Matthew 12:38 (KJV)** Then certain of the scribes and of the Pharisees answered, saying, Master, we would see a sign from thee.

**Matthew 12:39 (KJV)** But he answered and said unto them, An evil and adulterous generation seeketh after a sign; and there shall no sign be given to it, but the sign of the prophet Jonas:

**Matthew 16:4 (KJV)** A wicked and adulterous generation seeketh after a sign; and there shall no sign be given unto it, but the sign of the prophet Jonas. And he left them, and departed.

**2 Thessalonians 2:9 (KJV)** *Even him*, whose coming is after the working of Satan with all power and signs and lying wonders,

**2 Thessalonians 2:10 (KJV)** And with all deceivableness of unrighteousness in them that perish; because they received not the love of the truth, that they might be saved.

# CHAPTER 15

## LESSONS ON SPIRITUALITY THROUGH THE ACT OF TITHING

========================

### KETE PA

"Good bed"

Asante philosophical symbol of Good Marriage

========================

1.  The paramount importance of any contribution lies in the "readiness" and "enthusiasm" with which it is made

    **Genesis 4:3 (KJV)** And in process of time it came to pass, that Cain brought of the fruit of the ground an offering unto the LORD.

    **Genesis 4:4 (KJV)** And Abel, he also brought of the firstlings of his flock and of the fat thereof. And the LORD had respect unto Abel and to his offering:

2.  As depicted in **Genesis 4:3**, the initial act of giving to God Almighty was executed "willingly," free from any form of compulsion, necessity, or pressure.

3.  Subsequently, the practice of tithing became a requirement in the Old Testament narrative. However, the New Testament reemphasized the principle of giving "willingly," highlighting the essential belief that contributions to God should never be compelled, mandatory, or forced. Thus, the mandatory collection of tithes as described in Malachi 3:10 (KJV), practiced in many churches today, is deemed inappropriate, incorrect, and contradictory to the teachings of Jesus Christ!

    **Exodus 25:2 (KJV)** Speak unto the children of Israel, that they bring me an offering: of every man that giveth it willingly with his heart ye shall take my offering.

**1 Chronicles 29:9 (KJV)** Then the people rejoiced, for that they offered willingly, because with perfect heart they offered willingly to the LORD: and David the king also rejoiced with great joy.

**Malachi 3:10 (KJV)** Bring ye all the tithes into the storehouse, that there may be meat in mine house, and prove me now herewith, saith the LORD of hosts, if I will not open you the windows of heaven, and pour you out a blessing, that *there shall* not *be room* enough *to receive it.*

**1 Corinthians 9:17 (KJV)** For if I do this thing willingly, I have a reward: but if against my will, a dispensation *of the gospel* is committed unto me.

**Philemon 14 (KJV)** But without thy mind would I do nothing; that thy benefit should not be as it were of necessity, but willingly.

**1 Peter 5:2 (KJV)** Feed the flock of God which is among you, taking the oversight *thereof,* not by constraint, but willingly; not for filthy lucre, but of a ready mind;

4.  The primary rule of tithing stipulates that:

    it should be contributed not from one's existing possessions but from their growth or profit, as illustrated in Genesis 14

5.  The tithing law in Leviticus 27 refers to a portion of agricultural produce and livestock that the Israelites were commanded to give as a tithe, or tenth, to support the Levites, who served in the temple and had no land of their own. This law specified that the tithe should come from the seeds of the land (crops), the fruit of the trees, and the livestock (such as cattle and sheep).

Here's how it worked:

*   Crops and Fruits: Farmers were to give a tenth of their harvest, including grains, fruits, and vegetables, to the Levites. This contribution was a way to acknowledge God's provision and to support the religious and communal leaders.

*   Livestock: Herders were to count off every tenth animal from their herds and flocks as they passed under a rod, designating these as tithes. This tenth animal, regardless of its quality or condition, was set apart for the Levites.

*   The purpose of this tithe was not only to provide for the Levitical priesthood but also to teach the people to put God first in their lives and to rely on Him for their sustenance. It was a practical way of ensuring that those who worked full-time in religious service were taken care of, allowing them to focus on their duties without the burden of securing their livelihood.

- The emphasis in Leviticus 27 is on the source of the tithe: it should come from the increase of the land and the breeding of the livestock, symbolizing the fruits of one's labor and the blessings from God. This practice reinforced the idea that everything belongs to God, and by giving back a portion, the Israelites acknowledged His sovereignty and expressed gratitude for His abundance.

6. In the context of the Old Testament, the Levites were members of the tribe of Levi, one of the twelve tribes of Israel, assigned to perform various religious duties and rituals in the Tabernacle (and later in the Temple in Jerusalem). Unlike the other Israelite tribes, the Levites did not receive a specific territory to farm and live on. Instead, they were dispersed throughout Israel and lived in Levitical cities, including some cities of refuge.

7. The tithing system was established as a means to support the Levites economically. Since they were dedicated to serving in the Tabernacle, handling the religious ceremonies, and later maintaining the Temple services, they did not have the time or land to generate their own income through farming or other common means of livelihood in ancient Israel.

Here's how the process worked:

- Nature of Service: The Levites' responsibilities included assisting the priests (who were also Levites, from the family of Aaron), managing the day-today operations of the Tabernacle, teaching the laws of God to the people, and performing music and other duties during religious ceremonies.

- Source of Compensation: The tithe, which was a tenth of the produce and livestock from the other Israelites, was given to the Levites as their main source of sustenance. This system ensured that the Levites could fully commit to their religious duties without worrying about their material needs.

- Redistribution: Although the Levites received these tithes, they were also required to give a tenth of what they received as a tithe to the priests, specifically for the high priest and his family.

- This tithing system emphasized the communal responsibility of supporting those who were dedicated to religious service. It acknowledged the vital role that the Levites played in the spiritual life of Israel and ensured that their material needs were met so that they could focus on serving God and the community.

8. In the Old Testament, the Levites and priests received material compensation for their service to God, primarily through tithes and offerings given by the other Israelite tribes. This system of support is well-documented in passages like **Numbers 18,** where God

instructs the Israelites to give tithes to the Levites as a reward for their service in the Tabernacle (and later the Temple).

The Levites, who had no inheritance of land among the Israelites, were set apart for religious duties. Their work included performing sacrifices, maintaining the sanctuary, and teaching the law. In return, they received tithes (a tenth of the produce and livestock) from the people, which served as their livelihood.

This arrangement is different from the teaching found in the New Testament, particularly the principle "freely ye have received, freely give," as taught by Jesus in the Gospels. Jesus' teaching emphasizes the idea of giving and serving without expecting material compensation, reflecting a shift from the more structured, obligatory system of the Old Testament to a more voluntary, heart-driven approach in the New Testament. In this context, Jesus encourages his disciples to share the blessings they have received from God (like knowledge, healing, and spiritual gifts) generously and without charge, mirroring the unconditional grace and generosity God shows to humanity.

The absence of a direct Old Testament counterpart to this New Testament principle highlights the evolution of religious thought and practice from a system of prescribed levies and duties to a new covenant ethos of grace, charity, and voluntary service motivated by love and gratitude, rather than obligation.

In Deuteronomy 12, the concept of tithing is primarily discussed in the context of agricultural produce and livestock, reflecting the economic realities of ancient Israelite society, which was largely agrarian. The tithe was a portion (traditionally one-tenth) of a person's crops or livestock, given as an offering to God, which was then used to support the Levites, the priests, and the sanctuary.

- The passage suggests that the tithe was to be brought in the form of edible goods—grains, fruits, vegetables, and meat from animals—rather than monetary wealth. This is because, in the ancient Near Eastern context, wealth was largely measured in physical assets like land, crops, and animals, rather than in currency or money as we understand it today.

- The instruction in Deuteronomy emphasizes consuming the tithes as part of communal meals in a sacred place, signifying a shared celebration of God's provision among the givers, the Levites, and the poor. This practice was meant to remind the Israelites of their dependence on God's blessings for their livelihood and to foster a sense of community and shared blessing.

- The idea that collecting tithes as money is sinful and cursed may stem from the concern that transforming the tithe from a physical, consumable product into money could distort the purpose of the tithe. Instead of being a direct share of the produce and a means to support the religious and communal life directly, monetizing the tithe could lead to misuse or misallocation of the resources, potentially neglecting the needs of the Levites and the poor.

- The underlying principle is that tithing was meant to be a tangible act of worship and community support, directly linking the people's agricultural success to their spiritual and communal obligations. This approach ensured that the act of giving was not just a financial transaction, but a meaningful contribution to the sustenance of the community and the worship of God.

9.  In **Deuteronomy 14**, tithing is described as involving food that the giver would consume together with the Levite. This practice was part of a communal meal that celebrated God's provision. The tithe consisted of agricultural produce or livestock, not money, and was shared in a communal setting to reinforce the bond between the worshippers and the Levites, who had no inheritance of their own and depended on these tithes for sustenance. This form of tithing was more about community and shared worship than a monetary transaction to religious leaders.

10. In the Old Testament, tithing and offering of first fruits were practices carried out by landowners, who would give a portion of their crops or livestock as tithes and first fruits. These offerings were in the form of food, reflecting the agricultural basis of the society at the time. Landowners, who harvested crops or raised animals, provided these physical goods to fulfill their religious obligations and support the Levites and the temple services.

11. Ethical Consideration for the Indebted: Accepting tithes or first fruits from someone in debt is viewed as unethical and sinful because it exacerbates the financial burden on individuals who are already struggling.

12. Tithe Allocation in the Third Year: Every third year, the tithe was specifically allocated to support the needy, strangers, widows, orphans, and Levites who lacked personal inheritance, emphasizing social responsibility and community support.

13. Social Welfare Role of Tithing: Tithing functioned as a social welfare system aimed at helping the poor and vulnerable, rather than serving as a means for clergy to accumulate wealth.

14. Misappropriation of Tithes: Pastors or prophets who misappropriate tithes intended for the poor are seen as committing theft against God, with such actions leading to severe spiritual consequences.

15. Nature of Tithes and First Fruits: In the agricultural society of ancient Israel, tithes and first fruits were typically food products, reflecting the direct yield of the land God provided.

16. Selective Adherence to Tithing Laws: Individuals who selectively follow the tithing laws of the Old Testament, ignoring certain aspects, are considered to be under a divine curse.

17. Full Ceremonial Practice: Those who collect tithe money without following the complete ceremonial practices, such as animal sacrifices, are viewed as violating the law and thus are cursed.

18. Exemption Criteria: Individuals lacking land or surplus income are exempt from the obligation to give first fruits and tithes, acknowledging their financial capacity.

19. Teaching on Forced Payments: Jesus taught against the forced payment of tributes, including tithes, indicating that such obligations should not be imposed upon God's children, as highlighted in **2 Chronicles 8.**

   > **2 Chronicles 8:7 (KJV)** *As for* all the people *that were* left of the Hittites, and the Amorites, and the Perizzites, and the Hivites, and the Jebusites, which *were* not of Israel,

   > **2 Chronicles 8:8 (KJV)** *But* of their children, who were left after them in the land, whom the children of Israel consumed not, them did Solomon make to pay tribute until this day.

   > **2 Chronicles 8:9 (KJV)** But of the children of Israel did Solomon make no servants for his work; but they *were* men of war, and chief of his captains, and captains of his chariots and horsemen.

20. Tithe and first fruits are not money, but food. This refers to the traditional understanding and practice in many religious contexts, particularly within Judaism and Christianity. Tithing and offering first fruits originally involved agricultural produce rather than monetary payments.

A tithe traditionally means one-tenth of one's harvest or income. In ancient times, this often meant the produce of the land or livestock, not money. The concept comes from practices where farmers would give a tenth of their crops or animals as a form of religious offering or duty, supporting the religious institutions and the needy.

First Fruits refers to the practice of offering the initial yield or first harvested portion of crops to a deity or as a religious offering. The idea was to dedicate the first and best produce to God as an act of gratitude and recognition of divine providence. This practice emphasized giving from the very start of the harvest, symbolizing faith and trust in divine provision.

These practices emphasized the importance of agricultural produce in the lives of the people who followed these customs, reflecting an agrarian society's dependence on successful harvests and herds.

Over time, as societies evolved and economies changed, the nature of tithing and offerings also adapted, with money becoming a more common medium for these religious obligations. However, the original essence of these practices was about the physical goods directly obtained from farming and herding activities.

> **2 Chronicles 31:4 (KJV)** Moreover he commanded the people that dwelt in Jerusalem to give the portion of the priests and the Levites, that they might be encouraged in the law of the LORD.

> **2 Chronicles 31:5 (KJV)** And as soon as the commandment came abroad, the children of Israel brought in abundance the firstfruits of corn, wine, and oil, and honey, and of all the increase of the field; and the tithe of all *things* brought they in abundantly.

> **2 Chronicles 31:6 (KJV)** And *concerning* the children of Israel and Judah, that dwelt in the cities of Judah, they also brought in the tithe of oxen and sheep, and the tithe of holy things which were consecrated unto the LORD their God, and laid *them* by heaps.

> **2 Chronicles 31:7 (KJV)** In the third month they began to lay the foundation of the heaps, and finished *them* in the seventh month.

21. The funding of the Gospel includes provisions that exempt the Church from various forms of taxation and financial obligations such as taxes, tolls, customs, tithes, and tributes. This exemption is based on the belief that the Church holds a superior position relative to the government. As such, the government should not claim a portion of the Church's finances. This perspective is reinforced by the practice of government officials taking their oath of office on the Holy Bible, symbolizing their commitment to the truth and, implicitly, their recognition of the Church's higher authority. This concept is supported by references such as Ezra 7, which discusses the privileges and immunities granted to those serving in the Temple.

22. Here is Jesus Christ affirming spiritual tithing in **Luke 18:10-14 (KJV)**?

The passage below tells the parable of the Pharisee and the tax collector, illustrating a lesson on humility and the spirit of true worship, rather than directly affirming the practice of tithing. Here's a breakdown of the passage and its implications regarding spiritual tithing:

**Verse 10:** "Two men went up into the temple to pray; the one a Pharisee, and the other a publican."

This introduces the characters and setting. The Pharisee is a member of a religious group known for strict adherence to Jewish law, while the publican (or tax collector) is often viewed negatively in Jewish society.

**Verse 11:** "The Pharisee stood and prayed thus with himself, God, I thank thee, that I am not as other men are, extortioners, unjust, adulterers, or even as this publican."

The Pharisee's prayer focuses on his own righteousness in comparison to others, displaying pride and self-righteousness.

**Verse 12:** "I fast twice in the week, I give tithes of all that I possess."

Here, the Pharisee mentions his religious practices, including tithing, to justify his perceived superiority. This is the closest the passage comes to mentioning tithing, but it's in the context of the Pharisee's self-righteousness, not as an endorsement of the practice itself.

**Verse 13:** "And the publican, standing afar off, would not lift up so much as his eyes unto heaven, but smote upon his breast, saying, God be merciful to me a sinner."

Contrasting with the Pharisee, the tax collector shows humility and repentance, recognizing his unworthiness and seeking mercy.

**Verse 14:** "I tell you, this man went down to his house justified rather than the other: for every one that exalteth himself shall be abased; and he that humbleth himself shall be exalted."

Jesus concludes that the humble tax collector, rather than the proud Pharisee, was justified before God, emphasizing the value of humility and sincere repentance over outward religious practices like tithing.

In summary, while the Pharisee in the parable mentions tithing as part of his religious observance, the primary focus of the passage is on the attitudes of the heart with which one approaches God. Jesus Christ uses this story to affirm the importance of humility and sincere repentance over mere adherence to religious duties like tithing. The passage suggests that spiritual integrity and humility are more valuable in the eyes of God than the mechanical performance of religious acts, including tithing.

Below is the scripture for your edification:

> **Luke 18:10 (KJV)** Two men went up into the temple to pray; the one a Pharisee, and the other a publican.
>
> **Luke 18:11 (KJV)** The Pharisee stood and prayed thus with himself, God, I thank thee, that I am not as other men *are*, extortioners, unjust, adulterers, or even as this publican.
>
> **Luke 18:12 (KJV)** I fast twice in the week, I give tithes of all that I possess.
>
> **Luke 18:13 (KJV)** And the publican, standing afar off, would not lift up so much as *his* eyes unto heaven, but smote upon his breast, saying, God be merciful to me a sinner.

**Luke 18:14 (KJV)** I tell you, this man went down

23. Failing to act righteously before the LORD God Almighty is akin to theft! Similarly, neglecting to observe God's Law also constitutes a form of robbery!

> **Malachi 3:7 (KJV)** Even from the days of your fathers ye are gone away from mine ordinances, and have not kept *them*. Return unto me, and I will return unto you, saith the LORD of hosts. But ye said, Wherein shall we return?

> **Malachi 3:8 (KJV)** Will a man rob God? Yet ye have robbed me. But ye say, Wherein have we robbed thee? In tithes and offerings.

24. To reiterate, traditionally, tithes were given as food rather than money.

> **Malachi 3:10 (KJV)** Bring ye all the tithes into the storehouse, that there may be meat in mine house, and prove me now herewith, saith the LORD of hosts, if I will not open you the windows of heaven, and pour you out a blessing, that *there shall not be room* enough *to receive it*.

25. The Almighty God did not promise blessings from tithing in the form of money, but rather through the yield of agricultural produce!

> **Malachi 3:11 (KJV)** And I will rebuke the devourer for your sakes, and he shall not destroy the fruits of your ground; neither shall your vine cast her fruit before the time in the field, saith the LORD of hosts.

> **Malachi 3:12 (KJV)** And all nations shall call you blessed: for ye shall be a delightsome land, saith the LORD of hosts.

Based on the previous discussion, I am informing you that the concept of paying tithes is a misconception, and I am emphatically urging you, using scriptural references from Genesis to Revelation, to completely abstain from paying tithes!

# NEW TESTAMENT SPIRITUAL TITHING
## HEBREWS 7

1. Abraham is recognized as the first individual to offer a tithe according to the Holy Scriptures, as documented in **Genesis 14:17-20** and **Hebrews 7:1-2!**

   **Genesis 14:17 (KJV)** And the king of Sodom went out to meet him after his return from the slaughter of Chedorlaomer, and of the kings that *were* with him, at the valley of Shaveh, which *is* the king's dale.

   **Genesis 14:18 (KJV)** And Melchizedek king of Salem brought forth bread and wine: and he *was* the priest of the most high God.

   **Genesis 14:19 (KJV)** And he blessed him, and said, Blessed *be* Abram of the most high God, possessor of heaven and earth:

   **Genesis 14:20 (KJV)** And blessed be the most high God, which hath delivered thine enemies into thy hand. And he gave him tithes of all.

   **Hebrews 7:1 (KJV)** For this Melchisedec, king of Salem, priest of the most high God, who met Abraham returning from the slaughter of the kings, and blessed him;

   **Hebrews 7:2 (KJV)** To whom also Abraham gave a tenth part of all; first being by interpretation King of righteousness, and after that also King of Salem, which is, King of peace;

2. Upon delving into the narrative of tithing found in **Genesis 14:17-20** and **Hebrews 7:1-2**, the details unravel as follows:

**Wealth and Devotion:** Abraham is depicted as not just wealthy, but also a devout follower, underscoring his capacity and willingness to give.

**Conflict and Triumph:** The backdrop of a war sets the stage, highlighting Abraham's involvement in significant, tumultuous events.

**Victorious Return:** Abraham's success in battle and his safe return signify his favor and strength, possibly divine in nature.

**Divine Encounter:** The appearance of Melchizedek, king of Salem and priest of the Most High God, introduces a sacred interaction, as he provides sustenance (bread and wine) to Abraham, symbolizing both hospitality and spiritual nourishment.

**Blessings Exchanged:** Melchizedek's blessing to Abraham signifies divine approval and favor, while his blessing to the Most High God emphasizes his priestly role and reverence.

**Tithe as Acknowledgment:** Abraham's act of giving tithes to Melchizedek from the war spoils illustrates a profound acknowledgment of Melchizedek's spiritual authority and gratitude for divine assistance in his triumphs.

This passage not only depicts the historical roots of tithing but also illustrates its role as a gesture of respect, acknowledgment, and the spiritual bond between humanity and the divine, embodied in the figure of Melchizedek.

3. The scrutiny of Abraham's tithing uncovers discrepancies with the modern practice of tithing in churches, suggesting a deviation from the biblical precedent:

   - **Reciprocal Blessing Principle:** The pattern established by Abraham's tithing indicates that tithing is an act that follows the reception of blessings from God. Abraham only tithed after being blessed by Melchizedek, the priest of the Most High God, highlighting that tithes are given in response to divine provision.

   - **Post-Blessing Tithing:** The biblical template suggests that tithing is an act performed after one has been blessed by God, reinforcing the notion that tithing is a response to, not a precursor of, divine blessing.

   - **Surplus-Based Tithing:** The principle illustrated by Abraham's actions suggests that tithes are not meant to come from one's existing possessions or regular means, but rather from the surplus or additional bounty one receives, indicating a form of giving that is above and beyond regular sustenance or income.

   - This analysis points to a potential misalignment in contemporary tithing practices with the original scriptural examples, emphasizing the need for tithing to be a reflection of received blessings and surplus rather than a compulsory levy on one's basic resources!

4. In contemporary church practices, it is observed that pastors often require tithes from impoverished individuals who have not received any tangible assets from God Almighty. This contrasts with the biblical instance of Abraham, whose tithe was not derived from his personal wealth but from the spoils of war. This discrepancy highlights a shift from the original context of tithing, where it was a voluntary offering of surplus gains rather than a mandatory levy on personal or scarce resources!

   **Hebrews 7:4 (KJV)** Now consider how great this man *was*, unto whom even the patriarch Abraham gave the tenth of the spoils.

5. Asserting that tithing in the New Testament context is deceptive, it's argued that the genuine and accurate teaching of tithing for this era should be understood differently. Specifically, just as the tangible aspects of the Old Testament worship (like the tabernacle, temple, lamp, shewbread, oil, mercy seat, and the physical lamb of God) have transitioned into intangible, spiritual counterparts in Christ Jesus, so too should the act of tithing. It should evolve from a physical obligation to a voluntary, spiritual offering, varying in measure (hundredfold, sixtyfold, thirtyfold) according to individual capacity and willingness. This shift aligns with the New Testament's spiritual orientation, epitomized in **2 Corinthians 4:18** where the focus is on the unseen, spiritual realities rather than the tangible, material ones.

6. The authentic and accurate teaching of tithing for the New Testament period can be summarized as follows: Just as the Old Testament's tangible elements like the tabernacle, temple, lamp, showbread, oil, mercy seat, and the literal lamb of God have transitioned into spiritual entities in Christ Jesus, the concept of tithing too should evolve. It should move from being a physical act of giving specific percentages of one's income to a spiritual practice of voluntary generosity, where the amount given (be it a hundredfold, sixtyfold, or thirtyfold) is determined by the giver's heartfelt willingness and capacity!

7. In the spiritual context of the New Testament under Jesus Christ, the principle found in **2 Corinthians 4:18** emphasizes shifting our focus from the visible, material world to the invisible, spiritual realities, encapsulating the essence of the New Testament's perspective: "we look not at what is seen, but at what is unseen."

> **2 Corinthians 4:18 (KJV)** While we look not at the things which are seen, but at the things which are not seen: for the things which are seen *are* temporal; but the things which are not seen *are* eternal.

8. Thus, within the New Testament's spiritual framework, the concept of tithing has evolved from the Old Testament's physical contributions to a spiritual form, as depicted in the parables Jesus Christ shared in **Matthew 13:3-23**. In this new era, tithing transcends the physical offering of agricultural produce and becomes a nourishment for the soul, embodying spiritual sustenance rather than material provisions!

> **Matthew 13:3 (KJV)** And he spake many things unto them in parables, saying, Behold, a sower went forth to sow;

> **Matthew 13:4 (KJV)** And when he sowed, some *seeds* fell by the way side, and the fowls came and devoured them up:

> **Matthew 13:5 (KJV)** Some fell upon stony places, where they had not much earth: and forthwith they sprung up, because they had no deepness of earth:

**Matthew 13:6 (KJV)** And when the sun was up, they were scorched; and because they had no root, they withered away.

**Matthew 13:7 (KJV)** And some fell among thorns; and the thorns sprung up, and choked them:

**Matthew 13:8 (KJV)** But other fell into good ground, and brought forth fruit, some an hundredfold, some sixtyfold, some thirtyfold.

**Matthew 13:9 (KJV)** Who hath ears to hear, let him hear.

9. In essence, when Jesus Christ referenced the Scripture in **Matthew 4:4,** stating that "man shall not live by bread alone, but by every word that proceeds from the mouth of God," He was fundamentally transitioning the concept of tithing from a physical contribution of food to a spiritual offering of God's word. This transformation signifies a shift from material sustenance to spiritual nourishment!

**Matthew 4:3 (KJV)** And when the tempter came to him, he said, If thou be the Son of God, command that these stones be made bread.

**Matthew 4:4 (KJV)** But he answered and said, It is written, Man shall not live by bread alone, but by every word that proceedeth out of the mouth of God.

**Luke 4:3 (KJV)** And the devil said unto him, If thou be the Son of God, command this stone that it be made bread.

**Luke 4:4 (KJV)** And Jesus answered him, saying, It is written, That man shall not live by bread alone, but by every word of God.

10. Therefore, if we adhere to Abraham's example of tithing from his surplus or excess, then the individual described in **Matthew 13:19**, who lacks excess or surplus from the seed/word received, should not and does not pay tithes. This aligns with the principle that tithing should come from abundance, not from scarcity or basic sustenance!

**Matthew 13:18 (KJV)** Hear ye therefore the parable of the sower.

**Matthew 13:19 (KJV)** When any one heareth the word of the kingdom, and understandeth *it* not, then cometh the wicked *one*, and catcheth away that which was sown in his heart. This is he which received seed by the way side.

11. Similarly, the person mentioned in **Matthew 13:20-21**, who lacks additional or surplus resources from the seed/word they have received, should not and indeed does not pay tithes. This is consistent with the concept that tithing should be an act of giving from one's abundance, rather than from a position of lack or insufficiency!

**Matthew 13:20 (KJV)** But he that received the seed into stony places, the same is he that heareth the word, and anon with joy receiveth it;

**Matthew 13:21 (KJV)** Yet hath he not root in himself, but dureth for a while: for when tribulation or persecution ariseth because of the word, by and by he is offended.

12. Likewise, the individual referred to in Matthew 13:22 (KJV) should not and does not pay tithes, as they lack any overflow or surplus resulting from the seed/word they received. This illustrates that tithing, according to the principle laid out in these passages, is contingent upon having excess or additional resources beyond one's basic needs!

> **Matthew 13:22 (KJV)** He also that received seed among the thorns is he that heareth the word; and the care of this world, and the deceitfulness of riches, choke the word, and he becometh unfruitful.

13. Finally, the individual who should and does pay tithes is the one who has an overflow or surplus from the seed/word they have received. This person exemplifies the ideal scenario for tithing, where the giver has abundance beyond their immediate needs, aligning with the principle of giving from one's excess!

> **Matthew 13:23 (KJV)** But he that received seed into the good ground is he that heareth the word, and understandeth *it*; which also beareth fruit, and bringeth forth, some an hundredfold, some sixty, some thirty.

14. This final category of God's children practices tithing from the abundance they have gained, which can be hundredfold, sixtyfold, or thirtyfold, stemming from the seed/word they received. Their abundance and surplus align with that of Abraham, who acquired his excess from warfare. Similarly, New Testament believers engage in spiritual battles, exemplifying a good warfare, and from their victories, they accrue surplus, which they then offer as tithes!

> **1 Timothy 1:18 (KJV)** This charge I commit unto thee, son Timothy, according to the prophecies which went before on thee, that thou by them mightest war a good warfare;

15. In the Old Testament, Abraham utilized physical and carnal weapons in warfare, which led to his accumulation of surplus and excess possessions. From this abundance, he was able to give tithes to God Almighty!

> **Genesis 14:8 (KJV)** And there went out the king of Sodom, and the king of Gomorrah, and the king of Admah, and the king of Zeboiim, and the king of Bela (the same *is* Zoar;) and they joined battle with them in the vale of Siddim;

> **Genesis 14:9 (KJV)** With Chedorlaomer the king of Elam, and with Tidal king of nations, and Amraphel king of Shinar, and Arioch king of Ellasar; four kings with five.

**Genesis 14:10 (KJV)** And the vale of Siddim *was full of* slimepits; and the kings of Sodom and Gomorrah fled, and fell there; and they that remained fled to the mountain.

**Genesis 14:11 (KJV)** And they took all the goods of Sodom and Gomorrah, and all their victuals, and went their way.

**Genesis 14:12 (KJV)** And they took Lot, Abram's brother's son, who dwelt in Sodom, and his goods, and departed.

**Genesis 14:13 (KJV)** And there came one that had escaped, and told Abram the Hebrew; for he dwelt in the plain of Mamre the Amorite, brother of Eshcol, and brother of Aner: and these *were* confederate with Abram.

**Genesis 14:14 (KJV)** And when Abram heard that his brother was taken captive, he armed his trained *servants*, born in his own house, three hundred and eighteen, and pursued *them* unto Dan.

**Genesis 14:15 (KJV)** And he divided himself against them, he and his servants, by night, and smote them, and pursued them unto Hobah, which *is* on the left hand of Damascus.

**Genesis 14:16 (KJV)** And he brought back all the goods, and also brought again his brother Lot, and his goods, and the women also, and the people

16. In contrast, the New Testament teaches that the weapons of our warfare are not physical or carnal, but are powerful through God for demolishing strongholds!

The phrase "the weapons of our warfare are not carnal but mighty through God to the pulling down of strongholds," found in the New Testament, refers to the concept that spiritual battles are fought with spiritual tools, rather than physical weapons. This idea is primarily based on passages like **2 Corinthians 10:4,** where the Apostle Paul emphasizes that the struggles and conflicts faced by believers are not to be combated with physical means or human strength. Instead, these battles are spiritual in nature and require divine power.

In this context, "strongholds" symbolize the deeply entrenched problems, sins, thoughts, or ideologies that oppose God's will and truth. These strongholds can include things like pride, greed, lust, false beliefs, or any other issue that keeps individuals or communities from fully embracing God's plans and purposes.

The "weapons" in the spiritual realm are tools like faith, prayer, the Word of God, the Holy Spirit's power, and other spiritual disciplines that empower believers to overcome these strongholds. Through these spiritual means, Christians are able to challenge and dismantle the barriers that stand against the knowledge of God, leading to spiritual victory and transformation.

17. This concept highlights a fundamental transition from the Old Testament, which frequently depicts physical confrontations and battles, to the New Testament's emphasis on spiritual warfare. In this newer testament, believers are encouraged to depend on God's power and heavenly resources to navigate life's challenges and engage in spiritual conflicts. The shift moves the focus from physical to spiritual realms, emphasizing that the true struggle is against spiritual forces rather than earthly ones, and that victory is achieved through faith, prayer, and the application of biblical truths.

> **2 Corinthians 10:3 (KJV)** For though we walk in the flesh, we do not war after the flesh:

> **2 Corinthians 10:4 (KJV)** (For the weapons of our warfare *are* not carnal, but mighty through God to the pulling down of strong holds;)

> **2 Corinthians 10:5 (KJV)** Casting down imaginations, and every high thing that exalteth itself against the knowledge of God, and bringing into captivity every thought to the obedience of Christ;

> **2 Corinthians 10:6 (KJV)** And having in a readiness to revenge all disobedience, when your obedience is fulfilled.

18. Furthermore, in the Old Testament, specifically in **Genesis 14:8-16** we observe that the kings defeated by Abraham aimed to plunder and acquire physical assets. In contrast, in the New Testament narrative, Satan's objective is to thieve not material possessions but rather the Word of God itself, highlighting its value as the most precious treasure one can possess. This shift from physical to spiritual theft underscores the elevated importance of spiritual goods in the New Testament!

> **Matthew 13:19 (KJV)** When any one heareth the word of the kingdom, and understandeth *it* not, then cometh the wicked *one*, and catcheth away that which was sown in his heart. This is he which received seed by the way side.

> **Proverbs 3:13 (KJV)** Happy *is* the man *that* findeth wisdom, and the man *that* getteth understanding.

> **Proverbs 3:14 (KJV)** For the merchandise of it *is* better than the merchandise of silver, and the gain thereof than fine gold.

> **Proverbs 3:15 (KJV)** She *is* more precious than rubies: and all the things thou canst desire are not to be compared unto her.

> **Proverbs 3:16 (KJV)** Length of days *is* in her right hand; *and* in her left hand riches and honour.

> **Proverbs 8:10 (KJV)** Receive my instruction, and not silver; and knowledge rather than choice gold.

**Proverbs 8:11 (KJV)** For wisdom *is* better than rubies; and all the things that may be desired are not to be compared to it.

**Isaiah 33:6 (KJV)** And wisdom and knowledge shall be the stability of thy times, *and* strength of salvation: the fear of the LORD *is* his treasure.

**Matthew 13:44 (KJV)** Again, the kingdom of heaven is like unto treasure hid in a field; the which when a man hath found, he hideth, and for joy thereof goeth and selleth all that he hath, and buyeth that field.

19. Hence, in your spiritual battles against Satan, when you achieve victory, much like Abraham overcame the kings, you gain spiritual riches. These spoils of war differ from the Old Testament's physical and tangible assets, as they are spiritual, invisible, and manifest as the very Word of God that Satan seeks to steal. This comparison highlights the transformation from material to spiritual victories and treasures in the scriptural narrative!

**1 Timothy 1:18 (KJV)** This charge I commit unto thee, son Timothy, according to the prophecies which went before on thee, that thou by them mightest war a good warfare;

20. If you successfully engage in spiritual warfare and safeguard the initial measure of God's Word entrusted to you, God will increase what you have, multiplying it in measures of hundredfold, sixtyfold, and thirtyfold, fulfilling the promise made by Jesus Christ!

**Matthew 25:21 (KJV)** His lord said unto him, Well done, *thou* good and faithful servant: thou hast been faithful over a few things, I will make thee ruler over many things: enter thou into the joy of thy lord.

**Matthew 25:23 (KJV)** His lord said unto him, Well done, good and faithful servant; thou hast been faithful over a few things, I will make thee ruler over many things: enter thou into the joy of thy lord.

**Luke 19:24 (KJV)** And he said unto them that stood by, Take from him the pound, and give *it* to him that hath ten pounds.

**Luke 19:25 (KJV)** (And they said unto him, Lord, he hath ten pounds.)

**Luke 19:26 (KJV)** For I say unto you, That unto every one which hath shall be given; and from him that hath not, even that he hath shall be taken away from him

21. Once you have successfully protected and preserved the initial portion of God's Word given to you, and God Almighty has subsequently increased your share of His Word, you will then possess an abundance or surplus of spiritual wealth. From this surplus, you can offer a 'WordTithe' to Jesus Christ, who serves as your Apostle and High Priest.

This act of giving fulfills the spiritual principle outlined in **Hebrews 7:8**, demonstrating the practice of spiritual tithing in alignment with the teachings of the New Testament.

> **Hebrews 7:1 (KJV)** For this Melchisedec, king of Salem, priest of the most high God, who met Abraham returning from the slaughter of the kings, and blessed him;

> **Hebrews 7:2 (KJV)** To whom also Abraham gave a tenth part of all; first being by interpretation King of righteousness, and after that also King of Salem, which is, King of peace;

> **Hebrews 7:3 (KJV)** Without father, without mother, without descent, having neither beginning of days, nor end of life; but made like unto the Son of God; abideth a priest continually.

> **Hebrews 7:4 (KJV)** Now consider how great this man *was*, unto whom even the patriarch Abraham gave the tenth of the spoils.

> **Hebrews 7:5 (KJV)** And verily they that are of the sons of Levi, who receive the office of the priesthood, have a commandment to take tithes of the people according to the law, that is, of their brethren, though they come out of the loins of Abraham:

> **Hebrews 7:6 (KJV)** But he whose descent is not counted from them received tithes of Abraham, and blessed him that had the promises.

> **Hebrews 7:7 (KJV)** And without all contradiction the less is blessed of the better.

> **Hebrews 7:8 (KJV)** And here men that die receive tithes; but there he *receiveth them*, of whom it is witnessed that he liveth.

22. Hebrews 7:8 (KJV) explicitly indicates that Jesus Christ is the recipient of tithes.

23. The discussed doctrine of tithing suggests that as you faithfully participate in this practice, God Almighty will grant you greater revelations of His Word. This will lead to a deeper understanding of God, equipping you with substantial spiritual insight and enhancing your ability to discern spiritual matters.

24. Hebrews 5:6 (KJV) reveals to us that Jesus Christ holds the position of a perpetual, eternal, and everlasting Priest.

25. Hebrews 5:6 (KJV) discloses that Jesus Christ is identified as the perpetual, eternal, and everlasting Priest, according to the revelation given by God Almighty!

> **Hebrews 5:6 (KJV)** As he saith also in another *place*, Thou *art* a priest for ever after the order of Melchisedec.

26. God Almighty has disclosed that the priesthood of Jesus Christ is not temporary or fleeting; rather, it is an eternal appointment. This revelation indicates that Jesus Christ's

role as a priest transcends time, maintaining its significance and authority perpetually throughout history and into the future.

**Psalm 110:4 (KJV)** The LORD hath sworn, and will not repent, Thou *art* a priest for ever after the order of Melchizedek.

**Hebrews 5:6 (KJV)** As he saith also in another *place*, Thou *art* a priest for ever after the order of Melchisedec.

**Hebrews 6:20 (KJV)** Whither the forerunner is for us entered, *even* Jesus, made an high priest for ever after the order of Melchisedec

**Hebrews 7:17 (KJV)** For he testifieth, Thou *art* a priest for ever after the order of Melchisedec.

**Hebrews 7:21 (KJV)** (For those priests were made without an oath; but this with an oath by him that said unto him, The Lord sware and will not repent, Thou *art* a priest for ever after the order of Melchisedec:)

27. God Almighty has made it known that the priest has the right to receive tithes, a principle highlighted in **Hebrews 7:4**. This scripture illustrates that the entitlement to tithes is not just a customary practice but a divinely sanctioned aspect of the priestly role, emphasizing the priest's receipt of tithes as an integral part of their ordained duties and responsibilities.

**Hebrews 7:4 (KJV)** Now consider how great this man *was*, unto whom even the patriarch Abraham gave the tenth of the spoils.

28. Therefore, Jesus Christ, as the High Priest, is entitled to receive tithes. However, the question arises regarding the nature of these tithes: Are they to be the physical, material offerings as seen in the Old Testament, such as agricultural produce, or should they align with the New Testament's emphasis on spiritual offerings, representing the soul food of God's Word? This query highlights the evolution from tangible contributions to spiritual sustenance in the practice of tithing.

**Deuteronomy 14:22 (KJV)** Thou shalt truly tithe all the increase of thy seed, that the field bringeth forth year by year.

**Deuteronomy 14:28 (KJV)** At the end of three years thou shalt bring forth all the tithe of thine increase the same year, and shalt lay *it* up within thy gates:

**Jeremiah 15:16 (KJV)** Thy words were found, and I did eat them; and thy word was unto me the joy and rejoicing of mine heart: for I am called by thy name, O LORD God of hosts.

**Ezekiel 3:1 (KJV)** Moreover he said unto me, Son of man, eat that thou findest; eat this roll, and go speak unto the house of Israel.

**Ezekiel 3:2 (KJV)** So I opened my mouth, and he caused me to eat that roll.

**Ezekiel 3:3 (KJV)** And he said unto me, Son of man, cause thy belly to eat, and fill thy bowels with this roll that I give thee. Then did I eat *it*; and it was in my mouth as honey for sweetness.

**Matthew 13:8 (KJV)** But other fell into good ground, and brought forth fruit, some an hundredfold, some sixtyfold, some thirtyfold.

**Matthew 13:9 (KJV)** Who hath ears to hear, let him hear.

**Matthew 13:18 (KJV)** Hear ye therefore the parable of the sower.

**Matthew 13:23 (KJV)** But he that received seed into the good ground is he that heareth the word, and understandeth *it*; which also beareth fruit, and bringeth forth, some an hundredfold, some sixty, some thirty.

29. Brethren, I share with you the knowledge I've gained and the teachings I've received from the Holy Spirit regarding tithing. Many pastors today, who insist on collecting monetary tithes from you, are not adhering to the true nature of tithing, which is not about money but about food. They have not revealed to you the New Testament's perspective on tithing. By doing so, they inadvertently let Satan influence and obscure their understanding of the true Gospel of Jesus Christ. The financial tithes they impose and collect from you serve as their reward for conforming to these misguided practices.

    **Hebrews 7:12 (KJV)** For the priesthood being changed, there is made of necessity a change also of the law.

    **Hebrews 7:15 (KJV)** And it is yet far more evident: for that after the similitude of Melchisedec there ariseth another priest,

    **Hebrews 7:16 (KJV)** Who is made, not after the law of a carnal commandment, but after the power of an endless life.

    **Hebrews 7:18 (KJV)** For there is verily a disannulling of the commandment going before for the weakness and unprofitableness thereof.

    **Hebrews 7:19 (KJV)** For the law made nothing perfect, but the bringing in of a better hope *did*; by the which we draw nigh unto God.

30. If these pastors were to present the true concept of tithing, transitioning from the Old Testament's physical food tithing to the New Testament's spiritual nourishment through the words of Jesus, they would have to forsake their sinful ways, lose their financial gains, abandon their extravagant lifestyles and private jets, and adhere to a life of righteousness.

31. In a notable event from 2022, Creflo Dollar, a televangelist who previously propagated a misleading doctrine of tithing, admitted he had encountered a transformative revelation of Jesus Christ's teachings. He publicly renounced his long-held erroneous views on tithing and urged his audience to discard all his related materials, including tapes, books, and teachings, acknowledging his past mistakes. This leads to the question directed at him and his current followers:

- Will he reimburse the funds collected through his misleading teachings on tithing?

- Does he intend to keep the wealth amassed from the wrongly obtained tithes?

- Has he spread other inaccuracies beyond the tithing doctrine during his years of ministry?

- What are the ramifications of his additional erroneous teachings?

- Considering those he misled potentially towards eternal damnation, who is responsible for their spiritual misguidance?

- At which moment did he recognize that the truths he now acknowledges were always present in the Scripture?

- Is it possible to deem him a reliable source of truth again? It seems unlikely!

32. Behold, I have imparted the genuine doctrine of tithing to you! Do not delay for many years only to realize that you have been misled concerning this or any other doctrine.

**2 Timothy 2:15 (KJV)** You must study to shew thyself approved unto God, a workman needeth not be ashamed, rightly dividing the truth unto thyself

**Hebrew 4:12 (KJV)** For the word of God is quick, and powerful, and sharper than any twoedged sword, piercing even to the dividing asunder of souls and spirit, and of the joints and marrow, and is a a discerner of thoughts and intents of the heart.

**Psalms 119:105 (KJV)** Thy word is a lamp unto my feet and a light unto my path

**Colossians 3:17 (KJV)** And whatsoever ye do in word or deed, do all in the name of the Lord Jesus, giving thanks to God and the Father by him

The LORD Jesus Christ be with your spirit. The LORD Jesus Christ give you understanding.

# CHAPTER 16

## THE NEGATIVE IN THE PROPHET AND IN THE TITHING!

========================

**KETE PA**

"Good bed"

Asante philosophical symbol of Good Marriage

========================

There are some two places where Jesus Christ used a double negative in His parable. One of them is generally correctly understood, but the other still has understanding issues with Christians! Let us consider the following verses to confirm our doctrine:

> **Matthew 13:57 (KJV)** And they were offended in him. But Jesus said unto them, A prophet is not without honour, save in his own country, and in his own house.

> **Mark 6:4 (KJV)** But Jesus said unto them, A prophet is not without honour, but in his own country, and among his own kin, and in his own house.

The sentence construction in **Matthew 13:57 (KJV)**, and as repeated in **Mark 6:4 (KJV)**, reveals:

A double negative:

- not
- without
- A single positive:
- save or but

In **Matthew 13:57 (KJV)**, as repeated in **Mark 6:4 (KJV)**, Christians generally understand that Jesus Christ meant that:

> "A Prophet has honour and respect only outside his own country and outside his own house and outside his own kindred"

210

"A true Prophet of God is not honored, respected, nor believed by his own country, by his own people, by his own house, and by his own kindred and siblings"

The final meaning from the above analysis is therefore the total negative statement that:

"A true Prophet of God is not honored, respected, nor believed by his own people …"

Let us apply the same analysis above to tithing to see what we shall find:

**Matthew 23:23 (KJV)** Woe unto you, scribes and Pharisees, hypocrites! for ye pay tithe of mint and anise and cummin, and have omitted the weightier *matters* of the law, judgment, mercy, and faith: these ought ye to have done, and not to leave the other undone.

The sentence construction in **Matthew 23:23 (KJV)** reveals the same double negative and one positive, as follows:

- A double negative:
- not
- undone
- A single positive:
- ought

In **Matthew 23:23 (KJV)**, if we clone the same understanding from **Matthew 13:57 (KJV)**, as repeated in **Mark 6:4 (KJV)**, since both sentence constructions for the Prophet and Tithing are the same, then the correct cloned understanding that we get, or the final meaning from the analysis of **Matthew 23:23 (KJV)**, is therefore the total negative statement that:

"In a true church of Jesus Christ, tithe is not to be paid!"

That total negative meaning for **Matthew 23:23 (KJV)** is now equal to the first total negative meaning that we got for **Matthew 13:57 (KJV)**, as repeated in **Mark 6:4 (KJV)**!

"A true Prophet of God is not honored, respected, nor believed by his own people …"

Therefore, if you are a true Christian or a true Minster of Jesus Christ and you accept the total negative meaning for **Matthew 13:57 (KJV)**, as repeated in **Mark 6:4 (KJV)**, as the correct and true Bible meaning that:

"A true Prophet of God is not honored, respected, nor believed by his own people …"

Then, you cannot, in a true conscience, reject the same total negative meaning for **Matthew 23:23 (KJV)** when you have already agreed that both sentences are of the same stylistic construction! You must be a hypocrite to apply two different meanings to two sentences that have the same identical sentence construction and the same grammatical structure!

In fact, you must be a deceiver to do that because, then, your only interest in changing the negative meaning of **Matthew 23:23 (KJV)** into a positive one, is so that you can reap the tithe money that the verse offers after you have twisted it!

Nevertheless, like Jesus Christ said in **Matthew 23:23 (KJV)**, no worries, just go ahead and enjoy your tithe money from **Matthew 23:23 (KJV)** if you believe in your church that Jesus Christ was giving you authorization to collect tithe money through **Matthew 23:23 (KJV)**, but remember also to pick up the curse that Jesus Christ added to the tithe money in the same **Matthew 23:23 (KJV)** saying: "Woe unto you"!

The authority to collect tithes from today's followers of Christ is not the Gospel of the LORD Jesus Christ. It is selective amnesia purported to deceive the children of God. The spiritual tithe paying, which is NOT money or any physical thing, emanates from the soul and spirit of the believer in Christ Jesus.

The LORD Jesus Christ be with your spirit. The LORD Jesus Christ give you understanding.

# CHAPTER 17
## GENERAL CONCLUSION

===========================

**MATE MASIE**

"What I hear, I keep

Asante philosophical symbol of Wisdom, Knowledge,

Prudence, Secrecy, Confidentiality, Oath of Secrecy

===========================

This book, titled "**Christianity Lost in Translation**: A Critical Look at Christianity," concludes with an exploration of biblical spiritual themes and doctrines. These insights, as revealed to me by the Holy Spirit, aim to accurately convey the teachings of Jesus Christ. The objective is to provide followers and ministers of Christ with the knowledge necessary for effective ministry. Our primary and sole source for this study has been the Holy Scriptures, spanning from Genesis to Revelation, adhering to the research and doctrinal methodology divinely disclosed within these sacred texts:

**Isaiah 8:20 (KJV)** To the law and to the testimony: if they speak not according to this word, *it is* because *there is* no light in them.

**Jeremiah 23:28 (KJV)** The prophet that hath a dream, let him tell a dream; and he that hath my word, let him speak my word faithfully. What *is* the chaff to the wheat? saith the LORD.

**Galatians 1:8 (KJV)** But though we, or an angel from heaven, preach any other gospel unto you than that which we have preached unto you, let him be accursed.

**Galatians 1:9 (KJV)** As we said before, so say I now again, If any *man* preach any other gospel unto you than that ye have received, let him be accursed.

In our study, we've reinforced the conviction that everything else may fade, but the Word of God endures eternally. This realization underscores the supreme importance and salvific power of God's Word for believers, essentially serving as a passport to Heaven. Consequently, God Almighty has not left the teaching or interpretation of the Scriptures to the whims of human understanding, nor has He allowed us to judge their wisdom or folly. Instead, He uses what the world considers foolish to outwit the wise, demonstrating the divine wisdom embedded in the Scriptures.

> **1 Corinthians 1:26 (KJV)** For ye see your calling, brethren, how that not many wise men after the flesh, not many mighty, not many noble, *are called*:
>
> **1 Corinthians 1:27 (KJV)** But God hath chosen the foolish things of the world to confound the wise; and God hath chosen the weak things of the world to confound the things which are mighty;
>
> **1 Corinthians 1:28 (KJV)** And base things of the world, and things which are despised, hath God chosen, *yea*, and things which are not, to bring to nought things that are:
>
> **1 Corinthians 1:29 (KJV)** That no flesh should glory in his presence.

This Christian Theological Research Textbook is an invaluable resource for the following groups:

1. Established ministers who are actively teaching the Word of God.

2. Newly ordained ministers seeking to enhance their sermon preparation and pastoral training.

3. Theological scholars engaged in the study of theological questions within the Holy Scriptures.

4. Students at Bible colleges and universities pursuing various levels of theological education, including:

   - Certificate in Theology (CT)
   - Diploma in Theology (DT)
   - Bachelor of Theology (BT)
   - Master of Theology (MT)
   - Doctor of Theology (Th.D.)
   - Diploma in Chaplaincy Training Program for Pastors
   - Diploma in Church Financial Management Training Program for Pastors
   - Diploma in General Counseling Training Program for Pastors
   - Diploma in Marriage Counseling Training Program for Pastors
   - Diploma in Sermon Preparation for Ministers of the Gospel

The Word of God, as conveyed in the Scriptures, comprises two essential components, and the absence of either nullifies its completeness. These two components are:

- The written Scriptures, and

- ii. The Holy Spirit

Without the integration of these two, one does not truly possess the Word of God. This situation is akin to acquiring a ship without having a professionally certified pilot to steer and navigate through perilous waters. Similarly, merely purchasing a Holy Bible from a store does not equate to possessing the Word of God if one lacks the guidance of the Holy Spirit, referred to here as the 'Driver,' to navigate the spiritual complexities contained within the Scriptures.:

**Luke 24:48 (KJV)** And ye are witnesses of these things.

**Luke 24:49 (KJV)** And, behold, I send the promise of my Father upon you: but tarry ye in the city of Jerusalem, until ye be endued with power from on high.

**John 14:15 (KJV)** If ye love me, keep my commandments.

**John 14:16 (KJV)** And I will pray the Father, and he shall give you another Comforter, that he may abide with you for ever;

**John 14:17 (KJV)** *Even* the Spirit of truth; whom the world cannot receive, because it seeth him not, neither knoweth him: but ye know him; for he dwelleth with you, and shall be in you.

**John 16:12 (KJV)** I have yet many things to say unto you, but ye cannot bear them now.

**John 16:13 (KJV)** Howbeit when he, the Spirit of truth, is come, he will guide you into all truth: for he shall not speak of himself; but whatsoever he shall hear, *that* shall he speak: and he will shew you things to come.

**John 16:14 (KJV)** He shall glorify me: for he shall receive of mine, and shall shew *it* unto you.

**Romans 8:9 (KJV)** But ye are not in the flesh, but in the Spirit, if so be that the Spirit of God dwell in you. Now if any man have not the Spirit of Christ, he is none of his.

**Romans 8:14 (KJV)** For as many as are led by the Spirit of God, they are the sons of God

# RESEARCH METHODOLOGY

Our research employed the Perfect Harmony Theory for Bible Translation and Interpreting (Pryce, 2011) as the guiding methodology. This theory posits that the act of teaching or interpreting the Bible must not contradict any section of the Scriptures from Genesis to Revelation. Consequently, the interpretation of a text should be derived from within the text itself, rather than external sources.

According to the Perfect Harmony Theory for Bible Translation and Interpreting (Pryce, 2011), there is a singular, definitive approach to teaching, translating, explaining, interpreting, writing, and expounding the Holy Scriptures, the Word of God. This approach mandates that the teaching of God's Word must consistently align with the entirety of God's Word, illustrating that the Scripture must interpret Scripture, thus maintaining its perfect harmony.

> **Proverbs 21:30 (KJV)** *There is* no wisdom nor understanding nor counsel against the LORD.

> **Isaiah 8:20 (KJV)** To the law and to the testimony: if they speak not according to this word, *it is* because *there is* no light in them.

> **Jeremiah 23:28 (KJV)** The prophet that hath a dream, let him tell a dream; and he that hath my word, let him speak my word faithfully. What *is* the chaff to the wheat? saith the LORD.

> **John 10:35 (KJV)** If he called them gods, unto whom the word of God came, and the scripture cannot be broken;

> **Galatians 1:8 (KJV)** But though we, or an angel from heaven, preach any other gospel unto you than that which we have preached unto you, let him be accursed.

> **Galatians 1:9 (KJV)** As we said before, so say I now again, If any *man* preach any other gospel unto you than that ye have received, let him be accursed.

Achieving proficiency in the *Perfect Harmony Theory for Bible Translation and Interpreting* (Pryce, 2011) entails harmonizing the communicative aims of translation and interpretation with in-depth biblical scholarship. This process is underpinned by extensive research and analysis of the Word of God, spanning from Genesis to Revelation, while preserving a methodological rigor akin to scientific inquiry. Here, 'scientific' implies that the interpretations are not only independently verifiable but also reproducible, much like how a text can be evaluated through systematic translation analysis and assessment tools.

The core principle of this approach is ensuring complete congruence between the interpreted meaning of a scripture and the overarching narrative of the Bible, from Genesis to Revelation. This consistency is crucial to meet the biblical injunction that believers should maintain unity of thought and purpose, reflecting a seamless alignment with the scriptural text.

> **2 Corinthians 13:11 (KJV)** Finally, brethren, farewell. Be perfect, be of good comfort, be of one mind, live in peace; and the God of love and peace shall be with you.

> **Philippians 1:27 (KJV)** Only let your conversation be as it becometh the gospel of Christ: that whether I come and see you, or else be absent, I may hear of your affairs, that ye stand fast in one spirit, with one mind striving together for the faith of the gospel;

> **Philippians 2:2 (KJV)** Fulfil ye my joy, that ye be likeminded, having the same love, *being* of one accord, of one mind.

> **1 Peter 3:8 (KJV)** Finally, *be ye* all of one mind, having compassion one of another, love as brethren, *be* pitiful, *be* courteous:

In other words, one interpretation at one part of the Bible should not contradict another interpretation at another part of the Bible. Due to the verse comparison and verification that is required, the *Perfect Harmony Theory* (Pryce, 2011) is also a tool to test *faithfulness* in Bible translation and interpreting.

Quite specifically, there is ONLY ONE spiritual law that governs how to translate, interpret, explain, teach, and understand the Word of God! That law is stated twice: one in the Old Testament and the other in the New Testament, as follows: "turn not from it *to* the right hand or *to* the left"! That was the spiritual approach that we adopted throughout our Bible research:

> **Proverbs 21:30 (KJV)** *There is* no wisdom nor understanding nor counsel against the LORD.

> **Isaiah 8:20 (KJV)** To the law and to the testimony: if they speak not according to this word, *it is* because *there is* no light in them.

> **Deuteronomy 28:14 (KJV)** And thou shalt not go aside from any of the words which I command thee this day, *to* the right hand, or *to* the left, to go after other gods to serve them.

> **Joshua 1:7 (KJV)** Only be thou strong and very courageous, that thou mayest observe to do according to all the law, which Moses my servant commanded thee: turn not from it *to* the right hand or *to* the left, that thou mayest prosper whithersoever thou goest.

**Galatians 1:8 (KJV)** But though we, or an Angel from heaven, preach any other gospel unto you than that which we have preached unto you, let him be accursed.

**Galatians 1:9 (KJV)** As we said before, so say I now again, If any *man* preach any other gospel unto you than that ye have received, let him be accursed.

In other words, the only approach to Bible Teaching that is acceptable in Heaven is the one that will "turn not from it *to* the right hand or *to* the left"!

# EXPRESSION OF PERSONAL OPINION

We trust that ministers and Christians will evaluate the teachings of this textbook against the Holy Scriptures, embracing its contents to the extent that they align entirely with the Holy Bible. In doing so, they will significantly progress in their spiritual journey, gaining a deeper understanding of the Gospel of Jesus Christ's truth and, most importantly, adhering to the Word of God for salvation.

Our aspiration is for readers to regard the Scriptures as the ultimate spiritual authority, with this textbook serving as an auxiliary resource in their earthly journey of spiritual education, enhancing their heavenly learning experience.

> **Ephesians 6:19 (KJV)** And for me, that utterance may be given unto me, that I may open my mouth boldly, to make known the mystery of the gospel,

> **Ephesians 6:20 (KJV)** For which I am an ambassador in bonds: that therein I may speak boldly, as I ought to speak.

> **Ephesians 6:21 (KJV)** But that ye also may know my affairs, *and* how I do, Tychicus, a beloved brother and faithful minister in the Lord, shall make known to you all things:

This book fulfills a multifaceted role in supporting the educational and curricular requirements of students at Bible Colleges and Theological Seminaries globally. It is designed to be a valuable asset for research, offering a rich source of material for teaching and providing deep spiritual enlightenment. Its content is crafted to enhance academic exploration and promote a deeper understanding of theological concepts, serving as a comprehensive resource for those pursuing scholarly and spiritual growth within these institutions.

> **Jeremiah 23:15 (KJV)** Therefore thus saith the LORD of hosts concerning the prophets; Behold, I will feed them with wormwood, and make them drink the water of gall: for from the prophets of Jerusalem is profaneness gone forth into all the land.

> **2 Corinthians 2:17 (KJV)** For we are not as many, which corrupt the word of God: but as of sincerity, but as of God, in the sight of God speak we in Christ.

> **1 Timothy 4:13 (KJV)** Till I come, give attendance to reading, to exhortation, to doctrine.

> **1 Timothy 6:5 (KJV)** Perverse disputings of men of corrupt minds, and destitute of the truth, supposing that gain is godliness: from such withdraw thyself.

> **2 Timothy 2:15 (KJV)** Study to shew thyself approved unto God, a workman that needeth not to be ashamed, rightly dividing the word of truth.

I earnestly pray that, through the profound knowledge and wisdom imparted by the Holy Spirit, I may persist in revealing the sacred mysteries of the Gospel of Jesus Christ, aligning with the divine will of the LORD God Almighty. My hope is to faithfully convey these spiritual truths, guided by the Holy Spirit's illumination, to unfold the profound depths of the Gospel in accordance with God's sovereign plan.

**Romans 16:25 (KJV)** Now to him that is of power to stablish you according to my gospel, and the preaching of Jesus Christ, according to the revelation of the mystery, which was kept secret since the world began,

**Ephesians 6:18 (KJV)** Praying always with all prayer and supplication in the Spirit, and watching thereunto with all perseverance and supplication for all saints;

**Ephesians 6:19 (KJV)** And for me, that utterance may be given unto me, that I may open my mouth boldly, to make known the mystery of the gospel,

**Ephesians 6:20 (KJV)** For which I am an ambassador in bonds: that therein I may speak boldly, as I ought to speak.

# FUTURE EXPECTATIONS

Moving forward, I objective is to obtain the funding required for research, interior and graphic design, as well as printing and publishing activities. We are committed to continuing our exploration of the Scriptures and addressing relevant topics under the guidance of the Holy Spirit. This effort is aimed at producing Christian Theological Research Textbooks designed for an international readership, with the specific goal of enhancing the Body of Christ with knowledge and truth.

I foresee these materials acting as comprehensive guides, offering intellectual, academic, and spiritual support to individuals globally who are in search of educational tools for Spiritual Pastoral Training. They are intended to enlighten Christians and contribute to the fortification of the Church.

> **2 Timothy 2:15 (KJV)** Study to shew thyself approved unto God, a workman that needeth not to be ashamed, rightly dividing the word of truth.

In the process of conducting research for this textbook, it is crucial to acknowledge that our sole reference was the Word of God, the Scriptures, allowing the Holy Bible to articulate its message independently, without deviation to extraneous texts. This approach adheres strictly to the guidelines for research in Bible translation and interpretation, as stipulated in **Deuteronomy 28:14** and further supported by subsequent Scriptural references, ensuring a pure and unaltered conveyance of the biblical message.

> **Deuteronomy 17:18 (KJV)** And it shall be, when he sitteth upon the throne of his kingdom, that he shall write him a copy of this law in a book out of *that which is* before the priests the Levites:

> **Deuteronomy 17:19 (KJV)** And it shall be with him, and he shall read therein all the days of his life: that he may learn to fear the LORD his God, to keep all the words of this law and these statutes, to do them:

> **Deuteronomy 28:14 (KJV)** And thou shalt not go aside from any of the words which I command thee this day, *to* the right hand, or *to* the left, to go after other gods to serve them.

> **Joshua 1:8 (KJV)** This book of the law shall not depart out of thy mouth; but thou shalt meditate therein day and night, that thou mayest observe to do according to all that is written therein: for then thou shalt make thy way prosperous, and then thou shalt have good success.

> **Luke 10 :26 (KJV)** He said unto him, What is written in the law? how readest thou?

**John 5:39 (KJV)** Search the scriptures; for in them ye think ye have eternal life: and they are they which testify of me.

**2 Peter 1:19 (KJV)** We have also a more sure word of prophecy; whereunto ye do well that ye take heed, as unto a light that shineth in a dark place, until the day dawn, and the day star arise in your hearts:

**2 Peter 1:20 (KJV)** Knowing this first, that no prophecy of the scripture is of any private interpretation.

May the LORD God Almighty cause His face to shine upon you, and may the LORD Jesus Christ grant you understanding. Let the Holy Spirit be present with your spirit... Amen.

THE END!

PRINCIPAL REFERENCE

The Holy Scriptures King James Version Ending.